Food and Beverage Management

Food and Beverage Management

Devesh Bhushan

RANDOM

RANDOM PUBLICATIONS

NEW DELHI (INDIA)

Food and Beverage Management

ISBN 978-93-5111-496-3

Published in 2015 in India by

RANDOM PUBLICATIONS

4376-A/4B, Gali Murari Lal, Ansari Road
New Delhi-110 002
Phone : +9111-43580356, 011-23289044, 011-43142548
e-mail: sales@randompublications.com,
info@randompublications.com, randomexports@gmail.com

Reprinted 2018

Type Setting by : Friends Media, Delhi-110089
Printed at : Sanat Printers

Preface

The food and beverage industry is probably the most diverse but specialized industry in the world. It is certainly one of the largest, employing millions of people in a bewildering array of jobs around the globe. The industry encompasses those places, institutions and companies that provide meals and drinks taken away from home. It continues to change dramatically, and businesses need to respond quickly to constantly evolving challenges and trends without losing focus on top-line growth and margin management

Global market forces are driving the continual evolution of the food and beverage industry. Consolidation, changing consumer preferences and increasing government regulations are dramatically impacting manufacturing and business strategy. In this fiercely competitive marketplace, you must offer a greater variety of products to meet consumer demand. At the same time, you must consistently and cost-effectively produce high quality products. In today's global marketplace, where growth via acquisition is prominent, the key to sustained positive financial performance is the ability to understand and respond to consumer demands and competitive pressures while reducing cost of production.

This comprehensive book aims to cover all relevant aspects and issues related to food and beverage management. The underlying thinking behind much of this book relies on the application of a systems approach to the management of operations. It proposes systematic approaches to the design, planning and control of food and beverage operations, and also recognises the need to manage operations as operating systems. Besides students, teachers and professionals of hotel and hospitality industry, this book will be a necessary read for all who concerned with the management of food and beverage in different establishments.

Author

Contents

1

Food and Beverage Operations

The hospitality industry is primarily known by its output products for satisfying the guests' demand of accommodation, food and beverages away from their homes. Usually the industry is split into two separate segments of accommodation and Food and Beverages (F&B).

There are various kinds of food and beverage operations designed to meet the demand of the consumers. Over the years, eating out has become a matter of choice rather than necessity. However, the primary reasons for eating out are:

- to celebrate a special occasion or treat,
- meeting friends,
- just for a change from home, and
- at times a necessity, e.g., eating out while travelling.

The food and beverage segment of hospitality industry is primarily concerned with providing food and beverages to their consumers. Various elements related in it's operations can be summarised in the catering cycle (Figure 1).

The fact that the catering cycle is not only concerned with operations but it is also a dynamic model in the sense that any one problem in one section of the cycle will caus e difficulties for other elements of the cycle. For example, problem in the purchase section will also affect production and service, while improper utilisation of raw materials during production would also affect control system and so on.

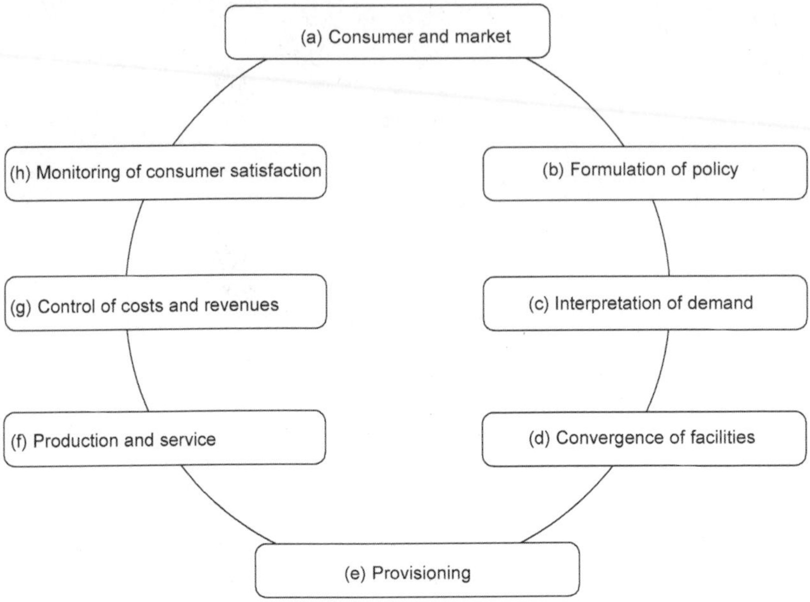

Figure 1. The Catering Cycle

We can infer from the cycle that an ideal food and drink service would be one which:

- provides food and drink on demand;
- has optimum utilisation of labour and skill, raw materials and equipments;
- has quick and simple methods of operational design; and
- has flexible system design allowing ease of adaptation.

To be able to establish and manage such an ideal food and beverage outlet one would require meticulous preparation, both at pre and post opening stages of the outlet. Yet the common assumption is that Food and Beverage outlet is the easiest way to earn a profit, since food always sells. It is also often assumed that if you eat well then you know how to run an eating joint. Well such thoughts are far from the truth. Let us now discuss various elements involved in the opening and running of a restaurant successfully.

Assessment of Consumer Needs

Market research should be the first activity to be performed once you decide to open food and beverage outlet. Figure 2 displays how you can decide upon creating a product based on the consumer needs.

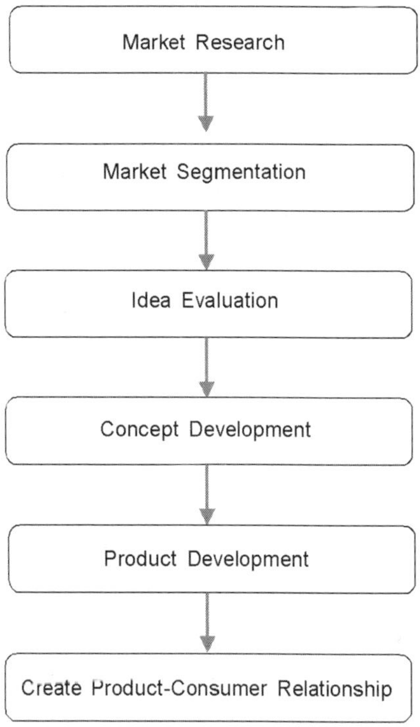

Figure 2: Product-consumer Relationship Development Framework

Market research requires investment of a lot of time and money. The methods used can be interviews, questionnaires, sales analysis, consumer panels, market information from specialises publications, specifically commissioned market information and other data available ordinarily. Large organisations try out all the avenues of market research while smaller outlets may perform their market research on their own. Market research is, therefore, concerned with human needs, wants, demands, goals and values.

Market research paves the way for market segmentation and the identification of the target consumers. As you know market segmentation can be demographic, geographic or others. You should know that the same product belonging to an international food chain can be priced differently in different countries.

Idea generation can be a brainstorming session or it can be based on the market research reports. It would be focussed on generating a product based on consumer needs, wants and demands. The generated ideas need to be screened. The type of outlet to the type of food that would be served needs to be generated and screened during this session.

Once an idea has passed the screening process, various products and parts of products need to be conceptualised. Various factors like price, quantity, amount of choice; consumer's quality perceptions and amount of product usage are used to position a conc ept. Once the idea is converted into a concept it needs to be tested in the identified market segment. Questionnaires and interviews regarding the conceptualised product, its price and location of outlet, etc. answered by the prospective clients would help in finalising the product(s).

Product Development Stage would involve turning this concept into a product. Food and Beverage products do not only mean providing food and drink but also involves decisions on the type of service outlet to be provided, the k ind of service whether a self-serving or speciality restaurant or a take-away meal outlet would also help in forming the complete product. It is essential to understand how we would like the consumers to view our outlet. The way we would want the consumers to view our outlet whether a Gourmet event or cheap meal outlet, etc. would define the ambience, price, service and food and beverage. Once we are definite on our product we need to launch our product with right promotion so as to reach our target consumers.

The consumer-product relationship, once built, needs to be maintained and improved upon. However, with the passage of time the needs, wants and demands of the consumer change. Therefore, market research should be an ongoing procedure to ensure a long al sting relationship with the consumer. In other words, feedback is necessary to maintain the old consumer relationships and to form new ones.

Food and Beverage Industry: Status and Trends

The food service industry generally encompasses those places, institutions, and companies responsible for any meal eaten away from home. This industry includes restaurants, school and hospital cafeterias, catering operations, and many other formats. Major foodservice providers include Compass Group, Sodexho, Aramark, and the Crown Group. The companies that supply foodservice operators are called foodservice distributors.

Some companies manufacture products in both consumer and foodservice versions. The consumer version usually comes in individual-sized packages with elaborate label design for retail sale. The foodservice version is packaged in a much larger industrial size and often lacks the colourful label designs of the consumer version.

Hotels

The hotel food and beverage department provides food-related guest services throughout a hotel, conference, or resort property. Outlets for food and beverage services can include the following:

- Full-service restaurant.
- Coffee shop.
- Catering facilities.
- Room service.
- Recreational areas.
- Lobby area bars.
- Food market or delicatessen.

Food items for these combined foodservice areas are provided from a central kitchen, with the exception of large hotel facilities where satellite kitchens provide auxiliary production and service areas. An executive chef supervises production for all areas, consulting with the manager of each foodservice area. Of the seven food service areas, catering affords the possibility for the greatest profit, in addition to providing much-needed cash flow during periods when room sales are slow. Hotel catering services are usually classified as:

- Business.
- Convention/conference.
- Social.

The volume of catering service available to a hotel is based on the size and number of facilities that can be used for private functions as well as the availability of production and service staff and related equipment. The primary catering market for a hotel is based on three factors:

— Location.

— Hotel facilities.

— Customer profile.

The location of a hotel determines the demand for in-house catering. In house catering is defined as guest-related foodservice functions associated with business meetings, conferences, conventions, and social concerns. A hotel with a remote location focuses its catering efforts on the business booked into the hotel. Resort locations often provide additional opportunities for catering services at sports facilities and landscape venues throughout the property.

A hotel with a suburban or downtown location can expect to develop a large volume of outside catering business, both business-related and social in addition to conferences and conventions. The amount of combined catering business that can be handled at any one time in a hotel is based primarily on the number and size of the facilities available. The major function rooms are usually referred to as the ballroom areas. These are complemented by a series of meeting rooms, some adjacent to the main ballroom area and some located in other areas of the hotel.

The customer profile for hotel catering services is made up of both business and social clientele. Customers who use the hotel as a location for a two or three-day meeting consider meal functions as part of the total meeting package. This arrangement not only enables customers to work within a budget that covers the entire project, but also fits with an approach to planning catering functions that considers the success of the overall meeting rather than each individual function.

The catering manager is generally given the responsibility of creating a menu plan for the entire programme along with theme functions and special events. The target market for hotel catering functions is a customer who reflects the social, business, and economic profile of the community. Hotel catering services attract a wide base of customers with a broad range of requests.

Customers who plan business functions on a regular basis are familiar with the catering staff and services of the hotel. Their needs are often quickly identified and provided for. Customers who plan social functions on a one-time basis, however, need more personal guidance throughout much of the planning stage. Pricing is a primary concern of this customer group.

Hotel food and beverage departments are often requested to handle the arrangements for functions to be held away from the hotel property. If a company wants to retain as much revenue as possible from business, convention, and social customers, an off-premise catering policy should be developed. Using the off-premise catering organisational guide, hotel catering departments can easily develop an off-premise catering programme.

Often, a hotel will have the facilities in place to offer a limited menu of take-out items. Items have been selected from the hotel dining room menu to offer to the general public on a take-away basis. Hotels have the advantage over many private catering companies of being able to use their own equipment. In addition, kitchen and storage facilities are available to handle large volumes of both food and beverage as well as equipment. If the volume of on-property business requires the use of hotel equipment, rentals can cover the additional needs, with costs being charged back to the customer.

Restaurants

A restaurant is an establishment that serves prepared food and beverages to be consumed on the premises. The term covers a multiplicity of venues and a diversity of styles of cuisine. Restaurants are sometimes a feature of a larger complex, typically a hotel, where the dining amenities are provided for the convenience of the residents and, of course, for the hotel to maximise their potential revenue. Such restaurants are often also open to non-residents.

The term restaurant (from the French restaurer, to restore) first appeared in the 16th century, meaning "a food which restores", and referred specifically to a rich, highly flavoured soup. The modern sense of the word was born around 1765 when a Parisian soup-seller named Boulanger opened his establishment. The first restaurant in the form that became standard (customers sitting down with individual portions at individual tables, selecting food from menus, during fixed opening hours) was the Grand Taverne de Londres, founded in 1782 by a man named Beauvilliers.

Whilst inns and taverns were known from antiquity, these were establishments aimed at travellers, and in general locals would rarely eat there. The restaurant became established in France after the French Revolution broke up catering guilds and forced the aristocracy to flee, leaving a retinue of servants with the skills to cook excellent food; whilst at the same time numerous provincials arrived in Paris with no family to cook for them. Restaurants were the means by which these two could be brought together—and the French tradition of dining out was born. In this period the star chef Antonin Carême, often credited with founding classic French cuisine, flourished, becoming known as the "Cook of Kings and the King of Cooks."

Restaurants spread rapidly to the United States, with the first (Jullien's Restarator) opening in Boston in 1794, and they spread rapidly thereafter. Most however continued on the standard approach of providing a shared meal on the table to which customers would then help themselves, something which encouraged them to eat rather quickly. The modern formal style of dining, where customers are given a plate with the food already arranged on it, is known as Service à la russe, as it is said to have been introduced to France by the Russian Prince Kurakin in the 1810s, from where it spread rapidly to England and beyond.

Types of Restaurants

Restaurants range from unpretentious lunching or dining places catering to people working nearby, with simple food served in simple settings at low prices, to expensive establishments serving refined food and wines in a formal setting. In the former case, customers usually wear casual clothing. In the latter case, depending on culture and local traditions, customers might wear semi-casual, semi-formal, or even in rare cases formal wear. Standardly customers sit at tables, their orders are taken by a waiter, who brings the food when it is ready, and the customers pay the bill before leaving.

In finer restaurants there will be a host or hostess or even a maître d'hôtel to welcome customers and to seat them. Other staff waiting on customers include busboys and sommeliers. Depending on local custom, a tip of varying proportions of the bill (often 10-20%) may be added, which (usually) goes to the staff rather than the restaurant. This gratuity might be added directly to the bill or it may be given voluntarily.

Restaurants often specialise in certain types of food or present a certain unifying, and often entertaining, theme. For example, there are seafood restaurants, vegetarian restaurants or ethnic restaurants. Generally speaking, restaurants selling "local" food are simply called restaurants, while restaurants selling food of foreign origin are called accordingly, for example, a Chinese restaurant and a French restaurant.

Depending on local customs and the establishment, restaurants may or may not serve alcoholic beverages. Restaurants are often prohibited from selling alcohol without a meal by alcohol sale laws; such sale is considered to be activity for bars, which are meant to have more severe restrictions. Some restaurants are licensed to serve alcohol ("fully licensed"), and/or permit customers to "bring your own" alcohol (BYO / BYOB).

Full-service restaurants

Full-service restaurants have the opportunity to offer a variety of catering services to their customers. Before any decision is made to offer these services, however, six important factors should be considered:

- Location
- Customer profile
- Restaurant style or concept
- Staffing capabilities
- Restaurant physical layout
- Cuisine and menu offerings

The proximity of the restaurant to office complexes and centralised business areas will help to establish whether its catering service will be focused on business or social marketing efforts. Businesses in the twenty-first century are spread from urban centres to suburban locations in office parks. Central urban locations offer a concentrated market for both office delivery and take-out. A significant factor in developing the market for business catering is that service is generally required during the business week, leaving weekend periods free to service social business. In addition, locations such as museums, concert halls, and historical sites offer interesting venues to catered functions for both local businesses and conventions.

Both urban and suburban restaurants can successfully develop social catering business. Suburban locations are generally more appropriate for social catering to private homes, clubs, churches, and other facilities. Delivery to urban locations can pose security and logistical problems, creating additional costs for transportation and service labour. Population density also affects the volume of anticipated catering business.

Restaurants situated in rural areas with low population density cannot expect immediate high volumes of catering business. Areas of high-density population yield a variety of catering opportunities that steadily increase in volume through referrals and reputation. The location of the physical restaurant building plays a role in the type of catering services to be offered.

Storage facilities, expansion possibilities, and access to major transportation routes are factors important to catering service production.

Restaurants have the advantage of a built-in customer pool to whom they can market in-house and off-premise catering services. In addition, the attraction of being associated with a restaurant's reputation will help to expand the possible market to include new business and social clients. The market profile should classify customers as business or social catering clients, designated by income bracket. In addition the range of activities for which each customer pool will need catering services should be researched as thoroughly as possible. This will help in developing package programmes along with potential menu programmes and accompanying pricing concepts.

The style, concept, and/or theme of the restaurant should be taken into consideration when planning potential catering services. Off-premise catering services do not necessarily have to blend with the facilities offered by the restaurant. On-premise catering services should, however, be designed to function within the restaurant facilities.

Restaurants facilities are a major factor in providing on-premise catering. The ratio of catering functions to restaurant services that can be handled at a given time is dependent on the size and flexibility of the physical plant. Small private parties are often incorporated into the general dining room setting. Large parties must, however, be given facilities that are separated from the general public. Many restaurants that offer in-house catering schedule large parties, such as weddings, anniversaries, luncheons, and dinners, on days and times when the restaurant is not otherwise open.

Often catering business must be refused because sufficient on-premise facilities are not available. When management is continually turning away catering business, a decision will need to be made as to how the restaurant will balance is future development of catering versus full-service dining services. Kitchen facilities play a major part in determining when and how catering service demands can be met. Kitchen equipment must be flexible, allowing for volume production to take place simultaneously with à la carte restaurant service.

The kitchen cooking load and holding capacity of ovens and auxiliary equipment is important to determine if a kitchen is to be used to its full capacity during busy times. Storage and refrigeration facilities determine the amount of food products available at any given time. The cost of waste from food spoilage due to lack of refrigeration and freezer space could dilute the profit from additional catering business.

The primary cuisine and menu offerings of a restaurant constitute one of the most important considerations for on-premise catering. Off-premise catering services do not necessarily need to be the same as those offered at the restaurant for full-service dining. Purchasing and production requirements are crucial to the successful development of catering services. On-premise catering should offer menu items that duplicate the established menu as closely as possible in order to enhance production capabilities.

Surrounding items, such as vegetables and starches, are the most effective area of the menu to duplicate. Kitchen production is more efficient when the number of surrounding menu items is limited. Profitable and effective purchasing for catering functions requires that the ingredients for menu items be the same or similar to those on the restaurant menu. This allows the purchasing agent to place orders for maximum volume pricing and quality.

Off-premise catering: The decision to participate in off-premise catering requires a thorough review of a restaurant's resources. A successful in-house catering programme can lead management into perceiving that taking on the challenge of off-premise catering will not cause operational difficulties. Several problems must be anticipated regarding the off-premise facilities in which the final production and service for functions takes place.

During in-house catering functions, service staff can often work between private parties and the dining room, filling in where needed, while the kitchen staff functions as usual, having planned ahead to handle the increased production load. In order to service off-premise functions, however, a separate wait-staff needs to be scheduled. In addition, at least one member of the kitchen production staff will be assigned to the function and therefore will be unavailable to the restaurant kitchen for the time period involved for the off-premise function.

Equipment as well as food will need to be transported both to and from the off-premise function location. Hot food and cold food must be kept at specific temperatures to prevent food spoilage. A refrigerator truck may be necessary at certain times of the year. Transportation routes and problems involving traffic congestion need to be considered in the timing of deliveries. Subcontractors may be necessary for equipment such as tables, chairs, dishes, glassware, linens, dance floors, and tents.

The extent to which a restaurant commits to a full-service catering business determines the amount of extra effort required to handle the increased business. Planning for offpremise catering requires attention to detail. Contingency plans for bad weather, delays in food transportation, and the failure of on-site equipment to function properly should be established in advance so that problems can be dealt with expediently as they arise. Additional costs are incurred when solutions to these situations are not planned for in advance. Contract prices must include these contingencies or management will find that overall costs are higher than the fees charged to the customer for food and services.

Take-out service: Take-out service is the most profitable way for restaurants and catering services to increase revenues without increasing costs. Because take-out service does not require extra seating, it generally will not require an operation to expand its facilities beyond accommodating take-out customers with a pick-up and waiting area. Kitchen production can plan and schedule to handle large increases in volume for short time periods. In addition, take-out does not require the additional expenses incurred by table service for glassware, linens, flowers, menus, and entertainment.

Disposable dishes, plastic flatware, and a carrying container are the basic requirements for take-out service. Successful take-out service does, however, require planning to assure that customers receive menu items in satisfactory condition. As with the catering menu, the selection of take-out menu items should be drawn from the restaurant menu in order to maximise purchasing and production efforts.

Brasserie, bistro, pub

In France, a brasserie is a café doubling as a restaurant and serving single dishes and other meals in a relaxed setting. A bistro is a familiar name for a café serving moderately priced simple meals in an unpretentious setting, especially in Paris; bistros have become increasingly popular with tourists. Mainly in the UK and other countries influenced by British culture, the pub (short for public house) today serves a similar dual menu, offering beer and other alcohol along with basic food fare. Traditionally, pubs were primarily drinking establishments, whereas the modern pub business relies on food as well, to the point where so-called gastropubs are known for their high-quality "pub food".

Dining car

A dining car or diner (but not "diner car", except in ignorant parlance) is a railroad passenger car that serves meals on a train in the manner of a full-service sit-down restaurant. It is distinct from other types of railroad food-service cars that do not duplicate the full-service sit-down restaurant experience, principally cars of various types in which one purchases food from a walk-up counter to be consumed either within the car or elsewhere in the train. (Grill cars, in which customers sit on stools at a counter and purchase and consume food cooked on a grill behind the counter, are an intermediate type, but on balance could be considered a type of dining car.)

Dining cars have always been prized for the way in which they enhance the familiar restaurant experience by offering a unique form of visual entertainment, namely the ever-changing views of the world outside. While dining cars are less common today than they were in the past, having been not just supplemented but in some cases replaced by other types of food-service cars, they still play a significant role in passenger railroading, especially on medium-distance and long-distance trains. In one of the most common dining car configurations, one end of the car contains a galley (with a side aisle next to it, so that passengers can pass through that end of the car to other cars of the train), and the other end contains table or booth seating on either side of a centre aisle.

Trains with high demand for dining car services have sometimes featured "double-unit dining cars", consisting of two adjacent cars functioning to some extent as a single entity, generally with one car containing a galley plus table or booth seating and the other car containing table or booth seating only. In the dining cars of Amtrak's bilevel Superliner trains, booth seating on either side of a centre aisle occupies almost the entire upper level, while the galley is below; food is sent to the upper level on a dumbwaiter.

Fast food restaurants

A fast-food restaurant is a restaurant characterised both by food which is supplied quickly after ordering, and by minimal service. Food purchased may or may not be eaten quickly as well. Often this food is referred to as fast food. In response to increasing backlash against "fast food", the industry has been trying to move the public away from that term over the past five years, shifting to the term quick service restaurant (QSR for short).

Consumers still refer to the restaurants as fast-food restaurants despite the industry's efforts to change them. The food in these restaurants is often cooked in bulk in advance and kept hot, or reheated to order.

Many fast-food restaurants are part of restaurant chains or franchise operations, which ship standardised foodstuffs to each restaurant from central locations. There are also simpler fast-food outlets, such as stands or kiosks, which may or may not provide shelter or chairs for customers. Because the capital requirements to start a fast-food restaurant are relatively small, particularly in areas with non-existent or poorly enforced health codes, small individually owned fast-food restaurants are common throughout the world.

Although fast-food restaurants are often seen as a mark of modern technological culture, they are probably as old as cities themselves, with their style varying from culture to culture. Ancient Roman cities had bread-and-olive stands, East Asian cultures feature noodle shops. Flat bread and falafel are characteristic of the Middle East. The modern history of fast food is connected with the history of the hamburger, as the earliest fast-food outlets sold hamburgers as their primary product.

The American company White Castle is generally credited with opening the first fast-food outlet in 1921, selling hamburgers for five cents apiece. White Castle later added five holes to each beef patty to increase its surface area and speed cooking times. White Castle was successful from its inception and spawned numerous competitors.

McDonald's, the largest fast-food chain in the world and the brand most associated with the term "fast food," did not appear until 1948 when a hot dog stand under the McDonald's brand name opened in San Diego. Ray Kroc, the distributor of an industrial milkshake mixer that the original McDonald's used, joined the founders of McDonald's in 1954 and began expanding the franchise. Wendy's, founded in 1972, is credited with pioneering the use of the "drive-thru" window to allow consumers to purchase fast food without having to park or exit their cars.

Fast-food outlets are take-away or take-out providers, often with a "drive-thru" service which allows customers to order and pick up food from their cars; but most also have a seating area in which customers can eat the food on the premises. Finger food comprises most fast food, and can be eaten without cutlery. Fast foods include fish and chips, sandwiches, pitas, hamburgers, fried chicken, french fries, chicken nuggets, tacos, pizza or ice cream, although many fast-food restaurants offer "slower" foods like chili, mashed potatoes, or salads. However, even though Western-style Chinese cuisine is most often served as take-away, it is seldom considered to be fast food.

Fast-food restaurants are popular in the United States, the source of most of its innovation. Many major international chains are based in the United States. Consequently, fast-food restaurants have often been the target of globalisation protests, the target of anti-Americanism sentiment and been subjected to attacks because of perceived cultural imperialism. Multinational corporations typically modify their menus to cater to local tastes. However, this practice has not quashed criticism. Additionally, multinational fast-food chains are not the only or even the primary source of fast food in most of the world.

Many regional and local chains have developed around the world to compete with international chains. Most fast food in the developing world is provided by small individual mom and pop eateries. In the developing world, multinational chains are considerably more expensive; they usually are frequented because they are considered chic and somewhat glamorous and because they usually are much cleaner than local eateries.

In the United Kingdom, while fast-food restaurant chains are now common, the British tradition of take-away foods such as fish and chips and steak and kidney pie with mash remain popular. Closer to the end of the 20th century, these have been joined by take-away outlets selling ethnic or pseudo-ethnic foods such as Italian, Chinese, and Indian.

Fast-food chains have come under fire from consumer groups (such as the Centre for Science in the Public Interest, a longtime fast-food critic) over the past decade. Some of the concerns have led to a Slow Food reaction. This movement seeks to preserve local cuisines and ingredients, and directly opposes laws and habits that favour fast-food choices. Among other things, it strives to educate consumers' palates to prefer what it considers richer, more varied, and more nourishing tastes of fresh local ingredients harvested in season.

Some of the large fast-food chains are beginning to incorporate healthier alternatives in their menu, e.g. salads and fresh fruit. However, some people see these moves as a tokenistic and commercial measure, rather than an appropriate reaction to ethical concerns about the world ecology and people's health. McDonald's has announced that in March of 2006, the chain will include nutritional information on the packaging of all of its products.

Cafeteria

A cafeteria is a type of food service location in which there is no table service, whether a restaurant or within an institution such as a large office building or school; a school dining location is also referred to as a canteen. Instead, there are food serving counters/stalls, either in a line or allowing arbitrary walking paths, and customers take food they require as they walk along, placing them on a tray, and pay at the check-out (buffet system). For some food items there may be the system that while at the counter one orders it and it is served by personnel behind the counter. Sometimes, for some food items and drinks, one collects an empty cup, glass, etc., pays at the check-out, then fills that after the check-out. This system may be combined with being allowed to take a free second serving.

Due to the consumption pattern of people, this system is rarely or never used for alcoholic beverages. As cafeterias require few employees, they are often found within a larger institution, catering to the clientele of that institution. For example, schools, colleges and their halls of residence, department stores, museums, and office buildings often have cafeterias. At one time, cafeteria-style restaurants dominated the dining-out culture of the Southern United States, and there were several prominent chains of them: Bickford's, Morrison's, Apple House, K&W, and Blue Boar among them. These institutions, with the exception of K&W, went into a decline in the 1960s with the rise of fast food and were largely finished off in the 1980s by the rise of "casual dining".

However, newer chains, notably Luby's and Piccadilly Cafeteria, have arisen to fill some of the gap left by the decline of the older chains. A cafeteria in a US military installation is known as either a chow hall, a mess hall, or, more correctly, a dining facility, whereas in common British armed forces parlance, it is known as a cookhouse or mess. Some monasteries and boarding schools refer to their cafeteria as a refectory. Students often refer to cafeterias as lunchrooms, though breakfast as well as lunch is often eaten there. Cafeterias serving university dormitories are sometimes called dining halls. A food court is a type of cafeteria found in many shopping malls and airports.

Private Clubs

Private clubs offer a self-contained facility that operates both full-service dining rooms and private function space along with a variety of food and beverage outlets. Private clubs are generally dependent on their membership for both dining room and catering business. Functioning as nonprofit organisations, clubs are, in many areas, prohibited by law from accepting or soliciting business from nonmembers. If such is the case private clubs may, however, cater functions that are sponsored by members and attended by nonmembers, allowing them to service both social and business activities.

Factors that influence the success of restaurant and hotel catering services, such as location, facilities, and customer profile, also affect private clubs. Off-premise catering services can also be offered to private club members. Private clubs may also contract out their foodservice operation to a contract foodservice operator.

Clubs are broken down into two general classifications: private clubs and country clubs. Private clubs are generally situated in the downtown areas of larger towns and cities. The club facility is used primarily as a location for meetings, private dining, social and business functions.

Country clubs require a suburban location and usually promote a combination of golf, tennis, and/ or boating as their primary recreational facilities. Private dining and catering facilities are located in the clubhouse. Acceptability of location is based primarily on general location and accessibility to major transportation routes. Downtown city locations can create problems regarding parking and security for people travelling into the city.

Contract Feeding Companies

Contract feeding companies provide institutions such as hospitals and schools, as well as businesses, with in-house meal programmes designed to meet specific needs. Food production and service is contracted for long-term periods with designated budget restrictions. The contract feeding segment of the foodservice industry has been steadily growing since the late 1980s. Major corporations such as Marriott International created large contract feeding companies to service a wide range of customers.

In the late 1990s a separate company, Host Marriott, was created and now operates independently of Marriott International, serving institutional customers internationally. As food costs have increased and available labour decreased, institutions and businesses have turned to outside contractors to operate their foodservice programmes. In most cases, these programmes function as a service to either patients, clients, or employees; they are subsidised benefits, not profit making operations.

By using a professional contract foodservice operator to handle this area of operations, businesses find that the quality of service increases significantly along with client and employee satisfaction. The major factors that can influence the success of catering services within a contract feeding location are:

— *Facilities*: Contract feeding can be offered in a wide variety of dining room and catering facilities. The type and number of facilities that can be used for function spaces within a business or institutional setting will help to determine the volume of in-house catering. Catering functions in these settings are usually business related, but open area spaces can be used by private groups for social functions.

— *Customer profile*: Identifying the customer profile for large and diverse groups of people in a business situation is initially done by job classification level. Private dining room service and business meeting menu selections should be based on the expectations associated with the job levels of the people who attend these functions. The types of food products that will be popular in a cafeteria area depend on the profile of the employee population group.

— *Off-Premise catering*: Contract feeding companies working for a business or institution are often called upon to produce foodservice functions in off-premise locations.

Charcuteries and Delicatessens

Charcuteries are food stores that offer take-out foodservice along with gourmet food products. Many of these products are used as ingredients in the preparation of the food line. In some cases a small seating area will be offered for eat-in customers. The trend for home-replacement food is significant to this type of operation. When customers want something beyond fast food for a take-home meal, they turn to establishments that can provide meals that they would like to have prepared for themselves.

Home-replacement food is being provided in a number of types of foodservice facilities, including upscale supermarkets. This type of foodservice operation usually specialises in a regional or national cuisine. Menu items range from salads and sandwiches to fully prepared meals. The success of a charcuterie depends on two major factors: location and customer profile.

Charcuteries should be located where the customer profile supports the level of cuisine offered. Pricing for this type of foodservice operation is generally higher than that of delicatessens and supermarket preprepared and packaged food items; hence it requires a customer base willing to pay for gourmet food products. Smaller independent caterers often operate out of this type of retail outlet, using the facility for both production and storage in addition to a means of advertising and promotion.

Delicatessens are food stores that provide a variety of food products and offer both eat-in and take-out food service. The location should be reasonably close to the targeted customer base. Menu item offerings range from sandwiches, salads, and pizza to preprepared meals-to-go. Take-out foodservice of preprepared foods is a major business segment for this type of foodservice operation.

The profile of customers for a charcuterie/delicatessen operation is drawn largely from the demographics of the population in the immediate area of the business. Primary customers can be identified as either employees of adjacent businesses or local area residents. A customer profile is determined for each of the two primary customer groups. The local resident profile, with an average check of twelve dollars or more two times a week, may be in the mid-30s to 50s age group, middle to upper income bracket. Further investigation may show that the business employee is a morning coffee and lunch customer while the local resident is an evening customer for home-replacement meals.

References

Cichy, Ronald F. *Managing Service in Food and Beverage Operations.* Lansing: Educational Institute of the American Hotel and Motel Association, 1998.

Raymond J. Goodman, Jr., *The Management of Service for the Restaurant Manager*, 2nd Edition

Waller, Keith. *Improving Food and Beverage Performance.* Oxford: Butterworth-Heinemann, 1996.

West, Bessie Brooks and LeVelle Wood, *Food service in institutions,* New York; London: J. Wiley & sons inc; Chapman & Hall limited, 1938.

2

Designing the Restaurant

The term *restaurant* (from the French *restaurer*, meaning : to restore) first appeared in the 16th century, meaning "a food which restores", and referred specifically to a rich, highly flavoured soup. According to the Guinness Book of Records, the Sobrino de Botin in Madrid, Spain is the oldest restaurant in existence today. It opened in 1725.

The modern sense of the word was born around 1765 when a Parisian soup-seller named Boulanger opened his establishment. The first restaurant in the form that became standard was the *Grand Taverne de Londres*, founded in 1782 by a man named Beauvilliers. Whilst inns and taverns were known from antiquity, these were establishments aimed at travellers, and in general locals would rarely eat there.

The restaurant became established in France after the French Revolution broke up catering guilds and forced the aristocracy to flee, leaving a retinue of servants with the skills to cook excellent food; whilst at the same time numerous provincials arrived in Paris with no family to cook for them. Restaurants were the means by which these two could be brought together — and the French tradition of dining out was born. In this period the star chef Auguste Escoffier, often credited with founding classic French cuisine, flourished, becoming known as the "Cook of Kings and the King of Cooks."

Restaurants then spread rapidly across the world, with the first in the United States (*Jullien's Restarator*) opening in Boston in 1794. Most however continued on the standard approach (*Service à la française*) of providing a shared meal on the table to which customers would then help themselves, something which encouraged them to eat rather quickly. The modern formal style of dining, where customers are given a plate with the food already arranged on it, is known as *Service à la russe*, as it is said to have been introduced to France by the Russian Prince Kurakin in the 1810s, from where it spread rapidly to England and beyond.

Segments of Restaurant Industry

The restaurant industry has two distinct audience segments: full- and limited-service operations. Both segments attract a certain clientele as well as various promotional products.

Full-Service Segment

The full-service segment of the restaurant industry can be categorised as sit-down restaurants that cater to the customer with a sense of personal attention. For example, an Italian restaurant with a hostess, a choice of wines and Italian music playing softly in the background is a full-service experience. Many full-service restaurants are competing for customers, not only in the full-service market, but with the fast-food or limited-service segment of the industry as well.

Full-service restaurants are generally categorised in terms of price, menu, or atmosphere.

- *Price*: When the focus is on price, restaurants can be categorised as luxury, highpriced, mid-priced, or low-priced establishments.
- *Menu*: Restaurants such as steak houses and seafood restaurants are full service restaurants defined in terms of menu. For example, Outback Steakhouse specialises in beef; Red Lobster features shrimp, crab, and lobster on its menu.
- *Atmosphere*: Some restaurants are known primarily for their atmosphere that is, for their unique architecture, decor, and / or setting. Show business and sports motifs-currently very fashionable in the industry-provide themes for a growing number of popular restaurants. The Hard Rock Cafe chain, which started in London and now has restaurants in major cities around the world, features Elvis Presley, the Beatles, and other rock-star music memorabilia.

Full-service restaurants can be categorised in other ways besides price, menu, or atmosphere. For example, there are dinner houses. Dinner houses are distinguishable by their combination of decor, informal atmosphere, and eclectic menus that draw from ethnic and traditional offerings. Family restaurants serve breakfast, lunch, and dinner, offering traditional menu items. Their pricing falls between casual dinner houses and quick-service restaurants. A major source of revenue for some family restaurants-such as Cracker Barrel—is an on-site gift shop.

To compete against its market segment as well as other establishments, the fullservice restaurant prides itself on customer appreciation. To survive, full-service restaurants must have a loyal customer following. This is accomplished by offering unique menu choices and a creative atmosphere that will entice the customer not only to return, but also to inform his or her acquaintances of the establishment. The biggest challenge for full-service operators is to attract customers, then maintain their loyalty. The 90s brought the theme restaurants. These include restaurants catering to music, movies, sports or environmental enthusiasts. Many theme establishments have the advertising and physical appearance to draw customers from all walks of life. Many are tourists who want an opportunity to view memorabilia and catch a glimpse of the creative interior that mirrors the establishment's theme.

Most full-service restaurants, especially theme establishments, will include logoed merchandise as a method of advertising. Customers will find T-shirts and a host of other items with a restaurant's logo on them. These items play an important role in earning customer loyalty and promoting the name of the establishment. Distributors have an advantage servicing the restaurant industry because they simply need to walk inside an establishment to get a hint of its décor and customer base, thus receiving a better idea as to what promotional products would be most appealing to the customers. On the other end of the scale, limited-service restaurants cater to a much fasterpaced clientele.

With corporate downsizing, employees are working longer hours and having meals ordered at the workplace. Longer hours and lack of time have transformed family mealtime into "home meal replacement." Fast-food restaurants and delis offer convenient alternatives to people on the go. The drive-up window has replaced the dining room in many limited-service establishments. In US, the National Restaurant Association states that nearly

30 percent of all retail establishments are eating and drinking places. Both the retail and bookstore markets are incorporating food services as a marketing tool to keep customers in the stores longer.

The grocery stores already have used food to entice its customers to stay and shop; however, many customers will purchase a carryout meal to avoid preparing a meal when they get home. Gasoline convenience stores are growing tremendously because of the possibility for additional revenue from drivers traveling on a trip or returning home from work. Many are building in residential areas in order to be easily accessible to nearby residents. The limited-service segment opens many doors to food-on-the-go suppliers who are interested in testing unique products specifically designed for the customer on the move. With intense competition between limited-service establishments, owners must rely on creative ideas to separate themselves from the rest of the competition.

For example, a product that fits in the automobile to serve as a reminder to visit a convenience store for gasoline and sandwiches is a marketing tool appropriate for people whose car has taken the place of the kitchen table. With thousands of restaurants to choose from, distributors must understand the establishment, its clientele and the competition to offer promotional products that will make a lasting impact. Whether it is full- or limited-service establishments, there are differences in the needs of restaurants within these segments. What works for the Italian restaurant may not work for the Mexican restaurant down the street.

Promotional products are heavily based on customer demand or the usefulness of the product for the market's customers. Two full-service restaurants that have survived the times and made a lasting name for themselves both nationally and worldwide are Ithaca, New York-based Moosewood Restaurant and Driftwood, Texas-based The Salt Lick. Despite outside competition and slow seasons, both restaurants have retained customer loyalty by listening to the needs of its customers. The Moosewood Restaurant is a vegetarian restaurant established in 1973 at a time when people were asking themselves if they could eat just vegetables. Situated in the same spot in Ithaca, New York, the restaurant has undergone several design changes over the years.

What is interesting about the successes of the Moosewood Restaurant and The Salt Lick is the creative uses of cookbooks and barbecue sauce to promote the restaurant on a grand scale. While it may not have been apparent to the establishments at the time, the cookbooks and sauce were innovative promotional products that continue to generate revenue for the restaurants more than 20 years after their inception. Several years later, both establishments have incorporated common-day promotional items to promote themselves.

Limited-Service Restaurant

It is for this segment of the population that limited-service restaurants were created. Whether it is a fast-food chain, coffeehouse or stop-and-go, the limitedservice establishment is providing customers with a demanding convenience. In US, the National Restaurant Association indicates that one out of five takeout food consumers is a daily user. Those customers represent half of all takeout occasions. Major growth in quick-service restaurants continues to come from hamburger chains as well as chicken, sandwich, and Mexican-food chains. Much of the growth is outside the United States. The type or number of menu items alone does. not determine the winners. A commitment to good service and providing nutritional menu choices has taken center stage.

McDonald's now guarantees hot food; fast, friendly service; and double-check drive-thru accuracy. A survey of 27 restaurant chains-including 19 quick-service chains-with 50,000 outlets found that at least three-quarters of them offered menu choices for health-conscious consumers. Examples included low-fat milk, skinless chicken, and reduced or low-calorie salad dressing. Nine out of ten chains said they used vegetable fats instead of animal fats for frying. While a limited-service establishment may not have all the personal touches of a full-service restaurant, there is a loyalty among limited-service customers that promotional products can reach.

With intense competition emerging between limitedservice establishments, it is becoming increasingly important to maintain a loyal customer base. An important method of accomplishing that is incorporating promotional products into the customers' orders. For fast-food restaurants such as McDonald's and Burger King, children have enjoyed kid's meals that include plastic toys depicting the establishment's mascots. Coffeehouses have used creative ideas such as cooking a muffin in a logoed coffee mug that the customer keeps for refills during repeat visits. Other limited-service establishments include logoed T-shirts, matchbooks, coasters, magnets and buttons.

The limited-service market has many opportunities for promotional products. The National Restaurant Association notes that in an average month 78 percent of U.S. households use some form of carryout or delivery. It is obvious that the limitedservice market has a large audience that can be reached via promotional products. For example, ast-food restaurants have been offering logoed glasses and toys to customers for many years. Promotional products are an inexpensive medium that limited-service establishments can utilise to promote their name and logo to the public. The full-service market is custom-oriented; therefore, it is essential that distributors create a promotion that leaves a sense of appreciation in the customer. Full-service establishments want and need customers to return and a well-crafted promotional product could be the difference between a high turnover or a loyal customer base.

The limited-service market works in a similar manner. Although limited service establishments need customers, the focus is to create name and logo recognition to a mass audience. With millions of people who enjoy hamburgers, limited-service operators must separate themselves from the rest of the competition that sells hamburgers. To accomplish this, promotional products with a relatively low cost and function can create long-term exposure to a large audience.

Concern of Restaurant Designing

The designing of the sitting area of restaurant depends on the type of restaurant. For example, if the restaurant is only for breakfast buffet, then the sitting arrangements needs to be centred around or near the buffet table for easy access by the customers. While designing the guest sitting area one needs to choose the correct furnishing and furnitures. The guest sitting area should provide some form of privacy to each guest table and at the same time have optimum utilisation of space. Each table should be easily accessible by the serving staff and thus save on serving time. The décor should be pleasant as well as attractive. The ambience of the restaurant contributes towards the customer satisfaction. Over -doing the décor is not advisable. Lighting plays an important role for giving the correct ambience, but one should remember there's a difference between deductive lighting and eating one's meal in almost total darkness. Soft music, if played completes the relaxed ambience and environment. Air conditioning, though not a must a few years back, has now become a necessity so as to provide clean and cool air to the guests.

Designing the kitchen also forms an important part since major work is done there. The primary areas of kitchen can be distinguished as:

a) *Storage*: where the raw materials are stored. This would mean both dry storage and refrigerated storage area. Storage area is also dependent on the type of restaurant. For example, a speciality restaurant may require some special storage facilities for the ingredients.

b) *Pre -preparation Area*: Kitchen usually has a specified area for cleaning, peeling, chopping, mixing and combining ingredients.

c) *Production Areas*: The production areas or food preparation area is best situated. The production area has hot food and cold food area wherein main courses, soups and salads and other refrigerated food is prepared, respectively.

d) *Bakery:* If the manager decides on providing baked food, a separate bakery is useful.

e) *Holding and Service:* An area for holding the food prior to service is very essential.

f) *Ware Washing*: The washing area is usually near to the dining area but also close to the main production area.

g) *Pot and Pan Area:* A pot and pan area would enable the storing of the utensils when they are not in use.

The restaurant design must have an Office Area and Employees Area. The office area would be used to keep the record of various transactions both with the suppliers and the consumers. The employees need an area to change into work clothes and also an area to rest during breaks. It's the manager's duty to check the viability of a restaurant's final design and work out the viability of the plan.

Functional Areas

In the day-to-day operation, all foodservice facilities perform various functions. These functions common to most operations include receiving, storage, preparation, production, service, warewashing, and waste disposal. These functions can easily be related to the materials and products involved in the food facility. Other functions that are performed it are not easily related to materials or products include accounting, purchasing, management, and communications. Typically, each function can be broken down into more specific items. For example, the general storage function may be subdivided into storage of meats, dry foods, beverages, linens, dishes, silver, supplies, and trash. The functional planning for the various areas of foodservice facilities may be accomplished in different ways. Experienced foodservice consultants have developed their own techniques of planning and can an areas fairly rapidly.

The first step in functional planning is to visualise all the necessary functions to be performed in the proposed foodservice facility. This obviously comes easily to experienced planners, but persons unfamiliar with planning may find it helpful to make a list of the functions. Each function consists of a number of tasks. For example, the tasks involved in the preparation function may include weighing, cutting, mixing, blending, panning, moving, and judging quality. These tasks vary from one facility to another depending upon the method of operation desired by the owner or manager. The method of performing the tasks also depends on the type and form of materials involved, the kind of equipment to be used, the quality of finished products, and the skill of the persons involved.

The evaluation and selection of these variables that affect the tasks are a part of the designer's responsibility. Hopefully, the best choice of materials, equipment, and processes will be made, to facilitate performance of these tasks. Thus functional planning begins with identification of functions and visualisation of the tasks to be performed for each function.

Physical Requirements

The basic requirements considered are equipment and space. For each function or task, the planner will determine the type of equipment to be used, and this in turn leads to the development of space requirements. The capacity of the equipment is not usually determined at this time because a careful analysis of the menu and scheduling are required. In the development of equipment and space requirements, the planner has to decide how each of the tasks for a particular function is to be performed in terms of the materials and processes involved.

To illustrate, consider the task of making a stew as one of the components of the cooking function. Some of the variations of the materials that may be used in making the stew are:

1. Entirely from fresh raw ingredients; both meat and vegetables
2. Partially fresh vegetables and partially canned (i.e., fresh potatoes and other canned)

3. Partially fresh vegetables and partially frozen vegetables
4. All canned vegetables and fresh meat
5. All frozen vegetables and fresh meat
6. Fully processed canned stew
7. Fully processed frozen stew

It can be seen that each of these variations in the ingredients will require different tasks and different processes for production. This in turn leads to different equipment types. The planner will evaluate the menu items to be produced and make the decisions regarding the type of production equipment to use. This same concept is used for all the other functions and tasks required to operate the facility. Considerations of space requirements are also evaluated in a similar manner. The mere identification of the functions and tasks alerts the planner to the fact that some kind of space will be needed.

The planner does not necessarily need to determine the final square footage of space now, but does consider whether a particular task requires floor space, work space, and/or storage space. The designer is essentially developing the basic concepts for the operation of the facility. This is done prior to the planning of the actual physical areas. In other words, the planning of the operational methods is the key to the functional planning for the facility. A short discussion of some of these functional areas will illustrate and clarify the concept.

Receiving Function

The receiving function is very similar for most: foodservice operations. The receiving of incoming foods, beverages, and supplies is planned according to the types and volumes of different materials handled. The frequency of deliveries and the type of delivery service are considered for each type of material to be received. For large facilities, materials-handling systems may be utilised to simplify the movement of materials into and out of the receiving area. Many suppliers offer their products in palletised form, which simplifies the movement. The use of carts, trucks, and conveyors will solve most materials-handling problems. Planning of the materials-handling system for the receiving area is only a part of the total system for the entire facility, and the planner should consider all the various components of the handling system before making a final decision.

Some may decide to use a single type of handling equipment for everything from the initial receiving to final service. Other planners may conceive a system which uses several types of equipment, each selected for its characteristics for handling certain types of materials. For example, mobile carts and trucks may be selected for handling food items, while conveyors may be chosen to handle dishes and other nonfood items. The availability of a wide variety of materials-handling equipment enables the designer to develop many different systems. Some temporary storage in the way of floor space and table space is required to check deliveries for quantity and quality. This space is designed on the basis of the larger amounts of frequently delivered materials.

Additional space is planned for scales, storage of skids and hand trucks, and for other necessary equipment for the receiving function. Consideration of waste disposal is also a factor in planning for the receiving function, since some partial trimming and cleaning of materials may be needed before they are placed in storage. Disposal of boxes, cartons, and other packaging materials removed during the receiving function is also involved. Architectural features, including the size and location of unloading docks and doors, may be developed at this time.

Storage Function

Planning for the storage function in food facilities includes dry storage, refrigerated storage, freezer storage, beverage storage, and storage for nonfood supplies.

Dry storage: The dry storage function, like other storage functions, is necessary for the on-the-site storage of frequently used materials. Storage requirements will depend upon the types of materials, frequency of delivery and the volume of each delivery. These variables are evaluated before functional planning of the storage area begins. Dry storage areas for food items are planned to maintain temperatures between 50° and 70°F (10° and 21.1° C).

The desired relative humidity is approximately 50%. For this reason, heat-generating equipment, such as motors and compressors, should not be planned for this area. Pipes carrying steam or hot water are insulated to minimise heat gain of the storage area. Protection against moisture from sweating cold water or refrigerant lines is also important. Planning for protection of the foodstuffs from insects and vermin is required for sanitary reasons. Some space for storage of frequently used dry items can be provided in various work areas of the facility. This concept will reduce the amount of movement required to obtain the materials.

Refrigerated storage: Refrigerated storage areas maintaining temperatures of 32°-37° F (0.0°-2.8° C) are required for fresh meats, vegetables and fruits, dairy products, beverages, and carry-over foods. Many planners are specifying smaller but more numerous reach-in refrigerators strategically located throughout the facility instead of one large walk-in storage. The use of reach-in units minimises employee movements in obtaining items. A combination of walk-in and reach-in refrigerators seems to be a good design for many types of foodservice facilities.

The reach-ins are usually located adjacent to preparation and production equipment or may be built-in under tables and counters. The design of walk-in refrigerated areas is similar to the dry storage areas except for the refrigeration system required to maintain the desired temperature. The size and type of foodservice operation and the frequency and volume of deliveries will determine whether a walk-in refrigerated space is needed. It is thought that a walk-in refrigerator is feasible for operations serving over 300-400 meals per day.

Reach-in refrigerators are generally designed to store for a shorter period of time and are ideal for smaller operations. Pass-through refrigeration units may be specified where their use will simplify the storage and movement of foods. The increased use of frozen foods necessitates planning refrigerated space for thawing purposes. Requirements will depend on the volume and type of frozen foods to be used in the operation. Thawing space is generally designed to handle one day's production.

Freezer storage: Temperatures of -10° to -15°F (- 23.3° to - 26.1° C) are needed to safely store frozen foods. Designers are aware of the increased use of frozen foods that are partially or fully preprocessed, and plan accordingly. Some operations have gone almost exclusively to frozen foods. Freezers may be walk-in or reach-in, and requirements are dictated by several factors including the availability of seasonal items. The possibility of buying seasonal items in volume lots should be evaluated before the design of freezer storage is finalised.

Storage of nonfood items: The design of storage areas for nonfood items like dishes, glasses, flatware, utensils, paper goods, linen, cleaning supplies, and furniture can take many different forms. They may be stored in rooms, on shelves, in cabinets, or on specially designed racks. In smaller operations, some items may be incorporated in the dry food storage area, but separate areas are best for larger operations. All chemicals, soaps, sanitising compounds, and other cleaning supplies should be stored separately because of their danger to foods. Separate areas are also desirable for cleaning equipment such as brooms, mops, pails, scrubbers, and polishers. In-process storage of items may be accomplished by special equipment such as self-levelling dispensers. The self-levelling dispensers are a very satisfactory method of providing storage for dishes.

Preparation Functions

The preparation functions for a foodservice facility are meat/fish/ poultry preparation, vegetable preparation, salad preparation, and sandwich preparation. Speciality restaurants may have different or additional functions depending on their menu items. An example is Le fish and shellfish preparation function for seafood operations. The various preparation functions are sometimes combined and performed in one area. Smaller facilities frequently combine the salad and sandwich preparation areas. Combined vegetable and salad preparation areas are also common.

Meat/Fish/Poultry Preparation Functions

The meat/fish/poultry preparation function consists of cutting, lopping, grinding, and portioning of these items and their products ready them for further processing. The preparation function has fanged drastically over the years with the advent and increasing use of fully preportioned products. Some operations may have minimal [eat/fish/poultry preparation areas where the only tasks involved are to opening of packages and the panning of the items. Larger operations and commissary operations may still require a full meat/fish/poultry preparation function. The planning for the meat/fish/poultry preparation function varies with the amount of preparation that will be done on the foodservice pemises.

Function of Vegetable Preparation

The vegetable preparation function historically involved preparing primarily fresh vegetables for cooking and salad production. Typical tasks associated with fresh vegetable preparation are trimming, peeling, washing, cutting, and chopping. As with meat preparation, the vegetable preparation function can be minimised by utilising various types of preprocessed vegetables. Canned arid frozen items are generally used as alternatives to fresh vegetables. Design and planning for the vegetable preparation function depends on the state of the raw materials and the subsequent tasks to be performed. Large operations choosing to use fresh vegetables will require the use of cutters, choppers, slicers, peelers, and similar equipment. Type and capacity will be designed to handle the volume of vegetables to be prepared. Holding refrigerators are used if the preparation is done a day prior to usage. Waste disposal is another aspect in planning for the vegetable preparation function.

Function of Salad Preparation

The function of salad preparation is that of combining and assembling ingredients prepared in the vegetable preparation area, or obtained from fruit and vegetable areas, into finished salads. Various quantities of meat, fish, and dairy products are used in certain salads. The preparation of some appetiser items may also be a part of this functional area.

Design for the salad preparation function will depend upon the type and volume of salads to be produced. Salad and vegetable preparation functions are frequently combined in smaller facilities. Another alternative is to combine the salad preparation with the sandwich preparation function.

Large foodservice operations, especially those serving banquets, will design for a separate mass production salad area. In this situation, assembly line concepts and related equipment can be utilised. The perishibility of salads necessitates planning of refrigerated holding facilities. Mobile refrigerated carts are selected by some designers as a method of transporting and holding the finished salads. Pass-through refrigerators are frequently specified for cafeteria operations.

Functions of Sandwich Preparation

The design of the area for sandwich preparation is based on the need for fast and efficient work methods. The work areas are planned to provide ample space for the ingredients used in the sandwiches, and tools, and a normal flow of work.

Custom-designed sandwich preparation areas are used for operations handling a large volume of sandwiches. In some cases the sandwich preparation area may be in part of the serving area, as in cafeteria or counter-service operations. Assembly-line techniques and automatic wrapping machinery are typical designs found in institutional and in-plant feeding operations.

Cooking Function

The heart of all foodservice facilities is the main cooking function, and special care in planning for it is required. In addition to cooking ill meat and vegetable items, the cooking area serves as the hub between the production and service functions. In many table-service operations, for example, the pick-up of food for serving is directly adjacent to the main cooking area. The design of cooking areas varies from very limited facilities, as in fast-food and limited-menu operations, to the very extensive facilities of luxury table-service operations or in large institutional food-services. In all cases, the design of cooking area is closely correlated with the various menu items to be processed.

Baking Function

Except in a relatively few cases, foodservice operations will not be involved in the production of a full line of baked goods. Even many large institutional operations in universities and hospitals confine heir baking function to cakes, cookies, and pastries, other items being obtained from commercial bakeries. Even the operations that do a good portion of their own baking will use basic mixes that simplify he tasks of the baking function. Full bakerics arc occasionally planned for commissaries or central kitchens that supply several outlets. These may be planned to handle the conventional tasks of formulation, scaling, mixing, handling, and make-up.

The advent of high-quality pre-prepared unbaked goods that require only thawing and baking has also had an impact on the design of baking areas. Many of the pre-prepared items can be processed in the main cooking area, eliminating the need for a separate baking area completely. An economic analysis of the cost of full baking on the premises versus the use of pre-prepared baked goods may also influence the design of the baking system.

Serving Function

The different ways of performing the serving function result in a variety of serving facilities that may be planned. Basic table-service operations require pick-up areas immediately adjacent to the cooking battery. Separate pick-up areas are used for salads, beverages, and desserts. Some items, including rolls, bread, butter, and water, are stored at waiter or waitress stations located in dining areas. Serving-line facilities are planned for cafeterias, employee feeding, and school or university feeding operations. Several- configurations of serving lines can be used, depending on the total number of people to be served and the time allowed for serving.

Straight-line configurations, are the most basic and are characterised by easy access and well-defined traffic flow. The major problem with the straight-line configuration is its limited serving capacity per line. Variations of the straight-line include the U-shaped counter and the herringbone design. These configurations give more linear space and increase serving-line capacity. The sopping centre or scramble serving line system is characterised by an open-square configuration of counters at the perimeters that allow traffic to flow freely in the centre.

Total serving capacity of the shopping centre or scramble system is much greater than that of the basic straightline configurations. Other types of serving functions that may be planned are tray make-up conveyors for hospitals, cart assembly areas for banquets, and room service facilities for hotels. Each of these has special requirements and should be planned for efficient handling of the food to be served.

Dishwashing Function

The dishwashing function is usually performed in a separate room or area that has to be well ventilated and illuminated. Acoustical tile and noise-absorbing materials are used to aid in lowering the high noise levels associated with this function. Modern dishwashing machines can be obtained to handle any volume of dinnerware. Glass washing, which used to be a major problem in food facilities, now better accomplished through the control of washing, rinsing, ad water additives.

In many cases it is possible to wash glasses satisfactorily if they are washed shortly after the water has been changed their operators may prefer to have a separate glass washer. Large hotel foodservice operations find it desirable to provide a separate silver room where silverware can be cleaned and polished the separate silver room provides a better means of control over the expensive silverware. The design of the dishwashing area is dependent upon the total volume of dinnerware to be washed and the time required to accomplish the washing. Some operations may prefer to carry a large dinnerware inventory in order to spread the washing over a long period of time. This usually occurs between the meal periods. Others may wide to carry a minimum dinnerware inventory and must therefore ash the items as soon as they are soiled so they can be returned to service immediately. Regardless of the system to be used, the designer will provide methods of sorting, soaking, washing, and drying of the various dinnerware items. Appropriate handling and storage methods are also devised for both soiled and cleaned dinnerware.

Pot and Pan Washing Function

The pot- and pan-washing function is also preferably done in a separate area instead of combining it with other areas as some small operations may be inclined to do. The basic pot- and pan-washing function can be handled with a three-compartment sink and sufficient space for storing the soiled utensils. In some operations, a large storage area for soiled utensils may be required because they are not washed as soon as they are received. This occurs when the same personnel who wash dishes also wash the pots and pans. Pot-washing machines are considered for large food facilities if they can be economically justified.

Waste Disposal Function

Every foodservice operation has different requirements for waste disposal and many factors should be evaluated before designing a system to handle this function: amount of waste generated, type of waste paper, plastic, garbage, cans, etc.), cost of hauling and dumping, frequency of pickups, and stricter air and water pollution laws. Some of the waste disposal systems that may be used are described as follows.

— *Compaction*: The use of compactors is usually considered where large volumes of disposables are to be handled. Compactors quickly reduce the volume of waste so that it can easily be handled in smaller nits. The weight of the compacted waste should preferably be less than 50 lb. (22.7 kg) for convenience in handling.

— *Incineration*: Incinerators can be used to some advantage if the cost of equipment needed to comply with local codes is not prohibitive. Pollution ordinances should be checked for requirements.

— *Grinding*: Garbage grinding is generally allowed in areas with municipal sewerage systems. However, some communities may not allow garbage grinding if they experience problems with nonbiodegradable materials such as completely plastic or plastic coated materials.

— *Pulping*: Waste pulping creates a liquified waste by using heavy-duty rotary grinders with a recirculating water system. The liquified waste is then processed through a water extractor where it is reduced to a semi-dry pulp and then stored in bins. The semi-dry material has very little odor and is trucked away periodically. Metal or glass cannot be handled by a waste pulping system and therefore these materials have to be disposed of separately. In many cases, different systems for different types of waste will have to be designed.

Space Requirements

The space required for each functional area of the facility is dependent upon many factors which are not constant for all types of operations. The factors involved include the number of meals to be prepared; the functions and tasks to be performed; the equipment requirements; the number of employees and corresponding workplaces required; storage for materials; and suitable space for traffic and movement. The importance of accurately evaluating these factors cannot be overemphasised. Overestimating or underestimating any of them can lead to an excess or a shortage of space for the facility.

Preliminary Space Estimation

Rules of thumb used for preliminary space estimates only. They are to be regarded as strictly tentative and subject to easy change. The "rules of thumb" are used to get a general idea of the overall size of a facility in order to make preliminary cost estimates for feasibility studies, or to determine approximate land requirements for the building. One problem with using guides and "rules of thumb" is that the figures given are usually based on existing operations and do not reflect newer methods of foodservice operation. Another difficulty is that these figures are not given for all types of foodservice operations and consequently they would be of little use for certain types of projects.

Facility Size

Depending upon the type of foodservice to be planned, a general estimate of the total building size can be obtained by relating it to the number of seats to be provided. The estimated square footage of total space per seat is given in Table 1. These figures can be related to the number of meals to be prepared by considering the turnover rate for a particular meal period. A range of space estimates is given to allow for variations in the methods of operation.

The smaller figures are used for limited menu and limited-space operations; the larger figures are suitable for operations with extensive menus and allow more spacious areas. Figures for estimating the total facility size of other types of foodservice, such as tray service, car service, or take-out service, are not available because of the great variations that exist in these types of operations.

Space for Dining Areas

The space required for dining areas is based on the number of persons to be seated at one time and the square feet of space allowed per seat. The number of persons to be seated at one time is determined by considering the total number of customers to be served for a given time period, and the turnover. Turnover refers to seat usage and is expressed by the number of times a seat will be occupied over a given time period. Turnover is usually expressed on a per-hour basis, although it can be determined on a per meal basis.

Table 1. Estimated total facility space for foodservice facilities

Type of operation	*Area per seat (ft^2)*	*(m^2)*
Table service	24-32	2.23-2.97
Counter service	18-24	1.86-2.60
Booth service	20-28	2.04-2.79
Cafeteria service	22-30	

The turnover is determined by estimating the average time a seat is occupied for the time period desired. For example, if the turnover is to be expressed on a per-hour basis and the average estimated time the seat is occupied is 20 minutes, the turnover is 3. If the average seat occupancy time is 30 min, then the turnover rate is 2 per hour. Determining the turnover rate per meal period is useful for determining the total seating capacity based on estimated sales volume. Turnover rates are affected by the method of serving and serving time as well as by the type of customer, menu offerings, and the dining atmosphere. Turnover rates can be increased to some extent by many design and operational factors. This is not to suggest that all facilities should be designed for high turnover rates. However, if high turnover is one of the basic objectives, then the planner and subsequent manager can use the following to accomplish this:

Use menu items that require short processing times, or use predominately preprocessed items. Provide ample production space and equipment to handle the peak periods. Use well-lighted and light-coloured painted areas for serving and dining. Arrange dining tables in close proximity to each other. Develop a somewhat uncomfortable dining seat design. Provide sufficient service personnel so guests are served promptly after they are seated. Provide for prompt clearing of the tables when a customer is finished with a course or the entire meal. Make sure guest checks are presented to customers as soon as they are finished eating. Note that a number of factors identified above are characteristic of the management policy after the facility has been built. This again emphasises the close working relationship that has to exist between the owner or manager and the planner during the planning process.

A foodservice facility designed for high turnover must also be managed for high turnover if the anticipated volume of sales is to be generated. The square feet of space allowed in the dining areas is governed by the amount of comfort desired. Crowding in dining areas is not desirable except in some quick-service fast-food operations. Most individuals would like to have sufficient elbow room and table space to enjoy their meal.

The estimates for dining areas include space for tables, chairs, aisles, and service stations. They do not allow for waiting areas, rest rooms, rather similar areas. Space requirements for these areas have to be determined separately. The size and arrangement of tables, chairs, booths, and counters selected for the dining area are important to the efficient use of the space allowed.

Space for Production Areas

The space estimates for production areas include room for all the functional areas, such as receiving, storage, preparation, cooking, and warewashing, that are required to produce the menu items. Facilities that will be processing primarily fresh items should use he higher space estimates. This allows for the additional equipment and worker space needed. The smaller figures are used for operations using preprocessed foods and require minimal production space. A suggested percentage breakdown of the production space for general table service operations is shown in Table 2.

Table 2. Estimated production space for foodservice facilities

Type of facility	Space per seat (ft^2)	(m^2)
Table service	8-12	0.74-1.11
Counter service	4-6	0.37-0.56
Booth service	6-10	0.56-0.93
Cafeteria service	8-12	0.74-1.11

Determination of Space

The problem of determining space requirements is to calculate the space needed for each of the functional areas separately. This is done by identifying and determining the pertinent variables involved for the different functional areas. It is assumed at this point that the individual workplaces and pieces of equipment for the facility have been determined and will now be grouped together.

The space required for the flow of materials and workers between the workplaces and pieces of equipment is added as needed to develop the space to allow for each function. Some of the functional areas and the variables affecting their space requirements will be given to illustrate this procedure. Computational examples are presented as applicable. Consideration of the traffic aisles is one of the common variables for all areas and is therefore included.

Traffic Aisles

Traffic aisles are used for the movement of materials and workers, and should not be confused with work aisles that provide floor space for the worker to perform the task. The primary purpose of traffic aisles is to allow easy movement between workplaces, equipment, and functional areas. Since traffic aisles are not productive space, they should be kept at a minimum both in numbers and size. In general, work aisles and traffic aisles should be separated as much as possible. This can usually be accomplished by locating traffic aisles perpendicular to the work aisles.

In some instances, combined work and traffic aisles may be used if the traffic is light and if they offer a better solution to the design problem. Traffic aisles that serve two or more functional areas will minimise the amount of space required. Placement of traffic aisles along walls and other perimeter locations is not desirable for the same reason. The width of traffic aisles is dependent upon the type of traffic to be accommodated. If it consists of only people who are not carrying anything, a minimum aisle width of 30 in. (762 mm) will allow persons to pass without difficulty.

For workers who will be carrying containers and materials or pushing mobile carts and trucks an aisle width of 24 in. (610 mm) plus the width of the container or material carried or the mobile cart width will allow enough space. For example, if one worker has to pass another worker pushing a 20-in. (508 mm) wide cart, an aisle width of 44 in. (1118 mm) (24 plus 20) would be needed. The traffic aisle widths required for special types of movement such as carrying large trays have to be sized accordingly. In those instances where a combined work and traffic aisle is needed, a minimum of 42 in. (1067 mm) is required to allow one person to pass another person at the workplace. Aisles where there are persons working in a back-to-back arrangement have to be a mimimum of 48 in. (1219 mm) wide to allow passage of people between them. An important point to remember is that the less movement required to operate the facility, the less aisle space is needed.

Space for Receiving Area

The main variables affecting the amount of space needed for the receiving function are the number, type, and size of deliveries that are to be handled at one time. Many operations can have deliveries scheduled so they will have to handle only one delivery at a time. The types of materials to be received are considered because of the variety of containers and packaging methods available. Ease of opening, checking, moving, and stackability all have a bearing on the space required. The size of deliveries to be handled may depend on the storage space available in the facility, and is determined in conjunction with storage space requirements. Storage space in turn can be modified by the frequency of deliveries. A greater frequency of deliveries can reduce the size requirements of the receiving area as well. Therefore, storage space and receiving space requirements should be determined together after these factors have been evaluated.

Space for Storage Areas

The amount of dry, refrigerator, and freezer space required for the facility is determined by the number of days of storage to be provided for. A general recommendation for dry storage of foods is to provide space for 2-4 weeks supply, depending on the availability of the food items. The total volume of goods to be stored can be estimated as follows. First determine the number of meals for which storage is to be provided. An operation planning on serving 600 meals per day and desiring a two weeks supply will need storage for 8400 (600 meals per day $\times$ 14 days) meals. Next, estimate the weight per meal of items that will be stored in the dry storage area. This calls for an evaluation of all menu items.

A general estimate between l/4 and 1/2 lb (0.113 and 0.227 kg) per meal may be used; it is based on a total weight estimate per average meal of 1-11/2 lb (0.454-0.680 kg). These figures are for full meals and adjustments for partial meals have to be made. If an estimate of 1/2 lb (0.227 kg) per meal is used, then the total weight to provide storage for is 4200 lb (1905 kg) (8400 meals $\times$ 0.5 lb per meal).

Then the total weight computed is divided by an average density of 45 lb per ft^3 (721 kg per m^3), which will give the total volume of goods to be stored. In this example, the total volume in cubic feet is 4200 lb = 45 lb/ft^3 = 93.3. This indicates that space for 93.3 cubic ft (2.64 m^3) of goods, exclusive of aisle space, will be needed. If the goods are to be stored on shelves, the total square footage of shelving can be computed by considering the height to which the materials can be stored on the shelf. If the materials can be stored to a height of 1 ft, then 93.3 (93.3 ft^3 = 1 foot) ft^2 (8.67 m^2) of shelving will be needed. If a height of 11/2 ft (0.457 m) can be used, then 62.2 (93.3 =1.5) ft^2 (5.78 m^2) of shelving is required. The length of shelving is computed by dividing the square feet by the width of shelving to be used.

This same method of computation can be used for the refrigerator and freezer storage areas. The weight per meal of items that will be stored in the refrigerators and freezers will vary between 0.75 and 1 lb (0.340 and 0.454 kg). The average density of refrigerator items can be assumed to be 30 lb/ft^3 (481 kg/m^3). Items that will be stored in freezers can be assumed to have a density of 40 lb/ft^3 (641 kg/m^3).

The number of days of storage for refrigerator items may vary from one day to a week or more, depending on the method of operation used for the facility. Freezer items can be stored for longer periods of time and are determined by the frequency of deliveries available. An economic lot size analysis may be made to determine the optimum size of storage to provide.

The analysis compares ordering, purchasing, and receiving costs to the cost of the storage.

Space for Serving Areas

Serving areas for most table service facilities are planned as a part of the main cooking area and separate space determinations are not usually needed. Additional serving stations for table service can be considered in computations for the dining area. Cafeteria operations require separate space for the serving function to allow room for the serving counter, room for guests, and room for servers.

Variables affecting the size of the serving area are the number of people to be served and the serving time allowed. Serving line rates vary from 2 to 10 persons per minute for straight-line cafeteria counters. The serving line rate is dependent on the number of choices and the number of servers. Shopping-center counter arrangements can handle up to 20 or more persons per minute. The length of cafeteria counters is determined by the variety and volume of food items to be displayed.

The space required for straight-line counters may be roughly estimated at 10-15 ft^2 (0.929-1.39 m^2) of floor space for each linear foot (0.305 m) of counter. This provides room for the counters, customer aisles, room for servers, and back-bar equipment. Shopping-center arrangements generally require 18-20 ft^2 (1.67-1.86 m^2) of floor area for each linear foot (0.305 m) of counter.

The sizing of serving facilities for cafeterias is directly related to the capacity of the dining area. Ideal design results when the flow of people from the serving facility is balanced with the seating available in the dining room. At equilibrium conditions, the flow rate of people leaving the serving areas and entering the dining area should equal the flow rate of people leaving the dining area. In other words, the number of seats provided in the dining area has a direct relationship to the rate of people leaving the serving line for a given average eating time.

For example, the maximum serving rate for a given type of serving area design can be estimated with a fair degree of accuracy if the variables affecting the serving rate are known. Another characteristic that is easily established for cafeterias is the average dining time for various types of customers or patrons. Although cafeterias may operate at different capacities during a meal period, a model can be developed to describe the peak period of operation since this is the most critical period for efficient design.

Layout of Food Service Facilities

The layout process described in two separate stages that occur at the same time. One stage deals with the arrangement of individual pieces of equipment, work tables, and sinks into a unit which comprise a functional area or a functional department. The term department is sometimes associated with separate rooms, but this is not necessarily the case with food service operations. In essence, the designer is developing an area where related functions will be performed and may include as many or as few functions as deemed appropriate for the project. To illustrate, one particular area may be developed for the functions of dessert preparation, salad preparation, and sandwich preparation, whereas another project may require three separate areas for these functions.

The second stage of the layout process involves arranging the functional areas or departments into the total facility. For example, the receiving, storage, preparation, production, and warewashing areas and the nonproduction areas, such as rest rooms, lounges, and offices, are brought together to form the basic floor plan for the facility. There may be some question as to whether these two stages of layout are done at the same time. Even though the planner may be working on one stage or the other at any given moment, layout decisions must be considered in terms of both stages.

In essence, the layout of the total facility must be considered when laying out the component areas; and in turn, the layout of the component areas must be considered when laying out the total facility. The layout phase of planning is critical because it integrates most of the factors that affect the food service facility when it is operational.

Flow of Variables

The planning of individual workplaces is followed by a logical grouping of several workplaces to develop work centers and departnents. The combining of workplaces including tables, sinks, and equipment is guided by different concepts of flow. The criteria involved may include employee flow, material or product flow, customer flow, or in some cases, combinations of these. For example, the layout of a short-order cooking area to be staffed by one employee is best done by evaluating the employee's movements. This can be done by determining the frequency of movements anticipated between pairs of equipment and then placing the pairs of equipment that involve the greatest frequency of movement next to one another in the equipment arrangement.

This analysis leads to arrangements that will minimise employee movement and leads to increased productivity. In some instances it may be possible to place equipment in the same vertical plane to completely eliminate employee movements. The use of salamanders above a range or a microwave oven above a work table are examples of this concept. Consideration of combined or multipurpose equipment where appropriate is warranted. The planning of a large dishwashing area to include a continuous dishwashing machine and where employees are primarily working in fixed areas such as the scrapping table, loading the dishwasher, or unloading the dishwasher may be guided by evaluating material flow.

In some situations, the flow of two or more variables may be evaluated to determine the best layout. A salad preparation area may require evaluation of both the flow of foods and the movements of employees in order to arrive at the best layout. In most cases, arrangements that minimise the flow of materials are also those that minimise the movements of employees. This is likely when the materials are moved primarily by workers, but may not be the case if mechanical conveyors are used. If there is any doubt, both flows should be evaluated. Regardless of the type of flow selected as the criterion for layout, the following principles can be applied:

— Flow should be along straight-line paths as much as possible.

— The amount of cross flow or cross traffic should be minimised.

— Backtracking should be minimised.

— Bypassing should be minimised.

These principles of flow, whether applied to the movement of materials or of people, can be used for all types of layout problems. The concept of keeping flow in a straight line is the most important because it results in movements over the shortest distance. To utilise this concept, the designer will visualise or chart the flow involved with several different arrangements and select the one that gives the best straightline pattern. Flow analyses for layout problems involving only a few pieces of equipment are easy to do. Layout problems involving numerous pieces of equipment or areas will require more extensive flow analysis.

Some planners find flow diagrams or string charts a helpful tool in evaluating complex flow patterns. With the great variety of materials and activities found in food service operations, the concept of minimising cross traffic is important because it results in layouts that are free of bottlenecks and congestion. This concept is especially pertinent to fast-food operations, which have peak periods of flow. Cross traffic is minimised by the proper location of aisles, passageways, and doors. Some cross traffic can be tolerated if it results in shorter flow patterns.

However, if the cross traffic creates a hazardous situation, it should be eliminated, even at the cost of increased distance of movement. Cross traffic between employees and guests is undesirable and should be eliminated. Backtracking occurs when a material or person moves from one piece of equipment or an area back to the point where the movement originated. The flow is back along the same path that was just traversed. Of course, many of the tasks required in food service operations involve a sequence of movements that make it practically impossible to eliminate all backtracking. Many of the cooking and production tasks are of this nature. In those situations, minimising the amount of backtracking is all that can be done. This involves evaluating several different equipment or space arrangements to find the best one.

Bypassing is the result of a material or person passing one or more pieces of equipment to get to the next piece of equipment required in the sequence of movements. Several different arrangements of the equipment or areas may have to be evaluated to determine which one results in the least amount of bypassing. As with cross traffic, it is impossible to eliminate all bypassing except in the very simplest of layout problems. The ultimate goal of layout is to develop arrangements of equipment and spaces for the food facility that have primarily straight-line flow paths with a minimum of cross traffic, backtracking, and bypassing.

Layout Decisions

Although flow has been identified as the most important criterion of layout, other modifying considerations which may affect some layout decisions should be evaluated before the arrangement is finalised. These include the following items:

— *Efficient use of utilities.* All equipment requiring steam, for example, may be placed together to economise on installation and operating costs.

— *Efficient use of equipment*. Some individual pieces of equipment that will be used in two or more functional areas can be placed in central locations so they are easily accessible.

— Efficient use of skilled labour. This requires arrangements of equipment that will minimise the movements of skilled personnel. This may increase the movements of other employees or increase the movement of materials. The decision may be based on an economic analysis of different arrangements.

— *Safety*. Some layouts based on the concepts of flow alone may result in an arrangement of equipment that is hazardous. Placing a deep-fat fryer next to a sink creates a dangerous situation, and safety should override flow in this case. Other hazardous arrangements may result when high-temperature equipment is placed adjacent to a traffic aisle or near entrances and exits. If another location is not feasible, sufficient guarding and shielding of the equipment is an alternative solution.

— *Efficient use of space*. Building configurations and shapes may require rearrangement of some layouts to make full use of available space.

— *Environmental factors of noise and odor*. Some pieces of equipment or areas may be isolated from flow paths if they are objectionable and cannot be modified to render them environmentally acceptable. Garbage-can washers or incinerators illustrate this situation.

These modifying criteria may result in arrangements that are more expensive than those based on flow alone. They have to be used, however, to achieve many of the objectives of planning that were identified.

Arrangement of Equipment and Workplaces

The arrangement of equipment and workplaces for functional areas is usually in the form of a straight line or in combinations and modifications of straight-line configurations. The basic patterns that may be used include:

Single Straight-line Arrangement

This is the simplest of designs, but it is limited in the number of pieces of equipment or workplaces that can be arranged. The straight-line arrangement may be placed along a wall or take the form of an island.

Ell-shaped Arrangement

This is a modification of the straight-line arrangement to accommodate more equipment and workplaces; it is sometimes used where linear space is limited. The ell-shaped configuration is very suitable for separating two major groups of equipment. One group of equipment would be placed on one leg of the ell, the other group forming the second leg.

U-shaped Arrangements

The U-shaped configuration is ideal for small areas where only one or two employees are working. One disadvantage of this configuration is that straight-line flow through the area is not possible.

Parallel, Back-to-back Arrangement

This configuration is an arrangement of two parallel lines where the backs of the equipment and/or workplaces on each line are adjacent to each other. This arrangement centralises the utility lines required for equipment.

Sometimes a short wall is placed between the two rows of equipment, in which case provision for cleaning and maintenance has to be allowed. Parallel, back-to-back arrangement of cooking equipment that must be vented is ideal because a single canopy hood can be used. The separation of major groups of equipment is easily accomplished with this configuration.

Parallel, Face-to-face Arrangement

This arrangement utilises two straight lines of equipment and workplaces where the fronts face each other and are separated by an aisle space. This is a very common configuration that can be used in many areas of the facility. A variation of this configuration is obtained by arranging a straight line of worktables between the two rows of equipment. The parallel, face-to-face arrangement requires two separate utility lines for equipment, as compared to the single utility line used in the parallel, back-to-back arrangement.

Modifications of any of these configurations can be used to handle special cases and problems. Tee-shaped, open-square, or other configurations should be used if they result in the best solution to the layout problem. Curved or circular configurations are sometimes used, but they should be planned very carefully to fit straight-line configurations that may be used in the facility. Circular serving islands for shopping-centre cafeterias and curved cafeteria counters are examples of these configurations.

The final arrangement for most facilities is usually composed of a combination of configurations of equipment and workplaces. Only the smallest of operations would use a single configuration for the layout of the facility.

The consideration of flow patterns in conjunction with other criteria that may affect a layout may be evaluated by a relationship chart following the desired degree of closeness between pieces of equipment or areas. A relationship chart is made by listing all the items or areas to be arranged for a given facility. Closeness ratings for all pairs of trays are identified in the relationship chart. These ratings are based In any number of factors including flow, efficient use of equipment, efficient use of utilities, use of labour, safety, and even the personal references of the planner. In the majority of the cases flow will still be the primary basis for the closeness ratings. Closeness ratings may be expressed by a numerical scale as shown text. The ratings are used to express the desired closeness for the final arrangement of the areas.

The usefulness of the relationship chart is dependent upon the planners' awareness of the need to compromise. Indicating that all areas of a facility have to be close to all other areas negates the purpose of the relationship chart. It is important to note that other types of food service facilities may have a greater or fewer number of areas listed on the left side of the chart. In some cases areas may be combined as illustrated by this facility that will utilise one area for both salad and vegetable preparation.

In other instances, additional areas may be designated as occurs when a separate take-out area is to be planned for in addition to the regular service area. Thus each different project to be planned requires a different relationship chart depending on the defined areas to be considered. If the exact or approximate size and shape of each area including aisle spaces are known, a preliminary schematic can be developed from the relationship chart ratings. The relationship chart does not necessarily lead to just one layout of areas but may result in several alternative layouts.

Basic Guidings for Layout

The concepts of flow along with the modifying considerations give the planner the basic guides for laying out the facility. It is not possible to discuss the layout of all areas for all types of food facilities, but general guides to the arrangement of some areas common to most facilities will be given. Overall design of the facility is usually based on the flow of major food items. Since most food items are received and then stored before preparation, the dry, refrigerated, and freezer storage areas should be adjacent to receiving areas and also be readily accessible to the various preparation areas.

The main cooking area is so located as to receive the flow from the preparation areas and have an outlet directly the serving area. The salad and sandwich preparation areas may so placed that their flow of foods is directly into the serving area. Placement of the dining area adjacent to the serving area is obvious. The flow of nonfood items is next evaluated to locate other areas. The flow of dinnerware in a repetitive route from serving areas to tying areas and then back to serving areas requires the dishwashing area to be adjacent to both. Similarly, the flow of utensils dictates Being the pot- and pan-washing section near the main cooking, baking, and serving areas.

Design of Storage Area

Layout of storage areas is based on convenience and accessibility. Arrangements that allow heavy and bulky materials to be moved title and as easily as possible are preferred. Central storage facilities with several satellite locations are good arrangements for many types of facilities. The storage space in the preparation, processing, and other functional areas should be planned so they do not interfere with efficient work methods. The use of combination walk-in and each-in storage units may increase the convenience of these areas. It is best to plan walk-in storage areas in a manner which keeps the products at least 8 in. (203 mm) above the floor to facilitate cleaning.

An alternative would be to use mobile bins and containers that can be easily moved when the area is cleaned. Storage areas for non-food supplies may be located in the various functional areas as required. Storage space for china, glass, and silverware may be provided in serving or dining areas. Linen and paper goods used for service are also stored in or near these areas.

Design of Cooking Area

Laying out the main cooking area is the key to fast and efficient production of foods. The flow patterns affecting this area include inflow of foods from storage and preparation areas and utensils from the pot- and pan-washing area. Outflow of foods to the serving, salad preparation, and sandwich preparation areas is common. The cooking equipment should be arranged so that the most frequently used pieces ire close to the pick-up location. Other factors related to the design of the main cooking area include the following:

- All heat- and moisture-producing equipment, such as fryers, broilers, griddles, ranges, and steamers, should be placed under ventilating hoods or be equipped with individual venting systems.
- Steam cooking equipment requires special installation including depressed floors, or the use of curbs.
- Some types of equipment require air for ventilation or cooling of enclosed spaces; vents and grill openings should not be blocked by other pieces of equipment.
- Provision has to be made to permit venting of fuel-burning equipment directly to the outside.
- Location of the main building ventilation or air-conditioning inlets is important to effect adequate cooling of the air without cooling the cooking equipment or interfering with the equipment venting system.
- If remote banquet rooms are to be served, methods of transporting hot foods and appropriate space for loading have to be considered.
- The use of partially or fully preprocessed foods will increase the need for refrigerated space in the cooking areas.

Flexibility and efficient use of employees and equipment can be obtained in some operations where similar equipment is involved in baking and cooking. In this case the baking and cooking areas are placed in close proximity so that kettles, ovens, and mixers can serve both areas. This may even result in reduced exhaust requirements. Placing the baking and cooking areas adjacent to each other also guides the placement of the pot-washing area since these two areas generate the bulk of the soiled pots.

The layout of preparation areas is fairly easy because most of the functions performed in them follow a logical sequence, and thus the equipment is arranged in the same sequence. Vegetable preparation, for example, basically involves trimming, washing, and size reduction, in that order. A straight-line arrangement of a work table for trimming, a sink for washing and draining, and equipment for size reduction becomes the layout for the area.

Since the inflow of vegetables is from storage areas, the trimming table is placed close to them; consequently, the size-reduction equipment is placed near the main cooking and salad preparation areas. Provision for temporary storage of materials and removal of waste will complete the layout of the vegetable preparation area for a small facility.

Salad preparation areas are planned in a similar manner. The foods should flow in a continuous path from the start of the preparation tasks, through the various workplaces and equipment, which are arranged in the order of the steps required, and on to the serving area. Operations that prepare a large number of the same or very similar salads may be designed by the concepts of mass assembly.

Design of Baking Areas

The volume and variety of baked items that will be produced in a particular food service operation determines the layout to be used. Operations that produce a minimum number of items such as pastries and desserts can combine the baking area with the cooking area. Employees' work shifts may be scheduled to avoid problems of equipment usage. Operations that will be involved in the production of a moderate amount of baked goods frequently locate the baking area adjacent to the cooking area so some equipment can be shared. Food service operations that will produce the full line of baked items including breads, rolls, pastries, or even speciality items may need a separate baking area in order to minimise interference between the cooking and baking functions.

The design of baking area layouts should follow the typical processing steps to assure a smooth work flow. For example, a proof box located near the ovens simplifies the loading of items into the ovens. Similarly, a landing table placed near the ovens simplifies unloading. Baker's tables are centrally located with easy access to storage areas, mixers, and kettles, as well as the proof box and ovens. Sufficient space is provided for mixing, cutting, panning, rolling, and finishing the baked items. Storage space for baking supplies, utensils, and tools that are frequently used are best located at the work centers. Provision for storage of the finished baked items might take the form of mobile units for easy movement to the serving or pick-up areas. Another possibility would be to use pass-through storage units between the baking and serving areas. Special requirements such as the freezing and storage of some baked items are considered so that space for freezers is provided either in or near the baking areas. Refrigerators are required for the storage of highly perishable items such as custard-filled or whipped cream desserts.

Design of Serving Space

The layout of serving areas is based on the method and speed of service desired. Serving equipment should be arranged in the order of use, and should be located so they are easily accessible to serving personnel.

Table Service

Hot food pick-up areas are located adjacent to the main cooking battery. Provisions for maintaining the temperature of hot foods at pick-up areas should be considered. Additional serving stations or pantries for salads, desserts, rolls, and beverages are located nearer the dining area to avoid congestion. Linen, flatware, water, and butter used for setups are best placed in inconspicuous areas of the dining room. These stations may also include facilities for depositing soiled linen and tableware.

Counter Service

Most of the cooking and serving facilities in typical counter-service operations occur at the back bar opposite the dining counter. A common layout is to have a straight-line back bar with straight-line or a series of U-shaped dining counters. Some operations offering a more extensive menu may require additional preparation and cooking facilities that can be located in a separate area. An efficient layout in this case is to have the pick-up counter as a part of the back bar. This is also a good arrangement for operations having both counter and table-service sections. The pick-up area should be located for easy access to the table servers.

Cafeteria Service

Cafeteria counters are placed as close to the production areas as possible with due regard to the free flow of customers or users. The layout of cafeteria counters is based on the shape of the serving area and the anticipated traffic patterns. Counters may be arranged in a straight line, ell-shaped, U-shaped, hollow square, or combinations of these configurations, as dictated by the length of counter required. The design of the counter should allow displayed foods that are usually selected in combination to be placed together on the counter.

Merchandising concepts call for desserts and salads to be located at the beginning of the line; hot foods should be at the end of the line to minimise cooling. Special care is needed in providing for cashiering, since this is one of the bottleneck areas in commercial cafeterias. The entire design of the cafeteria service system is based on volume flow, and anything that will speed service should be incorporated into the layout. Silver, napkins, water, and condiments may be located in stations away from the main counter area.

Islands placed between the serving and dining areas are frequently used for this purpose. Self-dispensing equipment for beverages will also help speed the flow of people. Cook-to-order items cause delays and are best located in a separate area where patrons can pull out of the main stream of flow to wait for their orders. This can be easily accomplished with the open square arrangement of counters.

The layout of dishwashing areas should follow the sequence of operations performed in washing. The arrangement has to provide for sorting, scraping or preflushing, and stacking, prior to loading the dishwashing machine. If glasses and silverware are to be washed separately, provisions for these operations have to be planned. Preflushing of soiled dishes may be accomplished in one of two ways. One method is to use a continuous flow of water over the dishes as they are being scraped. A disposal unit is used to handle the food wastes. The other method uses an overhead spray and is suitable for dishes that are placed in dish racks. In either case, the soiled-dish table has to be designed so that water is quickly drained away. Raised edges on the table help prevent excess water spillage.

Regardless of the type of dishwashing machine used, space for loading and unloading must be arranged. Rack-type machines are frequently loaded in a straight-line flow from the soiled-dish table. Rackless or peg-type machines require space for the loader to handle the individual pieces of dinnerware. Clean-dish areas are arranged so adequate drying time is allowed before the removal and stacking of dinnerware takes place.

The flow of dinnerware through the dishwashing area is planned to be continuous and over the shortest possible distance. The layout of other areas for the food facility should be accomplished in the same manner as given in the above examples. When all the preceding steps of the planning process are satisfactorily completed, the layout step becomes fairly easy.

Designing the Food Service Atmosphere

The concept of atmosphere may be physical aspects such as unusual location, a spectacular view, the method of pouring a drink, or a combination of interior colours, fabrics, spaces and textures, as well as such nonphysical aspects as the attitude of service personnel as exhibited in courtesy, ability, pleasantness, and promptness. The architect, consultants, and designers can develop the physical components of the atmosphere, but it is up to management to provide and maintain its nonphysical components.

Every individual experiences some type of reaction to the atmosphere that may be desirable or undesirable. If the individual response to the foodservice facility is favourable, the atmosphere has served to put that person into a good mood. Atmosphere has been identified as one of the inducements for people to dine out. Many people like to be in different surroundings to joy the dining experience. In addition to good food and courteous service, the diner is looking for a restaurant that offers luxury or excitement, or at least something pleasant. If customers experience a desirable dining atmosphere, they are more likely to come back because they remember that experience.

Atmosphere is one of the prime generators of repeat business and is an important aspect in the successful planning of foodservice facilities. In the highly competitive commercial restaurant field, the planning of the atmosphere for new facilities is going to be more important. The coming generation of potential customers is growing up in an environment that associates dining out with more than just good food. They will be expecting to experience a variety of feelings, and these feelings will be a direct result of the atmosphere. The planning of atmosphere may well include specialised audiovisual equipment and other electronic devices to help create a particular mood.

Many factors have to be taken into account when planning the atmosphere for a food facility, and they must be considered in light of the clientele who constitute the market. Just as food choice is a matter of individual preference, social custom, income level, needs of time, and so on, the individual's choice of atmosphere is related to many of these same factors. People from varying backgrounds and engaged in different activities will seek out different dining atmospheres. The atmosphere has to be planned to appeal to the particular segment of the market that the foodservice facility wishes to attract. A well-planned restaurant is characterised by both the right menu offerings and the right atmosphere. The most efficiently planned production areas are of little use if there are no customers to serve.

The foodservice industry continues to be more and more competitive, and the integration of marketing concepts into the creation of the atmosphere is desirable from the standpoint of increasing sales. One approach to this integration is to use attractive displays of food and beverages in the dining areas or lobby and lounge areas. Displays of wines, salads, desserts, or baked goods lend to the creation of a pleasing dining atmosphere as well as help increase the sales of these items. The use of salad bars, dessert carts, carving carts, and refrigerated display cases are some of the methods used to accomplish this integration. Among other things, the atmosphere to be developed for a food facility should attract attention, be pleasing to the eyes, and provide an interesting change of pace.

For example, an intimate, peaceful dining room provides welcome relief from noisy offices and industries. Likewise, a noisy cafeteria may actually be refreshing to students who are in quiet surroundings most of the day. The warmth and glow of a fireplace provides a welcome change in cold weather. The development of the physical and psychological aspects of the atmosphere depends in great part upon the planners selected to design the facility. They must have a clear understanding with the owner of the particular needs and goals to be accomplished in developing the atmosphere. In addition to knowledge of the functional operation of the facility, the planners should be keenly aware of the type of clientele to be attracted. Only then can they come up with a suitable design that will be attractive as well as functional. It is then up to management to develop the nonphysical aspects of the atmosphere to complete the total concept.

Comfort is one of the key considerations in atmosphere planning. If individuals do not feel comfortable in their surroundings, the atmosphere has not been properly designed. Comfort is created when individuals feel secure and at ease. Security may be psychologically imposed by the use of red and orange colours and by privacy, which can provided by booths and partitions. One way of sing dividers to create private areas in the dining room. Dining rooms which have an expensive look may create feelings of insecurity because individuals feel status-conscious in such surroundings. Atmosphere planning is dependent on an understanding of the perceptual awareness of individuals as sensed through sight, touch, caring, smell, temperature, and movement. The primary considerations of these perceptions as related to a dining experience are summarised as follows.

1. *Sight.* The perception of visual space involving lighting levels, colours, eye contact with fixtures and decorator items, and the use of mirrors and screens to expand or contract the visual space.
2. *Touch.* Perception of seat comfort, body contact, and contact with floor, tables, tableware, and upholstery fabrics.

3. *Hearing.* Perception of noise levels of conversation, kitchen sounds, Aside sounds, and music.
4. *Smell.* Perception of cooking aromas, body odors, and material odors from fabrics such as linen and leather.
5. *Temperature.* Perception of air temperature, relative humidity, Ay heat, cooking heat, radiant heat, and heat of cooked foods.
6. *Movement.* Perception of muscle activity required for access to tables and chairs, movement of servers and other customers, movement outside as viewed through windows.

It is important not to think of atmosphere as simply a combination of colours, lights, and spaces, but how the individual is affected by those factors. It is the perceptual concepts that should be kept in mind when developing atmosphere. To clarify the concept of perceptual environment, consider the matter of space. A person's perception of space is measured more in terms of freedom of movement than in terms of physical dimensions of feet and inches. A dining room one hundred feet long means very little to diners. If persons can walk across a smaller room without encountering obstacles, it will be perceptually large.

On the other hand, if they must make their way around closely faced tables and chairs, it will be perceptually smaller. This is due the feeling of crowding when their movements are restricted. Temperature works in much the same way. It is measured in terms of contrast rather than by degrees on a thermometer. An individual .just coming in from the cold will require less heat to perceive a feeling of warmth than someone who has been exposed to a heated room for a long time. The body heat of others is also an interrelated factor is how an individual perceives a crowded condition. Individuals who re in a cooler room may be seated closer together than those who re in a warmer room. A person's eyes are probably the most important yet deceptive tools of measurement in perceiving feelings. The structure of the eye exaggerates activity or movement that takes place on the periphery of vision. Consequently, individuals can be in an uncrowded room, yet feel as if it is crowded if there is a great deal of action or movement round them. When obstructions are used to block out the activity or movement on the periphery of their vision, they will perceive the area as uncrowded.

Thus, individuals measure the atmosphere with their senses and valuate it as desirable or undesirable. The atmosphere must be tanned so that the individual's perceptions result in a feeling of com-art, ease, and acceptability. With these concepts as a guide, the food facility planner should evaluate the many physical components of atmosphere that can be manipulated and arrive at a combination that ill give the desired sensations.

The following are the physical components that affect the perception of atmosphere:

1) Colours
2) Illumination
3) Noise
4) Ambient temperature, relative humidity, odors
5) Type of seating (tables, booths, counters)
6) Furnishings; floor and wall coverings, drapes
7) Table appointments; dishware, silverware, napkins
8) Shape and size of rooms
9) Layout of tables
10) Appearance and dress of employees
11) Menu design
12) Sanitary conditions
13) Exterior design
14) Landscaping
15) Age and dress of customers

Colour

This is one of the visual aspects of the atmosphere as perceived by individuals; it is also one of the best tools that planners have to create a variety of moods. Most people make a number of choices based on colour; they select their clothes, cars, houses, paints, and even foods by colour. Colour can be used to induce a feeling of happiness, to promote serenity, or to stimulate hunger. It can attract people to one type of dining room and drive them out of others. Certain colours are especially important to the development of dining areas.

Many experiments have shown that certain colours have a very strong emotional effect on most individuals. It is known that blue reduces excitability and therefore helps one to relax. Blue is also considered to be cooling and is "easy" on the eyes. Green is a colour that acts as a sedative. Yellow, on the other hand, is cheery, stimulating, and attention-drawing. On dull, sunless days, people exhibit mental and physical sluggishness which is partially attributed to the absence of yellow, red, and other stimulating colours. Red is associated with excitement and violence. Gray suggests coldness and is very depressing unless it is combined with livelier colours. Colour sensations can sometimes produce physical reactions that are not just of the visual system but affect the entire body. For example, persons exposed to predominately red colours exhibit increased blood pressure, quickened muscular reactions, and greater emotions.

Red also tends to produce restlessness and makes time seem to pass very slowly. In comparison, persons exposed to predominately blue and green colours have been found to exhibit slower muscle response and quicker mental and conversational response. Blues and greens also make time seem to go faster. Some of the common emotional responses caused by exposure to various colours. These may be used to develop the type of response desired in various areas of the food facility. The colours have to be predominant in an area and individuals must be exposed to them for a period of time.

The strong effect colours may have on individuals, care should be taken in selecting them to achieve the desired result. One if the aspects of good colour planning deals with contrast. A single predominant colour, no matter how pleasing, cannot function alone. A restful green that is predominant would strain the part of the eye susceptible to it and eventually lead to eye and body fatigue. With a single predominant colour individuals would have to look harder to distinguish objects because of the lack of contrast. Extreme contrast between very light and dark colours is also undesirable since they too result in eyestrain. Achieving the right amount of contrast along with maintaining the desired emotional responses is necessary to the creation of a pleasing environment for dining.

Red, yellow, and blue are the primary colours. They are referred to is primaries because other colours are derived from them. In their pure form the primary colours are too strong to use on large areas and therefore are used as accents. The secondary colours are green, orange, and violet and are mixtures of two of the primary colours. Green is obtained by mixing blue and fellow, orange by mixing red and yellow, and violet by mixing red and blue. Mixtures of primary colours and secondary colours result in the intermediate colours. Examples of intermediates are red-orange, yellow-green, and blue-violet.

Colours are also classified as warm or cool. Red, orange, and yellow are the warm colours; they seem to advance and convey a feeling of warmth. The cool colours are blue, green, and violet; these are retracting colours and are cooling and relaxing. A combination of one warm colour and one cool colour results in the complementary colours used in colour planning.

The problem of selecting colours that go well together or harmonise is solved by using one of five rules. These rules are related to harmonies and are identified as monochromatic, analogous, complementary, split complementary, and triad. Monochromatic harmony uses a single colour and is the simplest of colour schemes. The single colour can be expressed in the following ways.

- As the pure colour itself
- As a tint of the pure colour (a tint is the pure colour mixed with white) is a shade of the pure colour (a shade is the pure colour mixed with black)
- As a tone of the pure colour (a tone is the pure colour mixed with both black and white).
- Analogous harmony is obtained by using any three or four consecutive colours on the colour wheel. Examples of analogous harmony are red-orange, orange, and yellow-orange; or red, red-orange, orange, and Glow-orange.
- Complementary harmony results by using any two colours that are directly opposite each other on the colour wheel. Red and green, red-orange and blue-green, or yellow and violet are examples of complementary harmony.
- Split complementary or near complementary harmony involves three colours. Any one of the two complementary colours and two colours adjacent to the omitted complementary colour are used. On the colour wheel, the split complementaries are in the form of a Y. Examples of split complementary colours are yellow, blue-violet, and red-violet; green, red-orange, and red-violet; and red, blue-green, and yellow-green.
- Triad harmony also involves three colours. These are selected by king every fourth colour on the colour wheel. Two examples of triads are red, yellow, and blue; and yellow-orange, red-violet, and blue-green.

— After a particular harmony is selected, then a decision regarding the tints, shades, or tones of the colours is made. One or two of the colours selected will be used for the walls and other major surfaces. The other colours will be used as accents on smaller objects like drapes, table cloths, and dinnerware.

The important points in colour selection are as follows:

— Pure colours are usually too strong and brilliant when applied to large areas or surfaces.

— Colours should be selected under the kind of lighting that they will be used under. Colours selected under fluorescent lighting will appear different under incandescent lighting.

— Colours selected from a small sample will appear brighter when applied to large areas.

— Complementary, split complementary, and triad harmonies always result in a combination of warm and cool colours. The desired atmosphere will dictate which colour is to predominate.

— Black, white, brown, and gold usually go well with any of the colour harmonies.

— Texture is closely related to colour application and usage is best considered at the same time the colour choices are made.

As light modifies colours in many ways, the type of light source and systems of lighting should be considered when selecting colours. Pink lights, for example, have been shown to pale lipstick colours. Green lights have a tendency to show up wrinkles and should not be used in an atmosphere where a feeling of well-being is to be created. Another problem is the use of amber lights which tend to wash out colours. A well-chosen colour scheme can be easily spoiled by poorly selected lights. Lights and colours for work areas are quite different from those desirable for dining areas and should be planned separately.

The uses of colour in foodservice facilities are so numerous that space will not allow a complete presentation of all of them. Therefore, a guide to the uses of colour is presented below. Note that many of the uses of colour are related to other factors that affect an individual's perception of atmosphere.

1) The use of warm reds, browns, yellows, golds, and oranges enhances the appearance of foods.

2) Where emphasis is to be placed on fast service and high turnover, warm colours should dominate the major areas.
3) Use colours in dining areas that are flattering to people. Colours that tend to make people look pale (green and grey) should be avoided.
4) Use light colours in small areas to create the impression of size.
5) Use warm colours in rooms that are windowless.
6) High ceilings can be made to appear lower by using dark colours.
7) Emphasising horizontal lines by dark colours will make a ceiling appear lower.
8) Low ceilings can be overcome by emphasising vertical lines with dark colours.
9) The end walls of long narrow rooms should be a warmer or deeper hue than the other walls to make them approach and make the room seem squarer.
10) Undesirable features of a room can be painted the same colour as their background so as not to emphasise them.
11) Each room or area should have a mixture of warm and cool colours.
12) Adjoining rooms or areas are best painted in harmonious colours.
13) Avoid using too many different colours in one room or area.
14) Use light colours to make objects appear larger if they are to be emphasised.
15) Use dark colours to make rooms appear smaller.
16) Use brilliant colours to bring attention to signs or other features.
17) Dark-coloured objects appear to be smaller than they really are.
18) Maintain proper contrast to permit differentiation of objects from their backgrounds.
(19) Avoid highly reflective colours that tend to tire the eyes.

The selection of colours is a very difficult task that requires skill, taste, and experience. Colour scheming does not end with the blending of wall colours with upholstery, fabrics, and carpets, but includes the considerations of menus, dinnerware, uniforms, and even the type of decorations. Just as the right colours can be used to make a food facility more attractive, the wrong colours can focus attention on features that should not be accented. Also, since colour is so influenced by fashion and trend, these factors must be considered in the colour scheme chosen.

Lighting

As with colour, proper planning of lights can achieve dramatic effects and aid in the creation of the desired atmosphere. Both sexes enjoy a type of lighting that makes them look their best. This factor is of great importance in the planning and design of lights for dining areas, bars, rest rooms, and other public spaces. The best system of lighting for restaurants appears to be a combination of indirect, direct, and spot lights. These lights can be arranged to accomplish the desired flexibility required for the various meal periods. Areas should be well lit for breakfast and lunch, while less lighting is desired for evening meals. The installation of rheostats will provide this flexibility. In considering the lighting system, the amount of daylight entering an area should be considered. Total glass area can be specified by the architect to adjust for this factor. The use of tinted glass may be considered for some situations.

The ultimate type of lighting for dining areas has traditionally been considered to be candlelight. The reddish flame of candlelight is flattering to people and to most foods. The flickering of the flame adds to the creation of a desirable atmosphere. Alternatives to candlelight are incandescent and fluorescent lights. The economy of operation of fluorescent lights favours their installation in large areas. Incandescent lights would be the best choice in dining areas because of their red colour enhancement. Properly selected fluorescent lights may also be used in dining areas if sufficient red tones are used in the colour scheme. The deluxe warm white fluorescent tubes are the closest in colour tint to incandescent bulbs and would be recommended.

As with colour, lighting can do much toward creating atmosphere by correcting spacial deficiencies and accenting desirable areas. To illustrate, a low ceiling can be made to appear higher if it is well-lit; high ceilings will appear lower if they are dimly lit. Care should be taken not to light the long walls brightly in a narrow room since it will appear to be even narrower. Dark walls will show up better with bright lights, and if the colour is to be accented, the illumination level has to be high. Bright lights are placed above normal eye levels to minimise glare. The same concept applies to candles since they too can create glare. Candles may be placed in frosted globes if they are at eye level or slightly below.

In dining areas, it is best to concentrate illumination on the seats and tables and perhaps on special design features. The ceilings and walls should not be so brightly lit that they detract attention from the room. Bright lights may be used to create a brisk atmosphere which, if service is fast, results in a high turnover of customers. Serving areas, should be well-lighted. Some operations may use full lighting for a high turnover at lunch and then dim the lights for evening meals in hopes of attaining higher check averages.

Colourful Lights

Careful selection of coloured lights will enhance the total atmosphere. The first consideration is to coordinate the coloured lights with other coloured objects and colour schemes used in the room. This is important, since certain colours will take on strange off-colours when subjected to coloured lights. Red colours will appear very dark under blue or green lights and olive-green colours look brown under yellow lights. Coloured lights affect the appearance of the faces and clothes of people. Red lights have the advantage of flattering complexions and tend to enhance the colour of fabrics. Red lights also have a good effect on most foods.

Green and blue lights are undesirable for illuminating areas where people will be present. These lights tend to distort the red hues and are unflattering because of this. Green and blue lights may be used for inanimate objects that serve as accent pieces. The use of pink, ivory, or amber lights is suggested for areas where skin tone is important, as they are warm and impart a friendly and inviting feeling. It is better to use tints of colours rather than strong hues.

Lighting should not only provide atmosphere but should reach a satisfactory level of illumination from a practical standpoint. If the lighting level is too high, individuals will have a feeling of exposure; or if too dim, they may feel fearful. For these reasons, there should be enough light so persons can see, yet not so much that they feel uneasy. One method of attaining such an arrangement is to lower the height of ceiling fixtures. This provides a sufficient amount of light and at the same time results in a comfortable soft effect.

Foodservice lighting levels typically will range between 5 and 50 foot-candles (53.8-538 lux), with 30-50 foot-candles (323-538 lux) usually used for breakfast and lunch. A level of 5-30 foot-candles (53.8-323 lux), depending on the atmosphere desired, is used for evening meals. The lighting level in all areas must be sufficient to make the other elements of the atmosphere visible. It is senseless to spend a great deal of time and money creating a striking colour scheme and then ruin it with poor lighting. Any area with less than 5 foot-candles (53.8 lux) of illumination may as well be colourless.

In reality, the excitement of good lighting comes largely from its shadows and variations in brightness. Flat, shadowless lighting is dull and monotonous. The general lighting system for an area needs the accents of bright areas which come from direct light sources. These may take the form of wall brackets, chandeliers, downlights, or spot lights. Recessed ceiling downlights of low intensity are very satisfactory for lighting dining areas.

Sound

Aside from dinner music, sounds are to play a passive role and never attract attention. The design goal is to create a balance between quiet and noise. Many people are uncomfortable in a room which is very quiet. A noisy room creates tension and irritability. For dining rooms, a satisfactory acoustical environment has a reverberant sound level that is high enough to be heard, but not so high that individuals at nearby tables can distinguish what is being said. Correct planning for the acoustical environment contributes to the development of the desired atmosphere. The sensitivities of individuals to various sounds require control of undesirable noise and maintenance of desirable sounds at an acceptable level.

Sound may be considered to be a pressure wave and is compared to the ripples spreading out from a pebble dropped in water. If the sound is not restricted, it will spread out in all directions. The speed of sound in air is about 1100 feet per second (335 meters per second). Any sounds produced in open air will travel directly from the source to the listener. In a room, however, sound is reflected from the walls, floor, and ceiling and can build up a general sound level much greater than that which results from the same source in open space.

Sounds that are repeatedly reflected become noise or unwanted sounds. Noise at a high enough level causes irritation and fatigue. It can interfere with communication and concentration and become very distracting and disturbing. The intensity of sound is measured by the decibel. A sound intensity of one decibel is at the threshold of audibility for the normal human ear. A sound intensity of 20 decibels may be compared to a whisper.

The normal speaking voice has an intensity of about 60 decibels. Any sound intensities over 100 decibels for any length of time are undesirable, and constant exposure can cause partial loss of hearing. When there is a source of sound in a room, the level of noise at any position is made up of two parts. The first part is the direct sound travelling straight from the source to the position under consideration. The second part is the reverberant sound, which is the sound reaching the position after multiple reflection from the room surfaces.

The intensity of direct sound falls off as the distance from the source increases. Direct sound is reduced by about 6 decibels each time the distance from the source is doubled. Reverberant sound levels will generally be at a uniform intensity throughout the room. Direct sounds are predominant at positions close to the source, while reverberant sounds will dominate positions remote from the source.

Problem of Noise Controlling

The problem of controlling noise levels is basically a matter of suppressing the sounds from the source or reducing the amount of reverberant sounds. Sound-absorbing materials are used to minimise both types of sounds. In some instances, the source of the sounds can be isolated by coverings or baffles. Kitchen areas are very difficult to soundproof because of the materials used in the construction of the room and the large amount of metallic equipment present.

Hard, dense materials, like quarry tile or clay tile used for kitchen floors and tiled wall surfaces, reflect a large portion of the sound striking them. Stainless steel surfaces actually act as sound surfaces much like a drum. In these areas, it is desirable to increase the amount of sound-absorbing materials as much as possible to overcome the severe noise problem. Service doors leading to the kitchen can be vestibuled to reduce the noise level before reaching the dining room. This is a compromise between the additional square footage needed for the vestibule and the desirability of reduced noise levels. Thus a facility designed for professionals may include a vestibule while a facility to be designed for other segments of the market may not consider one.

The following things that can be done to minimise noise from the kitchen include the following:

1. Selecting mechanical equipment such as fans and compressors for quiet operation.
2. Using installation techniques that minimise duct noises, the sound of water flow, and water hammer.
3. Using silent closing devices on doors and drawers.
4. Providing rubber bumpers for mobile equipment.
5. Soundproofing walls between kitchen and dining areas.
6. Placing a service station between the entrance to the kitchen and the dining room.
7. Creating a quiet work environment to reduce employee noise.
8. Using the spread load dishwashing concept where an adequate inventory of china, silverware, and glassware are maintained to handle the entire meal period. Dishwashing begins after the meal period to clean the dinnerware for the next meal period. This concept has several ramifications in terms of soiled and clean dish storage requirements, dishwasher size, impact on employee scheduling, and the total size of the dishwashing area.

In addition to acoustical treatment of walls and ceilings, carpeting where permitted will also help. Local sanitarians should be consulted before specifying carpet for production areas. The sound-proofing of metal surfaces by undercoating will reduce the noise created. One method of handling noise problems in dining areas is to vary the spacing of tables. The distance between diners at one table should be appreciably less than the distance to diners at adjoining tables. If a greater density of seating is desired, the use of screens or partial partitions will reduce the sound levels.

Music

Music is a desirable sound is one way of enhancing the audible environment. Music has a direct effect on the mood of individuals. Background music should be selected so it does not attract attention. It should be soft, inoffensive, and as characterless as possible. The correct use of background music can put customers in a good mood for dining.

Climate

This is one of the important factors affecting the comfort of people. Most individuals are very sensitive to thermodynamic phenomena and variations from an ideal climate are easily noticed and quickly lead to discomfort. Customers will quickly respond to environmental conditions that are too hot, too cold, too drafty, too stuffy, or too damp. The ideal climate for dining consists of temperatures between 70 and 75°F (21.1 and 23.9°C) with a relative humidity of 50%. Thermodynamic comfort is a function of activity and other factors such as age, sex, and the amount of clothing worn. Needless to say, the climate should be designed for the particular type of patron that the facility is to be planned for. Higher-priced operations will usually attract people who are accustomed to slightly higher temperatures.

Women prefer higher temperatures than men, and children require less heat than both men and women. People who are in active occupations prefer lower temperatures. The amount of clothing worn during the different seasons reflects the needs of different temperatures. People will be wearing lighter clothing in the summer; therefore, slightly warmer than normal temperatures would be appreciated. Clothing worn in the winter is heavier and temperatures should not be allowed to get too high. The effects of colours and lighting are evaluated before a particular temperature level is decided upon.

Temperature can be used to some extent to affect a desired turnover of customers. Many fast-food operations may want lower temperatures to keep the customers on the move and thereby increase the turnover rate. The opposite is true in more luxurious dining rooms where turnover is not stressed. Customers are inclined to be more relaxed in a higher temperature, and the warmth is conducive to a leisurely meal of several courses. The ideal design is to have a system where the temperature can be precisely adjusted for the particular situation. Climate control in most regions requires both heating and air conditioning. The systems should have sufficient capacity to maintain the desired temperature and relative humidity.

Pleasant Odors

Climate control also includes the control of odors. Odors are an important part of the atmosphere, because smell usually evokes much deeper memories in individuals than either vision or sound. People are often uncomfortable in odor-free surroundings, and pleasant odors can contribute to the desired atmosphere. The popularity of display cooking areas in the dining room is partially caused by the cooking aromas that are emitted. Odors have to be controlled or they will blend and can become quite offensive. This is very noticeable in dining areas where the air circulation system may bring in varied kitchen odors. Mixing the odors of fish and steak, for example, is not at all appealing to the person eating the steak.

Odors are very disturbing to individuals when dining because taste is largely a matter of smell. If the odors cannot be controlled and separated, or if they are undesirable, they should not be allowed to seep into the dining room. One method of accomplishing this is to maintain the air pressure in the dining room at a higher level than the air pressure in the kitchen. Exhaust systems designed to rid the interiors of smoke, fumes, and odors should be positioned to avoid affecting the immediate exterior environment. This is especially important for exterior walks and entrances into the public areas.

Furnishings

Furnishings for the dining area are also correlated to the type of atmosphere to be planned. The first thing that an individual does upon entering a dining room is to look for a place to sit. Therefore, arrangement of tables, chairs, and auxiliary furnishings does much to affect the initial impression of customers. Many people do not like to sit at exposed tables because they feel observed. This problem is overcome by the use of booths or by planters that act as partitions.

Tables and Çhairs

Tables, chairs, and banquettes should be large enough to seat diners comfortably without crowding. Distances between tables are sized to enable waiters or waitresses to move through the area while serving and allow diners to eat and converse without being distracted. Selection of chairs is critical since the greatest body contact is made with them. Chairs must have suitable shape, angle of seat and back, size, relationship to table, and tactile qualities to be comfortable.

Table space of at least 26 in. (660 mm) should be allowed for chairs without arms to provide elbow room. Armchairs require a minimum table space of 28 in. (711 mm) for comfort. The preferred height of chair seats is 17 to 18 in. (432 to 457 mm), for adults. A minimum of 12 in. (305 mm) of space is needed between the top of the chair and the bottom of the table. The shape of the table should be considered in relation to the dining mood to be created. Round tables, for example, tend to promote communications among the diners and may result in a lower turnover but higher check averages. Square or rectangular tables tend to increase turnover and are more efficient in the use of dining space.Counter seating can be used to accommodate single customers and also increase turnover rates. Combinations of tables, booths, banquettes, and counters are frequently planned to appeal to a variety of market segments. Cashier areas should be placed for ease of access and in consideration of flow patterns. Bars, buffets, wine displays, or other merchandising setups are placed for maximum visibility and exposure to the customers.

Fabrics

The selection of drapes, carpeting, and fabrics is guided by the need for variations in textures, colours, and shapes. These materials may be chosen to blend with or contrast with the architectural features of the building. Drapes and floor coverings are selected to give an overall appearance of unity and balance. Various fabrics are selected to add warmth and cosiness to a room and to relieve any monotony in the shape of the room. Fabrics contribute not only by their visual impact, but by the fact that they are more pleasant to touch than hard surfaces. Designers may use grass wallpapers, ceramic tile, cork, linen, silk, brick, and other materials that are textured and appealing for wall coverings. Carpeting adds a feeling of intimacy and comfort because it is a point of contact.

Pictures and Prints

Pictures and prints used to decorate wall areas add considerably to the atmosphere. An advantage in using these items is that they can be easily changed. The pictures selected should not clash with the decorative scheme. The shape and size are correlated to the walls on which they will be placed. Colours within the pictures or on frames should blend with the overall scheme of the room to give a coordinated appearance.Table settings can enhance the appeal of the dining atmosphere. Customers notice the tableware they are using and will thus form an impression of the restaurant. Each item placed on the table is selected to add to the feeling and mood to be created in the room. This pertains to dishes, glasses, silver, napkins, and tablecloths.

Exterior Design

The term exterior, as used in food facilities design, is taken to include signs, landscaping, parking areas, building structure, doors, and windows. The objective of exterior design is to attract customers. To perform this function effectively, the exterior must convey the correct impression of the type of food facility into which the customer is being invited. Exterior design is to be coordinated with interior design to provide the total atmosphere.

One problem to be dealt with in exterior design is the matter of attracting initial attention. This is a problem of visibility as seen through the eyes of pedestrians and people in slow- or fast-moving cars. An attractive sign, large enough for the situation, is generally accepted as the best method of attracting attention. The placement of the sign must ensure that drivers are aware of the facility before it appears in view. In some locations, signs may have to be placed at considerable distances from the building. The most effective signs are those that are short and to the point.

Attraction is also gained by the exterior treatment of the building. This includes the size, shape, colours, and materials used in construction. The first impression of an interior of a facility is gained from the exterior. This impression- is derived not solely by the exterior design but from glimpses of the interior that are provided by windows. Windows are so located as to frame the parts of the interior that they expose.

Colour usage on the exterior can follow the same general guidelines presented for interior use. An additional consideration is to let any natural landscaping provide much of the colour. In this case, the building elements can be finished as plainly as possible so as not to compete.

Floodlighting is frequently used with success when the architectural features of the exterior are appealing or dramatic. Care must be used in sizing and placing windows in floodlighted areas to prevent glare into the building. Some designers may prefer to rely on the elegance of simplicity and use little, if any, decorative detailing. On the other hand, facilities with perhaps a national theme may require carefully selected exterior details to complete the concept of total atmosphere.

Parking Areas

Parking lots and areas is important in creating the right impression with the customers. The ease of entering and leaving the parking lot as well as the individual parking space is critical to good design. Consideration should also be given to the placement of walkways from the parking lot to the building. The locations of exterior trash and garbage containers have to be selected carefully. It may be desirable to sacrifice a parking space or two to give special treatment to these undesirable areas. The customers' first impression of a foodservice facility as they leave their cars should not be the sights and smells of trash and garbage. Management should stress the cleanliness of exterior areas at all times.

The entrance door to the facility can form the climax of the exterior attractiveness. It should be selected in accord with the overall design of the building exterior. Doors may be all glass, half glass, wood, or metal, plain or with panels. Separate entrances to the bar are provided if the bar will be used by nondiners. Entrance doors are located for easy access from streets or parking areas. Whether to provide an entrance area or not is largely a matter of choice. An entrance area can have several desirable functions: it can convey a sense of spaciousness and enhance the atmosphere. Entrance areas also provide a meeting place for people and can be used is waiting space during rush hours.

Landscaping provides the setting for -he facility. Another use of landscaping is to hide undesirable service areas or views from dining areas that are not pleasant. The landscape architect may use contours, plant textures, heights, rocks, pathway surfaces, or garden furniture to achieve the desired exterior appearance. In laying out the landscape, important views are selected and foregrounds and backgrounds are developed for them. The landscaping must harmonise with the exterior features of the building so that a good impression is created from all angles of view.

References

Brown, Douglas Robert. *The Restaurant Managers Handbook: How to Set Up, Operate, and Manage a Financially Successful Restaurant.* Lauderhill, Atlantic Pub., 1991.

Cournoyer, Norman G. *Hotel, Restaurant, and Travel Law: A Preventive Approach.* Albany: Delmar Publishers, 1993.

Katsigris, Costas. *Design and Equipment for Restaurants and Foodservice: A Management View.* New York: Wiley, 1999.

Livingstone, Helen, *Food service; for restaurant, coffee shop, hotel, cafeteria, home,* Blooming Ill: McKnight and McKnight Pub. Co., 1950.

Ware, Richard. *How to Open Your Own Restaurant: A Guide for Entrepreneurs.* New York: Penguin Books, 1991.

3

Food and Beverage Service Equipment

The operating equipments used in hotels/restaurants play an important role in attracting customers. The restaurant operating equipments include service equipments, furnitures, fixtures and linen all of which squarely reflect the standard and style of the restaurant.

Service equipments include attractive serviceware, clean dishes, plates and glassware. Glassware refers to glass and drinkware items besides tableware, such as dishes, cutlery and flatware, used to set a table for eating a meal. Many standard patterns and sizes of glassware are available to serve each drink which includes Collins glassware, highball glass, shot glass, pint glass, pilsner glass, beer stein, flute glass, goblet, snifters, wheat beer glass, tulip glass, cocktail glass, red wine glass, white wine glass, champagne flute, sherry glass, coupette glass, coffee-mug, Irish coffee cup, pitcher, old fashioned glass, yard glass, etc.

Chinaware is made of silica, soda ash, and china clay, glazed to give a fine finish. Chinaware is more resistant to heat than glassware. There are various classifications of chinaware which include porcelain, clay mixed with bone ash, earthenware, stoneware, etc. Tableware includes the dishes, glassware, cutlery, and flatware eating utensils (knives, forks, and spoons) used to set a table for eating a meal. Special table ware include asparagus holder, pastry slicer, pastry fork, oyster fork, lobster pick, snail tong and snail fork, snail dish, skewers, ice-cream scoop, nutcracker, etc. Stainless steel flatware and culery are available in a variety of grades.

Many different sizes and shapes of tables are used. They are generally round, rectangular and square. Chair are available in various shapes, colours and sizes to suit all occasions. The side station is also called the dummy waiter or service console. This is a very important piece of furniture in a restaurant. Various trolleys used in the food and beverage service outlets are: gueridon or flambe trolley, room service trolley, dessert trolley, hors d'oeuvre trolley, carving trolley, etc.

Linens are fabric goods, such as tablecloths, napkins and slip cloths. Linen is a material made from the fibers of the flax plant. The main items of linen normally found in a restaurant are: tablecloths; slipcloths; buffet cloths; trolley and sideboard cloths; and waiter's cloths or service cloths.

A food service without utensils is unthinkable and a well-equipped food service is every manager's dream. But since food service managers are also individuals, a list of food service equipment and utensils which may suit one may not suit another. However there are certain essential items that every food service needs and as such are identified by the number of times they are used.

Different pieces of foos service equipment exist for every purpose. While setting up a new foos service, certain amount of time and thought has to be given in choosing and buying equipment and utensils where utmost importance should be given to quality. Modern food service establishments are equipped with many efficient labour-saving devices. Machines make tasks such as chopping, shredding and pureeing easier and less time consuming. A food service appliance is a major investment, not only in the initial purchase cost but also in the use, care, energy consumption, and maintenance for the lifetime of the appliance.

Kitchen Equipment

Kitchen Stoves

A kitchen stove is used to cook food, and refers to a device which has both burners on the top (also known as a cooktop or range or hob) and an oven. Modern stoves are typically considered a basic appliance in homes in developed nations. Along with the refrigerator, a stove is typically located in the kitchen room.

Many modern stoves typically have from three to six burners or hotplates of various sizes and power levels, an oven, and knobs for controlling heat on burners, which may be located on the backsplash, on the cooktop, or on the front of the stove closest to one's hips. Middle to high-end models also may feature locking mechanisms for the oven door, convection cooking, automatic cleaning mechanisms that raise the oven temperature to over 260 degrees Celsius and reduce accumulated food spills to ash, one or more timers, a digital display, and may even be programmable such that they start and stop heating at preset times.

Halogen Cooking System: The halogen cooking system is one of the newest cooking units available. Its tungsten halogen lamps appear to produce virtually instantaneous heat and light. The halogen unit surface is made of vitro-ceramic. This new, smooth surface is also used for some of the induction cooking systems.

Induction Cooking System: The induction cooking system is quite new to many consumers. It is fast, safe, and energy efficient. Target temperatures can be instantly achieved and very low temperatures can be easily maintained to eliminate burning. The cooking surface stays cool, so less heat escapes into the kitchen. Only the cookware, which must be magnetic, and the food get hot-not the entire cooking surface.

Solid-disk Cooking System: The solid-disk cooking system is somewhat new and currently very popular. European design, ease of cleaning, and evenness of cooking are some of the reasons for its popularity. The disk requires frequent application of a special cleaning treatment to keep it looking new. Since the solid disk is made of cast iron, it is slow to heat-up, cooks evenly, and retains heat well. Energy can be saved by turning the element off and using the retained heat to complete cooking.

Convertible Cooking System: The convertible cooking system stoves can be custom designed simply by unplugging a module and plugging in a different one. There are modules for induction, halogen, solid-disk, conventional-coil, and glass ceramic cooking. Extra modules are also available for deep-fat frying, griddling, grilling, barbecuing, and wok cooking. Convertible cooking surfaces work well in open kitchen areas because an overhead exhaust unit is not needed due to the presence of down-draft ventilation systems.

Pilotless Gas Cooking System: Pilotless gas stoves are relatively new. Elimination of the continually burning pilot light results in big energy savings. It also keeps the kitchen cooler. The new gas stoves are easier to clean. On many of the new gas stoves, the top lifts up or off so burners can be easily removed and cleaned. In addition, the knobs, burner bowls, and cookware supports can be easily removed for cleaning.

Beverage Can Stoves: A beverage can stove is a homemade, ultra-light backpacking stove. The simple design is made entirely from cans and burns denatured alcohol. Countless variations on the basic design exist. Pepsi cans are often used because they have a bottom shape that lends itself to securing the stove's inner wall, and because of this the stoves are sometimes called Pepsi can stoves. The Pepsi can stove weighs 0.4 oz (10 g) and will boil two cups of water in five minutes with two tablespoons of fuel. Total weight, including a windscreen/stand can be less than one ounce (30 g). Due to the low weight compared to commercial stoves and their fuel canisters, backpackers can save about one pound (450 g) of pack weight with this stove. This advantage may be lost on long hiking trips however, because the stove is less efficient and requires more fuel, especially when cooking for more than one person.

The stove is made from two aluminum can bottoms. An inner wall is cut and rolled from can material. A ring of holes is pierced into the top with a pin. Parts are glued with high temperature epoxy, or sealed with thermal foil tape. Total height is less than two inches (50 mm), though dimensions can be increased to hold more fuel or decreased to take up even less space. The choice of aluminum has several advantages; light weight, low cost, and good thermal conductivity to aid vaporisation of fuel. Alternative construction materials have been used, including stoves made of tin cans such as cat food tins, tuna cans, and juice cans—the basic design is very similar. Windscreens/stands can be fabricated from tin cans, cut to size and with ventilation holes added.

The stove is designed for one or two people. When used to cook larger meals, it is less efficient than a more powerful stove that delivers more heat to a pot. This is because a longer cooking time is required, during which more heat is lost to the surroundings. To use the stove, a small amount of fuel is poured into the stove and ignited. The pot is then placed above the stove, on a windscreen or stand. The flame is small at first, only burning from the inner chamber. Once the fuel has warmed up, requiring about one minute, its vapour will pass through the perforations and form a ring of flame.

Portable stoves: A portable stove is a stove specially designed to be portable and lightweight, such as for camping. There are several main types based on the type of fuel used:

— Simple single-burner stoves, often without any controls at all, using solid or liquid fuel which is placed in the burner before ignition.

— Single-burner stoves using volatile liquid fuel in a pressurised burner-tank combination.

— Single or multi burner bottled gas stoves, providing controls for the heat setting similar to a kitchen cooktop.

— Gravity-fed spirit stoves, with priming pans.

Simple single-burner designs: The simplest stove is a burner that contains the fuel, and which once lit burns until either it is snuffed or the fuel is exhausted. The rise in the popularity of extreme light-weight equipment for extended backpacking, and the increasing restrictions on the use of campfires in most wilderness areas, have made these small stoves extremely popular. The two most popular of these are the solid fuel stove, using Hexamine tablets, and the liquid fuelled stove using methylated spirits. Both types are available commercially. There are also many designs published for similar home-built stoves, like the Pepsi can stove.

While solid-fuelled stoves may be refuelled while burning with care, with a liquid-fuelled stove it would be reckless to attempt this. Both solid alcohol fuel and stoves for using it are produced by Esbit, and fuel is produced by several other makers. While most brands of firelighters can be used in such stoves, some types will produce a troublesome residue that may be impossible to remove from cookware, and will taint any food exposed to the flame or fumes. One popular make of simple liquid-fuelled stove is the Trangia, available in many different models from a single bare burner to an integrated expedition cooking system. Some of these come with a sealing cover, allowing the burner to be packed while containing fuel.

Pressurised burner stoves: There is some controversy over the invention of the pressurised burner. Most have given the credit to F.W. Linqvist, who was granted a patent for a kerosene-fuelled burner in the late 1880s and went on to develop the Primus brand name of stove into a market leader. However, some have suggested that he bought the design. The Primus stoves and their imitators were a significant advance over previous designs that had used a wick to supply liquid fuel to the burner by capillary action.

Instead the Primus burner vaporised the fuel in a loop of pipe, and used this to both supply the fuel to the burner as a gas and to maintain pressure in the fuel tank. Initial pressure was provided by a small hand-operated pump. It was also necessary to pre-heat the burner with methylated spirits. This burner design was also successfully adapted to portable lamps, lighthouse lamps and blowtorches.

Pressurised burner stoves are now available to burn almost any volatile, inflammable liquid, including alcohol, diesel or other motor fuels, kerosene, jet propellant, and many others. Work is proceeding on vegetable-oil burners. Some can burn multiple fuels or even mixtures. Some require special low-residue stove fuel, others are either designed to resist clogging or to be easily and regularly cleaned of the residue. Most provide some control over the amount of heat produced. Some fuels permit preheating with the fuel, others require use of a more volatile fuel, such as methylated spirit or alcohol priming paste, for preheating the burner.

Most provide an integrated pump for initial pressurisation, others require the use of a separate pump, while a few need no pump but pressurise themselves when the burner is preheated. Although heavier than the simpler designs and more complex to maintain and operate, these stoves can heat food more quickly, and as standard issue to many units in the second world war they enjoyed a large base of competent users in the years immediately following. Another advantage is that hydrocarbon fuels have a higher heat content weight for weight than alcohol fuels, so for extended expeditions the weight advantage of alcohol-fuelled stoves is reduced or even reversed.

Gas-cartridge stoves and refillable gas-bottle stoves: The greatest variety in designs is in this category. They include gas-cartridge stoves and refillable gas-bottle stoves. In most of these the gas is stored as a liquid under pressure, but vaporises immediately it leaves the storage bottle and so arrives at the burner as a gas. Smaller, lighter designs tend to use non-refillable gas cartridges containing butane, propane or a mixture of hydrocarbons. There is little compatibility between different makers and systems, and cartridges for older stoves are often unobtainable. In addition, the single-use cartridges are considered objectionable by some on environmental grounds. Refillable gas bottles are heavier and tend to be used on larger stoves intended for car-camping or expedition base camps. However a great variety of gas-fired stoves is available, some integrating the gas cylinder, some connecting it by a hose.

Gravity-fed spirit stoves: The traditional "spirit stove" still found in many pleasure boats is a unique design, largely replaced by gas stoves but still with a following. It consists of a tank that supplies methylated spirit under gravity to the burner or burners, where it is vaporised and burned. Around each burner is a priming pan used to preheat the burner. To light the stove, the burner is first turned on to allow a small amount of fuel to pass through the burner and collect as a liquid in the priming pan. The burner is then turned off, and the fuel ignited to preheat the burner. When the fuel in the pan is almost all gone, the burner is turned on again, and fuel passes into the burner where it is vaporised and passes through the jets. These stoves look and even sound a bit like pressurised-burner stoves, but the fuel tank is under no pressure. They remain popular for small boats owing to the minimal fire risk they pose in a confined space.

Liquid-fuel and Gas-fuel stoves: Most stoves can use either liquid or gas fuel, but not both (One exception is Primus Omni/Multi-Fuel). Gas-fuel stoves are simpler to operate than liquid fuelled stoves. The gas, being already pressurised, flows from the fuel canister into the burner, where it ignites, in the same manner as a domestic kitchen stove. Liquid-fuel stoves are more complex because the liquid fuel must be vaporised prior to burning. To accomplish this, the stove design brings the fuel line containing the liquid fuel near the flame of the burner. The heat from the flames converts the liquid fuel to a gas before it reaches the burner, where it mixes with air and is ignited. Stoves operating with liquid fuels must be heated or primed before the burner is turned on.

Many stoves require the operator to open the fuel valve briefly without igniting the fuel, so that it flows into a small pan. This small quantity of fuel is then lit and allowed to burn down. When the fuel valve is opened again, the fuel vaporises from the heat of the pan. Some stoves do not have this apparatus, and must be preheated by the application of an external heat source such as a solid fuel block. In many stoves, the priming pressure is generated by a small hand pump that forces air into the fuel container. As the fuel is consumed, the pressure decreases according to Boyle's Law, so the pump must be operated occasionally during use to maintain steady stove operation. Liquid fuel stoves are the most popular for backpacking in United States.

Liquid fuel costs less than gas fuel generally. Some forms of fuel, such as kerosene or fuel oil, are readily available worldwide. Disadvantages to liquid fuelled stoves include they require priming, hence some skill is needed to operate them properly. Using liquid fuel stove in a tent is difficult or even dangerous. The fuel does not burn as cleanly as gas fuelled stoves. Soot builds up on cooking vessels eventually. Spilt liquid fuel poses a fire hazard, and can soil equipment. The odour of the fuel may also attract dangerous wild animals.

Gaseous fuels have many advantages; the fuel burns cleanly. They are quite simple to use, just adjust the fuel flow with a valve and light the burner. Since the gasious fuel quickly dissipates, the fire hazard associated with leaking fuel is reduced. Safety is also increased because there is no priming. Gas fuel bottles of a particular make may be widely available in some countries but not in others, so international travellers have to be particularly careful. Some disadvantages of gas fuel are the difficulty of transferring fuel from one container to another and the difficulty of accurately gauging how much fuel remains in a container.

Gas fuel is somewhat less efficient than liquid fuel, meaning more fuel volume is required for the same heat output. Gas fuelled stoves usually do not operate well in colder temperatures. Butane in particular, does not vaporise well at low temperatures which makes stoves fuelled with butane unsuitable for cold weather camping. Boiling point of butane under normal pressure is -1°C and under this temperature butane cannot be used as a fuel for gas stove. The temperature where use of butane becomes impractical is even higher (around 5°C). Propane-butane-isobutane mixtures used in most containers are suitable to temperatures of -10°C. Pure propane boils at -42°C which is the actual limit of usability of propane stoves. Gas fuel canisters tend to be heavier than liquid-fuel bottles, because it must be stored under greater pressure. When a canister runs out, it may have to be treated as hazardous waste. Canisters tend to deteriorate and leak if stored for several years.

Solid-fuel stoves: A quantity of liquid fuel sufficient to cook a meal, if simply placed in a container and ignited, would burn violently and consume itself in a matter of seconds, and a similar quantity of gas fuel would simply explode. The primary design principle of stoves that use these fuels is to provide a steady flame and prevent the fuel's escape. Solid fuel, however, is more manageable. A solid-fuel stove may consist of no more than a metal plate to hold the fuel, a set of legs to keep it out of contact with the ground, and some supports for the cooking vessel. This design is highly scalable, and may be used for anything from tiny backpacking stoves to large portable woodstoves.

While admirably simple, solid fuel has many disadvantages. First of all, its burn rate may be controlled only by varying the amount of fuel placed on the fire, while fluid fuels may be controlled precisely with valves. Second, no solid fuel burns completely. It produces considerable amounts of ash and soot, which soil both the stove and the cooking vessels. Some of the chemical energy of the fuel remains locked up in the ash and soot, so solid fuel releases less heat, gram for gram. Firewood may often be used in solid-fuel stoves, but manufactured fuels are also available. One type is sold in the form of small blocks, on the order of a centimeter in size. Sterno is a viscous fluid that is also used in solid-fuel stoves. Simple stoves are sometimes used in ice houses and large tents, both to provide warmth and for cooking. They burn wood, and have a small flue used to exhaust the smoke. When used in tents, they are used in a larger tent made of fabric that does not burn readily, and are most often used in base camps that move infrequently.

Ovens

One of the newest features found in ovens is convection cooking. It is available in portable, full-size, free-standing, and built-in wall ovens. In convection ovens, a fan blows the heated air over and around food, increasing the rate of moisture evaporation and thus decreasing cooking time. The oven temperature can be reduced 25 to 50 degrees when cooking with convection because of the air circulation and more even cooking. Shorter cooking times and lower temperatures add up to important energy and dollar savings. Because convection ovens use forced-air for cooking, noise level is a consideration. It should be low enough to not be irritating. Some manufacturers are making combination ovens as an option to conventional gas or electric ovens. These combination ovens allow microwave-convection, microwaveconventional, or convection-conventional cooking in a single large oven.

Microwave Oven

Microwave energy is a natural phenomenon that occurs when electric current flows through a conductor. Microwaves are a form of electromagnetic radiation that is very similar to sunlight and radio waves. The microwaves do not heat glass, ceramic, and plastic containers. One advantage of microwaving is that small amounts of food can be heated very quickly, making it useful for reheating leftovers. A disadvantage of microwaving is that food which is microwaved does not undergo some of the chemical reactions, such as browning, that make the food both visually attractive and give it a different flavour. Primitive microwave ovens often do not cook the food evenly, leading to a concern that bacteria easily killed by more traditional cooking methods may survive the quick cooking time in "cold spots", though the food item as a whole is cooked to a safe average temperature. This can be overcome by leaving the food to stand for a few minutes when cooking is completed. Some high-end microwave ovens are combined with a convection oven; they cook the food using microwaves and hot air simultaneously to achieve both the fast cooking time and the browning effect.

Using a microwave for cooking a large food mass is difficult due to limited penetration of microwaves. However, microwave ovens are used in some fast food chains, and special microwave bags are available for cooking fowl or large joints of meat. Professional chefs generally recommend using microwaves for a limited set of tasks, including melting fats (such as butter) and chocolate, cooking grains like oatmeal and grits, cooking rice, thawing frozen meats and vegetables before cooking by other methods, and quickly reheating already-cooked foods. A common myth is that a microwave oven cooks from the centre of the food outward. However, most foods only have their outermost inch heated by the microwaves, and the rest of the food is heated via conduction. Similarly, foods with both air and water content allow the microwaves to penetrate fully, heating the entire item with the microwave radiation.

Using a microwave to boil liquids is potentially dangerous, due to the possibility of superheating. In a microwave, liquids can be raised quickly to a temperature above the boiling point before major bubbles form, especially if the liquid is purified and in a very clean glass vessel. When a liquid in a superheated state is disturbed, it can suddenly and unexpectedly boil violently, leading to a risk of scalding. This effect is rare, even for scientists who try to deliberately recreate it, and any seed whatsoever for boiling is likely to prevent the problem.

Boiling water with, for instance, a teabag already in it will prevent any dangers by providing a seed, as will using a mug that is not perfectly clean. The risk greatly increases when the liquid has already been boiled once in the same container. This situation can occur if the user of the oven boiled the liquid once, forgot about it, then came back later to boil it again. The first time the liquid boils, the seed bubbles are used up and largely eliminated from the liquid as it cools down. When the liquid is heated again, the lack of seed bubbles allows superheating, and creates the risk of a steam explosion when the liquid's surface is disturbed. Placing something in the liquid before heating can mostly alleviate this risk.

If you are planning to mix something with the liquid you are heating, such as tea or hot chocolate, adding it before heating will ensure that the liquid boils properly. Otherwise, placing a wood object, for instance a chopstick, in the water before heating will also work. All that is necessary to prevent superheating is the presence of seed bubbles, so any liquid that has been allowed to sit undisturbed for a period of time is more prone to superheating. Care should be taken when removing heated liquids from a microwave. Make sure that the hands are protected from possible liquid boil-over, place the container on a level, heat-proof surface, and stir liquid with a warm spoon. Also, never add powdered substances to the container taken from the microwave, due to the addition of a large amount of seed bubbles and the potential for violent, spontaneous boiling. It is advised that the liquid be poured slowly into another container that already contains the powder.

Metal objects, such as metal utensils, in a microwave oven can lead to dangerous situations. Metals do not absorb microwaves effectively. Instead, metals reflect microwaves, thereby preventing the latter from reaching the food. If the microwaves are not absorbed inside the oven, the oven can be damaged by electrical arcs and overheating of the microwave source. Thin metal layers, such as metal foil and mugs with metal trim, can melt or burn due to the strong electrical currents that are generated in metal objects. However, small solid metal objects, such as spoons, in combination with a large amount of absorbing food or liquid, normally do not lead to problems. With wireless computer networks gaining in popularity, microwaves can disrupt wireless network transmissions because the microwave creates radio waves at about 2.4 GHz. This is about the same frequency that 802.11 wireless networks use, so microwaves in use may interfere with network signals, as the specific frequency varies slightly.

A microwave oven is a kitchen appliance employing microwave radiation primarily to cook or heat food. A microwave oven consists of:

— a magnetron,

— a magnetron control circuit,
— a waveguide, and
— a cooking chamber

Microwave oven

A microwave oven does not convert all electrical energy into microwaves. A typical consumer microwave oven could consume 1100 W, and deliver 700 W of microwave power. The remaining 400 W are dissipated as heat by components of the oven. The main source of energy loss is the magnetron tube which is much less than 100% efficient at generating microwave output from the power source. Lesser amounts of power are consumed by the oven lamp, AC power transformer losses, magnetron cooling fan, food turntable motor and control circuits. This waste heat does not end up in the food but is mostly expelled from the cooling vents on the oven and heats the air in the kitchen. Most of the actual microwave power will end up heating the food inside the oven, unless the microwave oven is loaded with a very small amount of absorbing food.

Solar Oven

A solar oven or solar cooker is a way of harnessing the sun's power to cook food. A metal box forms the simplest solar oven. A set of large mirrors or a large Fresnel lens to focus sunlight to a single point may also be added. On a sunny day a black baking tray or cooking pot can convert thousands of watts of light into heat, in addition to any infra-red. Temperatures in a typical oven can reach 400 degrees F (200°C). Apart from the obvious need for sunlight and the need to aim the solar oven before use, using a solar oven is not substantially different from a regular oven. However since they use no fuel they are free to run. Humanitarian organisations are promoting their use worldwide to help slow deforestation and desertification caused by the need for firewood with which to cook. The first known western solar oven was built by Horace de Saussure in 1767.

The available designs of solar ovens fall into three main categories: the box, parabolic, and panel designs. The feature common to each oven design is the shiny reflective surface that directs the sun's rays onto a dark cooking vessel. Each category has advantages when compared on their heating ability, ease of construction, ease and safety of use.

Box cookers: Box cookers are the most common type made for personal use. Despite the name "box" cooker, they are made in both circular and rectangular shapes. Box cooker consist of an enclosed inner box covered with clear glass or plastic, a reflector, and insulation. There is a wide variety of patterns and plans that can be adapted to work with available materials. While they do not heat quickly, they provide slow, even cooking. Box cookers are very easy and safe to use, and fairly easy to construct.

Parabolic cookers: Parabolic cookers reach higher temperatures and cook more quickly than solar box cookers, but are harder to make and use. Most commercial ovens are a form of parabolic cooker. Parabolic cookers require more precision to focus the sunlight on the cooking vessel. If the sunlight is not focused exactly on the cooking vessel, the food will not cook. When the parabolic oven is used, the temperature must be watched so the vessel does not overheat, burning the food. The risk of burns and eye injury is greater with homemade parabolic designs. While they provide excellent results when used correctly, they are not easy to build at home and require great care to use.

Convection Oven

Convection ovens use heated air that is forced into the oven by fans located in the back of the oven, generally for cooking food. By moving heated air past the food, convection ovens operate at a lower temperature than a standard conventional oven and they can cook food more quickly. They are mostly used in industrial and commercial applications, but can be purchased for the home as well. With a convection oven there will be about a 25 to 30% decrease in cooking temperature and a 20% decrease in cooking time as compared to a conventional oven.

Convection ovens are highly versatile units. They're ideal for cooking, warming, roasting, re-thermalising and baking. Whether you're roasting a turkey or baking croissants, convection ovens cook evenly and thoroughly. Convection ovens are available in gas or electric and in various configurations, including full-size, half-size, stackable, and as part of a traditional bake oven. Convection ovens are highly versatile and ideal for cooking, warming, roasting, re-thermalising and baking. Convection ovens work by forcing heated air, via fans located in the back of the oven wall, over and around the food racks. By moving heated air around the food product, convection ovens do the same job as a rotary oven in a lot less time and using a lot less space. Convection ovens operate at lower temperatures than standard conventional ovens and they cook faster, saving an operator both time and energy. In a convection oven, product that is placed with little space between pans will still cook evenly. Convection ovens offer the operator more flexibility to cook, bake, or steam inject.

Convection cooking reduces product shrinkage and, in some cases, can result in an extra serving. You can use a convection oven to bake and roast anything from meats to pizza, pastries, and crusty breads. One can bake delicate pies and pastries in a convection oven. When these ovens first came on the market, the moving air would create uneven meringues and custards. Today, with the "gentle bake" and diffused air circulation, uneven cooking is no longer a concern. Although both of these ovens use convection to carry heat, only one of them has the word "convection" in its name. The difference between them is that while a standard oven waits for natural convection to move heat slowly from the heat source to the food, a convection oven uses a fan to drive heat rapidly from source to food. While natural may sound appealing, a convection oven is simply better than a standard oven.

Dutch Oven

A Dutch oven is a thick-walled metal cooking pot with a tight-fitting lid. A camping, cowboy or chuck wagon Dutch oven has three legs and a flat, rimmed lid, so that coals from the cooking fire can be placed on top as well as below. This provides more uniform internal heat and lets the inside act as an oven. They are ordinarily made of cast iron, although some are aluminum.

Modern dutch ovens consist of a covered, shallow cooking pan set on legs and heated from below with a built-in electrical heating element. The dutch oven is also a slang name for a practical joke played on bedmates by restraining them under the covers after you have passed gas. Also refers to slang term used to describe the smoking of cannabis or marijuana in a sealed enviroment such as a small room or car for the purpose of inhaling the residual smoke long after the smoking implement has been emptied, thus providing a further high. This is also known as hot-boxing, clam-baking, or fish-bowling.

Cooking techniques such as roasting, baking simmering, stewing, frying, boiling, steaming, and many others are easily done on the campfire with only a single utensil, the dutch oven. Think of the possibilities, delicious fresh baked bread that will rise up and lift the lid, cobblers made from berries picked fresh at the campsite, incredible deep-dish pizzas, stews, quiches that melt in your mouth, cornish game hens roasted to perfection, and imagine a chocolate cake a foot in diameter. These and many, many more are very possible and sometimes easier than they are at home.

Cookware

Cookware comprises cooking vessels, such as saucepans and fry pans, intended for use on a stove or range cooktop. Bakeware comprises cooking vessels intended for use inside an oven. The terms cookware and bakeware are not exclusive, and it is possible for a single utensil to be used as both cookware and bakeware. Knowledge of cooking vessels before the development of pottery is minimal due to the limited archaeological evidence. It has been possible to extrapolate likely developments based on methods used by latter peoples. Among the first of the techniques believed to be used by stone age civilizations were improvements to basic roasting. In addition to exposing food to direct heat from either an open fire or hot embers it is possible to cover the food with mud or large leaves before roasting to preserve moisture in the cooked result. Examples of similar techniques are still in use in many modern cuisines. Of greater difficulty was finding a method to boil water. For people without access to natural heated water sources, such as hot springs, it was possible to prepare a small pit lined with stones and filled with water.

Types of Cookware

Cookware consists of different types of pots and pans that are used for specific purposes. Some of the pieces of cookware can be substituted for a type you may not have and still accomplish the type of cooking you need to perform. Pots and pans are available in different sizes and made of different types of material. Some materials are better than others when used for specific cooking methods. When selecting the cookware for your kitchen, you should take the following points into consideration:

— *Budget*: How much can you afford to spend on the pots and pans you purchase? You should purchase the best quality that you can afford. It will be well worth it in the long run. Otherwise, you will find yourself replacing them in a short time.

— *Cooking Habits*: How much will you be cooking? Do you eat out a lot and buy convenience food or do you like to prepare meals from scratch? Will you be entertaining a lot?

— *Cuisine*: Will you be making a lot of pasta, soups, or stir-fries? There are special pots and pans that assist in preparing these types of food.

— *Quantity*: Will you be cooking for 1, 2 or several? Having the right size cookware will be important when preparing your food.

Cookware is made from many different materials. Understanding the differences will assist you in making the best choice for your needs.

Lined copper: Copper is one of the more expensive materials used to make pots and pans. It conducts heat evenly and is very responsive to heat. It heats up quickly and will also cool down quickly when removed from the heat, preventing sautés and delicate foods from burning and becoming overdone. Because copper distributes heat so evenly and efficiently, it is the best choice for frying and sautéing, but it is also a good choice for many other cooking methods. One problem with copper is that it interacts with everything it comes in contact with. Moisture in the air causes it to form a film on it that is poisonous and salty food causes a chemical reaction that can make food have a metallic taste.

Stainless steel: Stainless steel cookware is moderately priced. It is the most versatile material to use because it keeps its bright shine and has good tensile strength, preventing it from denting easily. Stainless steel is a good material for any type of pan because it does not corrode and does not react with alkaline or acidic materials. The one problem with stainless steel is that it does not conduct heat well. To combat this problem, pots and pans made from stainless steel have should have a thick aluminum or copper core in the bottom of the pan to help conduct heat more evenly and make the pan more responsive to heat. In the better quality pans, the aluminum or copper core also runs up the sides.

You may find a stainless steel pan with an aluminum or copper plate on the bottom but if the plate is not thick enough, it will not do an efficient job of conducting heat evenly. To care for stainless steel cookware, wash with hot soapy water. A nylon scouring pad or nylon scraper can be used to remove stuck on food. There are stainless steel cleaners that can also be used to remove stains and bring a shine back to the cookware.

Aluminum: Aluminum cookware is fairly inexpensive in comparison to cookware made from other materials. Aluminum is lightweight but fairly strong. It is a good conductor of heat and does not easily distort when exposed to high temperatures. Aluminum works well for sautéing and frying foods because if its heat responsiveness. The drawback of aluminum is that it reacts to acidic and alkaline foods, causing it to corrode and affect the taste of the food being cook. Aluminum is generally used as a core heat conductor, or coated with stainless steel or an anodised coating to protect the food. To care for aluminum cookware, wash the pans with hot soapy water. Avoid washing the cookware in hard water because it tends to darken the aluminum. To remove stains, use a cream of tarter and water paste.

Anodized aluminum: This is aluminum that has been given a special finish to protect it from corrosion. It is a good conductor of heat and the special finish makes it stick-resistant. It is a good choice of material to look for in pots and pans for most any type of cooking. Pots and pans made from anodized aluminum are not dishwasher safe and can be dark in colour, making it hard to see slight colour changes in the food being cooked. To care for anodized aluminum pans, do not cook foods that are highly acidic or alkaline in them because they have a tendency to cause pitting in the coating. They should be washed by hand in hot soapy water rather than in a dishwasher where the strong detergent would damage the surface of the cookware. To avoid scratching the finish, do not use abrasive materials on the surface of anodized aluminum cookware.

Cast iron: Cast iron cookware is inexpensive to moderately priced. It is fairly heavy and conducts heat evenly. It heats slowly but once it is hot it holds the heat well. This makes it good for deep frying and slow-cooking. It can be used on top of the stove and in the oven. Drawbacks to cast iron are that it rusts, stains and becomes pitted when exposed to air, moisture and certain foods. To care for cast iron cookware, do not wash in soapy water but try wiping clean with a paper towel. Run hot water over stuck on food to help loosen and remove. After your cast iron pot has been washed it should be dried thoroughly. To prevent the pan from rusting, rid it of any excess moisture by setting it on the stove over high heat until all moisture has evaporated and coat with oil before storing.

Non-stick: These pots and pans have had a coating applied to them that prevents food from sticking and makes clean up easier. The non-stick surface is really an advantage when cooking some foods, such as omelettes, and when reheating sticky foods, such as rice. It also reduces the amount of fat that is normally required when cooking. The non-stick surface is less efficient when using certain cooking methods, such as sautéing, because the coating interferes with the transfer of heat from the underlying pan. To care for non-stick cookware, use hot soapy water and avoid using abrasive pads or powders. If food does stick to the pan, soak in hot water to loosen stuck on food. A nylon scouring pad, nylon scraper, or nonabrasive cleaner can also be used to help remove stuck on food. Do not wash in a dishwasher. Also protect the non-stick surface by only using wooden, plastic, or coated utensils when cooking.

Types of Pots and Pans

There are many types of pots and pans available for different cooking methods. Many of the types can be used for more than one method. Shown below are some of the different types and a brief description of each.

Braiser pan: A round or oval-shaped pan with two stay-cool handles and heavy domed cover. This is a heavyweight pan made of anodized aluminum or stainless steel. Both types of material contain an aluminum or copper core layer in the middle that runs all across the bottom and up the sides, which spreads heat evenly through the pan.

Braising pans

Braising pans can be used on the stovetop and in the oven. It is important that the cooking vessel has a tight fitting lid so that the liquid does not evaporate. They are available in depths ranging from 2 to 3 inches and in various sizes ranging from 10 to 13 inches in diameter or 2 ½ quarts to 6 quarts. This pan could also be used as a casserole pan.

Casserole: A round or oval pan with steep sides, which ranges in size from 2 quarts to 12 quarts. The casserole pan can be found made from many different materials. It is available made from the same high quality materials as a saucepan or you may find it made from glass, ceramic or earthenware. It may have a cover but many times the cover is not used when cooking the food in a casserole.

Casserole pan

Depending on the material it is made from, it may be used on the stove top but is generally used in the oven. It is used for cooking one-dish meals and the meal is served at the table in the casserole pan.

Chef's pan: A medium depth pan that generally has flared or rounded sides but is sometimes found with straight sides. It has a flat bottom and wide mouth, which accelerates the evaporation of liquids. A chef's pan most often will have a long handle and a tight fitting cover. It is made of a metal with a thick ground base that allows temperature changes to occur rapidly as the level of the heat applied to it changes, either increasing or decreasing for the best heat conduction.

Chef's pan

Chef's pans are available in a variety of sizes such as 2, 3, 4, 5, or 6 quart. The height of the sides make it easier for sautéing, frying or steaming greater amounts of foods, allowing sufficient space for turning and stirring of the contents. Chef's pans are very similar to saucier pans and either pan can be used interchangeably.

Double boiler: A double boiler consists of two pans where one sits inside of the other. The bottom pan is slightly larger so the top pan can fit inside. The bottom pan contains hot water and the top pan holds the ingredients that are being cooked. This type of pan is used when making delicate sauces that have a tendency to separate if cooked on direct heat.

Double boiler

Double boiler are often made from stainless steel but can also be found made from other materials, such as enamelled steel, aluminum, and glass.

Grill pan: A heavy metal pan that consists of ridges spaced evenly across the bottom that closely simulate the grilling process when cooking various meats and foods. They are available with shallow sides and with deeper sides similiar to a frying pan.

Omelette pan: An omelette pan is basically the same as a frying pan. It is available made from the same type of material as frying pans and is generally shaped the same. An omelette pan with a non-stick surface is beneficial when making omelettes because it allows the eggs to release from the pan, making them easier to turn or flip. The omelette pan is also available in an oval shaped pan that is generally 10 to 12 inches long. The oval pan works well for cooking foods such as omelettes, fish filets, and shell steaks. The most common sizes for round pans are 8, 10, and 12 inches.

Roasting pan: A rectangular shaped pan with low sides, which allows the heat from the oven to expose the entire surface of the meat to create a browned exterior. The pan is generally used with a rack to prevent the meat from sitting in its own juices and stewing instead of browning. There are several sizes available. Select a size that allows approximately 2 inches between the side of the pan and the meat. Also, be sure that there is at least 2 inches of space between the outside of the pan and the sides of the oven so that there will be proper air circulation.

Roasting pan

The roasting pans are available made from several different materials, such as stainless steel, stainless steel with an aluminum or copper core, aluminum with non-stick surfaces, anodized aluminum, lined copper and granite. An oval shaped pan with deep sides and a large domed cover. It generally has a flat rack included on the bottom of the pan. They are available in several sizes and material, such as granite, anodized aluminum, and stainless steel. The meat is cooked with the cover on, which acts as an oven in an oven, resulting in the meat cooking more quickly and in a moister environment. This results in moist, tender meat. The deep-sided roasting pan, generally without the cover, is also used for casseroles.

Saucepan: A round pot with high straight sides and a flat bottom that is used for several purposes, such as cooking vegetables, heating soup, and making sauces. The standard saucepan has straight sides but there are other styles available that are used for special purposes.

Saucepan

Sauteing pan: A pan very similar to the frying pan, only it has short, straight sides. It has a heavy gauge bottom and is made from a material that is heat responsive, such as lined copper, stainless steel with a copper or aluminum core, or anodized aluminum. It is used for sautéing foods but can also be used for frying foods. The pan should have a long handle and it generally comes with a cover. Some of the larger models have a loop handle opposite the long handle that is used to assist in lifting the pan.

Sauteuse pan: An round, lidded pan with small handles that is often used to sauté or braise a variety of foods. With short to medium height outward sloping sides, a sauteuse pan is a utensil for cooking casseroles, stews, and pasta dishes as well as meat and poultry dishes. Common in European households, this pan has a small curved handle on each side instead of a single straight handle and is typically available in sizes ranging from 2.5 quarts to 7 quarts.

Stir-Fry pan: A round, deep pan that may have straight sides with a slightly rounded base or more commonly a round base that slopes out and upward. Stir fry pans are available with several different sized handle lengths that can be selected to match the cooking process. The pan allows heat to be well distributed across the base while the sloping sides make it easier to stir and turn ingredients as they cook. The Asian pan referred to as a "wok" is one traditional type of stir-fry pan while other versions are often available with bases and sides that are thicker in substance, not as curved, nor as deep as the wok pan. Stir fry pans are often used to prepare and quickly sear multiple ingredients that go well together including various meats and vegetables mixed with sauces. The stir fry pan is good for cooking food in a small quantity of oil and for retaining the colours and textures of the various ingredients.

Stockpot: A deep, straight-sided pot that is taller than it is wide. It has two, securely attached, loop handles that are big enough to easily allow the use of potholders or oven mitts. It is used for simmering large amount of liquid, such as stock, soup and stews, but also works well for thick soups, chilli and for boiling pasta.

The pot does not need to be made of anodized aluminum or copper to promote responsive heat reaction but should have a heavy bottom to protect against burning and scorching. Stockpots are available in sizes ranging from 6 quarts to 20 quarts and generally include a cover. 10, 12 and 14 quarts are standard sizes that will satisfy many uses. You will find stockpots made of several different materials, such as stainless steel, aluminum, anodized aluminum, copper, and non-stick materials.

Wok: A bowl shaped pan that is used to quickly cook food over high heat. It is available with a rounded or flat bottom. The traditional type wok has a rounded bottom and is used over a flamed heat source, such as a gas burner. The flat bottom wok was designed to use on an electric burner or a ceramic stovetop but can also be used on a gas stove.

The rounded woks come with a ring that should be placed over the flames to hold the woks steady. Woks are available made from various materials, such as carbon steel, cast iron, stainless steal with aluminum inner layers, and metal with a non-stick coating applied. Cast steel and cast iron woks must be seasoned before they are used for the first time. Some varieties of woks have one long handle, some have two short handles and others have a long handle on one side and a short one on the opposite side.

Bakeware

There are many different types of bakeware, such as, round pans, square pans, rectangle pans, tube pans, bundt pans, jelly roll pans, loaf pans, springform pans, roasting pans, and casseroles. Your recipe will suggest that you use a certain size and type of pan. If you do not have the pan requested, you can generally substitute a similar size pan without any problem. The information below will help you make the appropriate substitution. Select a pan that is as close to the same size as the pan the recipe indicated to use. The pan should have approximately the same volume capacity and when filled, the ingredients should be close to the same depth as they would be in the original size pan.

Food Processing Equipments

Food processing takes clean, havested or slaughtered and butchered components and uses these to produce attractive and marketable food products. Similar process are used to produce animal feed. A food processor is a kitchen appliance used to facilitate various repetitive tasks in the process of preparation of food. It helps to chop, slice, shred, grind, and puree almost any food quickly and easily. Some models can also assist the home cook in making citrus and vegetable juice, beating cake batter, kneading bread dough, beating egg whites, and grinding meats and vegetables.

Today, the term almost always refers to an electric-motor-driven appliance, although there are some manual devices also referred to as "food processors". Food processors are similar to blenders in many ways. The primary difference is that food processors use swappable blades and disks (attachments) instead of a fixed blade. Also, their bowls are wider and shorter, a more appropriate shape for the solid or semi-solid foods usually worked in a food processor.

Its functions normally consist of:

— Slicing/chopping vegetables

— Grinding items such as nuts, meat, or dried fruit

— Shredding or Grating cheese or vegetables

— Pureeing

— Mixing and kneading doughs

Modern food processors come in three basic sizes: full, compact, and mini. No matter what size they are, however, the basic components are the same: a motor, a bowl with a lid and feed tube, and a set of attachments. The motor is housed in the base of the appliance, and it is the heaviest part of the device. Full-size machines generally have larger, more powerful motors, and can weigh more than 20 lbs (9 kg). This weight has a utilitarian value: The heaviness of the base gives the appliance stability and ensures that it doesn't move around while the motor is running.

Though the first food processor bases were clad only in white, hard plastic, today they are available in a range of stylish colours and with metal and plastic finishes, ensuring that your appliance will fit in with your kitchen decor. From the motor, a shaft extends upward to power the attachments. The bowl, which is usually made of durable, transparent plastic, fits onto this shaft and locks into position. The lid, usually made of the same material, locks onto the top of the bowl; in many older models, engaging the locking mechanism turns on the motor, but newer models generally have an on/off switch or button.

Mixers

A mixer is a kitchen appliance intended for mixing, folding, beating, and whipping food ingredients. Mixers come in two major variations, hand mixers and stand mixers. A hand mixer, as the name implies, is a hand-held device. It typically consists of a handle mounted over a large enclosure containing the motor, which drives two beaters. The beaters are immersed in the food to be mixed. Hand mixers are often battery-powered.

Blenders

A blender is a kitchen appliance used to blend ingredients or puree food. The term typically refers to a stationary, upright electrical device, which is to be distinguished from a hand-powered or electric mixer that may be used for similar purposes.

A typical blender is built around a vessel for the ingredients to be blended. At the top of the vessel is a cap to prevent ingredients from escaping when the blender is switched on. At the bottom is a blade assembly, typically removable for cleaning purposes. The bottom seal is most likely watertight. The vessel rests upon a base containing a motor (for turning the blade assembly) with controls on its surface. Most modern blenders offer a number of possible speeds.

Coffee Makers

Most people who are dependent on caffeine have breakfast with an old friend — the coffee maker! Every morning you scoop in the coffee, add the water and turn it on, but have you ever wondered what is happening inside? How does the water get from the little compartment where you pour it in to the top of the coffee maker, and what is that gurgling sound? A modern drip coffee maker is a surprisingly simple device. Manufacturers have had 25 years to hone their designs, so these coffee makers are pretty straightforward once you open them up.

Toasters

For lots of people, the toaster is a daily part of breakfast (and lunch and maybe even dinner). A toaster is a machine for toasting food such as sliced bread and bagels. Toasted bread is called toast. Other toastable products may be described as toaster pastry. A typical toaster uses infrared radiation to heat a piece of bread. The heat is usually produced by conducting electricity through nichrome wires (Joule heating).

The toasting process consists of reducing the bread's water content, raising its temperature, and slightly charring and caramelising its surface. The caramelisation process is a chemical reaction in which the complex starch molecules break apart into simpler sugar molecules upon heating. That is why toast is usually sweeter than normal bread.

Toaster ovens perform toasting functions of a pop-up toaster, however, the heating elements are positioned horizontally. A toaster oven usually has a glass door and a pull out tray upon which the object to be toasted is placed. Because of its design, a toaster oven can also perform some of the functions provided by a regular oven, but on a somewhat smaller scale. Toaster ovens are freestanding units, commonly placed on countertops or hung from cupboards (kitchen cabinets). It is highly recommended that no one attempts to retrieve toast and other objects from the toaster using silverware such as a knife because of the risk of electric shock.

The most common way for a toaster to create the infrared radiation is to use nichrome wire wrapped back and forth across a mica sheet. Toaster heating element, nichrome wire on mica sheet. Nichrome wire is an alloy of nickel and chromium. It has two features that make it a good producer of heat:

— Nichrome wire has a fairly high electrical resistance compared to something like copper wire, so even a short length of it has enough resistance to get quite hot.

— The nichrome alloy does not oxidise when heated. Iron wire would rust very quickly at the temperatures seen in a toaster.

The very simplest toaster would have two mica sheets wrapped in nichrome wire, and they would be spaced to form a slot about an inch (2.5 cm) wide. The nichrome wires would connect directly to a plug.

Pressure Cookers

A pressure cooker is often used by mountain climbers to compensate for the low atmospheric pressure at a very high altitude. Without it, water boils off before reaching 100 °C, leaving the food improperly cooked, as described in Charles Darwin's *Voyage of the Beagle*: At the place where we slept water necessarily boiled, from the diminished pressure of the atmosphere, at a lower temperature than it does in a less lofty country; the case being the converse of that of a Papin's digester. Hence the potatoes, after remaining for some hours in the boiling water, were nearly as hard as ever. The pot was left on the fire all night, and next morning it was boiled again, but yet the potatoes were not cooked. I found out this, by overhearing my two companions discussing the cause, they had come to the simple conclusion, "that the cursed pot [which was a new one] did not choose to boil potatoes."

A larger scale version of a pressure cooker, used by laboratories and hospitals to sterilise biological waste materials, surgical instruments etc. is known as an autoclave. Pressure cookers create healthier, tastier meals and yet have remained an enigma to American cuisine and cooks. Because food cooks faster at higher temperatures, this cooking utensil works its magic by creating the necessary pressure to increase the temperature without burning the food. For example, water (which at sea level normally boils at 212° Fahrenheit) boils under pressure when the temperature is 30-50° higher than normal. The food cooks thoroughly and evenly, the nutrients stay in the food, and you get risotto in 7 minutes, artichokes in 10 minutes, beef stew in 15 minutes, cheese cake in 30 minutes.

New pressure cookers, with their multiple safety features and improved vent systems, are once more catching on in The United States. These vessels offer a choice of a quick-release option, taking even less time to finish that meal and without the need for the water to cool down. Busy cooks with hectic schedules, demanding jobs, an active family and little spare time are looking for fast, economical ways for preparing home-cooked, nutritious meals. Television ads market overpriced cookers with fancy new names, touting the "latest, greatest new invention" to cooks who would never have considered buying a pressure cooker. Wide spread advertising has brought with it a resurgence of interest in pressure cookery, and now this old fashioned cooking method is suddenly new again!

The moral of the story is a moot one indeed. If you get a used pressure cooker, it is crucial to make sure that the gaskets (rubber seals) are still in the top of the pressure cooker. You must also make sure that the steam vent works properly. If you opt to buy a new cooker, keep in mind that the 6-quart size is the standard for most recipes. Select a cooker with a detachable pressure regulator that can adjust the pressure to low, medium and high. The higher the pressure, the higher the internal temperature and the less cooking time required. The safety valve automatically vents steam. Choose a pot with heat resistant handles, a locking lid that is easy to manoeuvre and a heavy bottom of stainless steel construction so that the same pot can be used to do preparatory sauteing.

Rice cooker: A rice cooker or rice steamer is a self-contained electrical appliance, used primarily for cooking rice. There are also microwave, gas and open flame variants. The preparation of rice has traditionally been a tricky cooking process that requires accurate timing, and errors can result in inedible undercooked or burnt rice. Rice cookers aim to avoid these problems by automatically controlling the heat and timing in the preparation of the rice, while at the same time freeing up a heating element on the range. Although the rice cooker does not necessarily speed the cooking process, the cook's involvement in cooking rice with a rice cooker is significantly reduced and simplified.

Typically, a rice cooker contains an insulated outer container containing a heating element, into which is fitted a non-stick or teflon-coated inner removable bowl, which often has graduations marked in cups of rice (white). Whereas less expensive and older models use simple electronics and mechanical and thermal sensors, high-end rice cookers use microchips to control the cooking process and often incorporate a timer which can be used to set the desired "ready time". Many rice cookers can keep rice warm safely for up to 24 hours. This helps to avoid the dangers of food poisoning due to Bacillus cereus. Rice cookers, when purchased, normally include a small "cup" measure and a plastic paddle for doling out the cooked rice.

Restaurants that serve a lot of rice, particularly those specialising in Asian cuisine, often use industrial size rice cookers that quickly and cheaply produce large quantities of cooked rice. A rice cooker is a standard appliance in kitchens around the world, especially in Asian countries. The bowl in the rice cooker is usually removable, and beneath it lies a spring and thermostat. These form the main components of the rice cooker. The spring in the bottom is simply to ensure contact of the thermostat to the base of the cooking bowl.

In a rice cooker the amount of rice and water are exactly measured. During cooking the mixture is continuously heated. The temperature cannot go above the boiling point of water—100°C (212°F)—as any energy put into the system at that point will only cause the water to boil. At the end of cooking all of the water will have been evaporated or absorbed by the rice. If the heating continues past this point the temperature surpasses the boiling point. The thermostat then trips, and switches the rice cooker to "warm" mode, keeping the rice no cooler than approximately 65°C (150°F) (simple rice cookers, like the one below, may simply turn off at this point).

To cook white rice, the rice is measured and optionally rinsed, then added to the inner bowl. Cold water is measured and added or simply added up to the appropriate graduation in the inner bowl. Sometimes there are separate scales for brown rice or for cooking other foods in the appliance. Once the lid is closed and the cooking cycle has been activated, the rice cooker does the rest. Fancy models give a countdown in minutes to the "ready time," and beep when done, whereas less expensive and older models simply click or ring a bell when done.

Rice cookers are typically used for the preparation of plain or lightly seasoned rice, but more elaborate recipes are possible using a rice cooker, and there are cookbooks devoted entirely to dishes prepared using a rice cooker. One of the more unexpected dishes that can be made in a rice cooker is a beef stew. By simply adding ingredients and setting it to "warm", a rice cooker would cook that at about 65°C (150°F). In few hours, the stew is fully cooked and ready to eat.

Some rice cookers are designed to accommodate a basket above the rice. This basket is generally used to steam vegetables, holding them in the steam coming off the rice. Some vegan cooks consider rice cookers to be an invaluable tool in the preparation of vegan meals. They find it extremely versatile, allowing a variety of meals to be cooked with minimal preparation and no attention during the cooking process, which suits contemporary busy lifestyles well.

Refrigerators

Refrigeration and freezing are used on almost all foods: meats, fruits, vegetables, beverages, etc. In general, refrigeration has no effect on a food's taste or texture. Freezing has no effect on the taste or texture of most meats, has minimal effects on vegetables, but often completely changes fruits (which become mushy). Refrigeration's minimal effects account for its wide popularity. The fundamental reason for having a refrigerator is to keep food cold. Cold temperatures help food stay fresh longer. The basic idea behind refrigeration is to slow down the activity of bacteria (which all food contains) so that it takes longer for the bacteria to spoil the food. For example, bacteria will spoil milk in two or three hours if the milk is left out on the kitchen counter at room temperature. However, by reducing the temperature of the milk, it will stay fresh for a week or two — the cold temperature inside the refrigerator decreases the activity of the bacteria that much. By freezing the milk you can stop the bacteria altogether, and the milk can last for months.

Refrigeration and freezing are two of the most common forms of food preservation used today. There are many options to choose from when shopping for a new refrigerator. Choices include a variety of models and styles that have new convenience and energy-saving features. Before purchasing a refrigerator, it is a good idea to measure the space available for the new refrigerator as well as door and hallway clearances. These measurements can be compared to the refrigerator's outside dimensions to make sure it will fit into the kitchen. When deciding what size of refrigerator to purchase, a rule-of-thumb is a minimum of 12 cubic feet for the first two persons in the household, plus 2 more cubic feet for each additional person.

A refrigerator (often shortened to fridge) or freezer is an electrical appliance that uses refrigeration to help preserve food. A domestic refrigerator is present in 99.5% of American homes. It works using phase change heat pumps operating in a refrigeration cycle. An industrial refrigerator or industrial freezer is simply a refrigerator used in an industrial setting, usually in a restaurant or supermarket. They may consist of either a cooling compartment only (a larger refrigerator) or a freezing compartment only (a freezer) or contain both.

Dishwashers

In some countries dishwashing is usually done with a brush instead of a sponge. Collect all of your cutlery into a pile. Remove food scraps and stack the plates and bowls neatly. Find all the coffee mugs, wine glasses, and what-have-you, and group them next to the sink. Arrange your dishes so that they are all in easy reach for when you are standing over the sink. Empty all glasses or other containers before filling the sink. In some European countries the dishes are always washed in a separate tub placed inside the sink. This was a matter of hygiene, as the kitchen sink was the only sink available for all the household water. The clothes were washed in the sink; the water used to wash the floor went down the sink, and so it made sense to separate the dishwater from the sink. There were two other possible reasons. Kitchen sinks tended to be very large in a time when heating water was considered to be a major household expense — a tub used less water. Also kitchen sinks were usually made of hard ceramic; any contact between the sink and plates was liable to cause chips, but a tub could be made of more forgiving material.

Using a separate washing-up bowl in the sink also provides a place to dispose of unfinished drink, soaking-water, etc. Washing up gloves may be worn when washing dishes. Also, modern devices which consist of a sponge mounted on a hollow plastic handle may also be used. The handle is filled with soap, which impregnates the sponge and is gradually released as the dishes are washed. This precludes the necessity of filling a sink or tub with soapy water, which eventually gets dirty. In cases where dishes are to be shared among many, such as restaurants, sanitising may be desirable. These are some steps to sanitise dishes.

- Scrape and rinse to remove visible food particles.
- Soak items briefly in soapy warm water, scrub, sponge.
- Rinse in clean water to remove soap.
- Rinse in dilute bleach solution.
- Allow to air dry.

Dishes are placed on large trays and fed onto rollers through the machine. The use of bleach is critical to sanitation when large groups are involved. While toxic to the environment and not to be used more than necessary, it evaporates completely, is cheap, and kills almost everything. Cabinets, refrigerators, countertops and anything else touched by people in a large group setting should be periodically wiped or sprayed with a dilute bleach solution after being washed with soapy water and rinsed in clean water.

Hand dishwashing: Hand dishwashing is probably subject to more variables than any other household clean-up job. In theory at least, any detergent or soap can be used for hand dishwashing, except an automatic dishwasher detergent. However, soap has become almost extinct as a dishwashing product and many laundry detergents are not very acceptable. Laundry detergents, may leave spots and streaks, the powders may not completely dissolve, or may discolour certain metals with soaking. A light-duty liquid hand dishwashing detergent is the best choice. Regardless of brand, certain characteristics are important in a hand dishwashing liquid: lasting suds, effective cleaning performance, mildness to hands, safety for dishes and other washables, storage stability, pleasant fragrance and appearance, convenient packaging and dispensing. In formulating a product to meet these criteria, manufacturers, in general, use certain basic ingredients. Surfactants or surface active agents are the primary ingredients in a liquid hand dishwashing detergent. Often a combination of surfactants is used to produce good grease cutting capability and soil suspension, mildness in water of varying degrees of hardness, and a high, stable suds level. All surfactants in these detergents are biodegradable. Stability and Dispensing Aids are added to keep the product homogeneous under varying storage conditions, and to provide desirable dispensing characteristics.

Alcohols, hydrotropes, and salts are often used. Fragrance and Colour Additives are what give a product its "personality," and are important, though present in extremely small amounts. Mildness Additives may include moisturising agents, certain oils and emollients, certain protein compounds, or other neutralising or beneficial ingredients. Preservatives are added, if needed, in small quantities to help prevent any microbiological growth in the product which could cause colour or odour change, poor performance and separation of the ingredients.

Mechanical dishwasher: The term dishwasher can represent either a person who washes dishes or a machine that performs a similar function. A dishwasher is a mechanical device for cleaning food utensils for preparation, keeping, serving and eating and drinking. They are found in restaurants and also in many kitchens of homes. The dishwasher therefore is mainly a device for spraying water on the dishes—first detergent-added water for cleaning purposes, then clean water to remove the detergent residue. Some dishwashers also contain a heating element to achieve fast drying of the dishes. In today's kitchens, an automatic dishwasher is no longer a luxury. Automatic dishwashers use less water and sanitise dishes far better than hand washing.

Service Equipments

Elegant and attractive serviceware, colourful and clean dishes, quality plates and glassware add to the decor of a restaurant. However, several factors have to be considered while selecting the equipment.

- Standard of the restaurant
- Types of service

- Décor and theme of the restaurant
- Type of clientele
- Durability of equipment
- Ease of maintenance
- Availability when stocks runout for replacement
- Storage
- Flexibility of use
- Price factors
- Standardization

A hotel / restaurant should be well stocked with appropriate equipment to provide quality service. For multipurpose use and to cut down costs, most hotels / restaurants standardise equipment in terms of size and colour.

Food and beverage service equipment may be divided into glassware, chinaware and tableware which are further subdivided into flatware, cutlery and hollowware.

Glassware

Glassware refers to glass and drinkware items besides tableware, such as dishes, cutlery and flatware, used to set a table for eating a meal. The term usually refers to the drinking vessels, unless the dinnerware is also made of glass. The choice of the right qulity glass is a vital element if the cocktail is to be invitingly presented and give satisfaction to the consumer. Well designed glassware combines elegance, strength and stability, and should be fine and smooth rimmed and of clear glass.

Types of Glassware

Many standard patterns and sizes of glassware are available to serve each drink. Most glass drinking vessels are either tumblers, flat-bottomed glasses with no handle, foot, or stem; footed glasses, which have a bowl above a flat base, but no stem; or stemware, which have a bowl on a stem above a flat base. Neither a tumbler, footed, nor a stem, yard (beer) is a very tall, conical beer glass, with a round ball base, usually hung on the wall when empty.

Collins Glassware

A Collins glass is a glass tumbler, holding 240 to 350 ml, used to serve a mixed drink, named after Tom Collins. This glass is somewhat narrower, and holds less than the similar highball glass.

Highball Glass

A highball glass is a glass tumbler, holding between 8 and 12 fluid ounces (240 to 350 mL), used to serve a mixed drink, or highball. This glass is taller than an Old-Fashioned glass, and shorter than a Collins glass.

Shot Glass

It is a small glass used for measuring or serving up to three ounces of liquor. Modern shot glass holds a thicker base and sides than the whiskey glass.

Pint Glass

A pint glass is a drinking vessel holding an imperial pint (568 ml) of liquid and is usually used for beer. Three common shapes of pint glass are found (conical, jug, and flared top), though others are available. Pints are considered good for serving stouts, porters and English ales

Pilsner Glass

A pilsner glass is a glass used to serve many types of light beers, but is intended for its namesake, the pilsner. Pilsner glasses are generally smaller than a pint glass, usually in 250 ml or 330 ml sizes. They are tall, slender and tapered. Wheat beer glasses are often mistakenly referred to as pilsner glasses, but a true pilsner glass has an even taper without curvature. Pilsner glasses are made to showcase the color, effervescence, and clarity of the pilsner, as well as to maintain a nice head.

Beer Stein

A beer stein is a traditionally-German beer tankard or mug, made of pewter, silver, wood, porcelain, earthenware or glass; usually with a hinged lid and levered thumblift.

Flute Glass

A flute glass is the preferred serving vessel for Belgian lambics and fruit beers. The narrow shape helps maintain carbonation, while providing a strong aromatic front. Flute glasses display the lively carbonation, sparkling color, and soft lacing of this distinct style

Goblet or Chalice

Chalices and goblets are large, stemmed, bowl-shaped glasses adequate for serving heavy Belgian ales, German bocks, and other big sipping beers. The distinction between goblet and chalice is typically in the glass thickness. Goblets tend to be more delicate and thin, while the chalice is heavy and thick walled.

Snifters

Typically used for serving brandy and cognac, a snifter is ideal for capturing the volatiles of aromatic beers, such as Belgian ales, India pale ales, barleywines and wheat wines. The shape helps trap the volatiles, while allowing swirling to agitate them and produce an intense aroma.

Wheat Beer Glass

A wheat beer glass is a glass used to serve wheat beer, known also as Weizenbier or Weibbier. The German glass generally holds 500 millilitres with room for foam or "head". It is much taller than a pint glass. It is very narrow at the bottom and slightly wider at the top. In other countries such as Belgium, the glass may hold 250 ml or 330 ml. The tall glass provides room for the often thick, fluffy heads produced by the style, which traps aromas and is visually pleasing.

Tulip Glass

A tulip glass not only helps trap the aroma, but also aids in maintaining large heads, creating a a visual and olfactory sensation. The body is bulbous, but the top flares out to form a lip which helps head retention. It is recommended for serving Scottish ales, barleywines, Belgian ales and other aromatic beers.

Cocktail Glass

A cocktail glass, martini glass, or champagne glass, or stem cocktail glass, is a drinking glass with a cone-shaped bowl (the tip of the cone forming approximately a 90 degree angle in the cross section) on a stem above a flat base, used to serve a cocktail or champagne. As with other stemware, the stem allows the drinker to hold the glass without affecting the temperature of the drink. One variation is the double martini glass which is taller and wider at the opening than a standard martini glass

Red Wine Glasses

Glasses for red wine are characterized by their rounder, wider bowl, which gives the wine a chance to breathe. Since most reds are meant to be consumed at room temperature, the wider bowl also allows the wine to cool more quickly after hand contact has warmed it. Red wine glasses can have particular styles of their own, such as:

- Bordeaux glass: Tall with a wide bowl, and is designed for full bodied red wines like Cabernet and Merlot as it directs wine to the back of the mouth.
- Burgundy glass: Larger than the Bordeaux glass, it has a larger bowl to accumulate aromas of more delicate red wines such as Pinot Noir. This style of glass directs wine to the tip of the tongue.

White Wine Glass

White wine glasses are generally narrower, although not as narrow as champagne flutes, with somewhat straight or tulip-shaped sides. The narrowness of the white wine glass allows the chilled wine to retain its temperature for two reasons;

- The reduced surface area of the glass (in comparison to red wine glasses) means less air circulating around the glass and warming the wine.
- The smaller bowl of the glass means less contact between the hand and the glass, and so body heat does not transfer as easily or as fast to the wine.

Champagne Flutes

Champagne flutes are characterised by a long stem with a tall, narrow bowl on top. The shape is designed to keep sparkling wine attractive and inviting during its consumption. The glass is designed to be held by the stem to help prevent the heat from the hand warming up the champagne. The bowl itself is designed in a manner to help retain the signature carbonation in the beverage. This is achieved by reducing the surface area at the opening of the bowl. Champagne flutes are often used at formal engagements, such as award ceremonies and weddings.

Sherry Glass

A sherry glass is a drinkware generally used for serving aromatic alcoholic beverages, such as sherry, port, aperitifs and liqueurs, and layered shooters. An ISO-standard sized sherry glass is 120 ml. The copita, with its aroma-enhancing narrow taper, is a type of sherry glass.

Coupette Glass

A modified version of the cocktail glass. Used for serving drinks where the rim of the glass is required to be coated in either sugar or salt or any other condiments used to make some of the more exotic drinks such as margaritas.

Pitcher

This larger container usually has a handle and a lip or spout for pouring the contents into several glasses. Available in glass or plastic. Generally used for serving beer for a beer keg for draft beer.

Old Fashioned Glass

The Old-Fashioned glass, rocks glass, or "lowball", is a short tumbler used for serving liquor "on the rocks", meaning over ice, or cocktails having few ingredients. It is named after the old-fashioned cocktail, traditionally served in such a glass. A White Russian is traditionally served in the Old Fahioned Glass.

Yard Glass

A yard (or yard glass) is a very tall glass used for drinking beer; a yard (or yard of ale) also refers to the (variable) quantity of beer held by such a glass. The glass is approximately 1 yard long (hence the name), and holds 2 imperial pints (1.14 litres) of liquid. The glass is shaped with a bulb at the bottom, and a widening shaft which constitutes most of the height. Because the glass is so long and in any case does not usually have a stable flat base, it is hung on the wall when not in use.

Coffee-Mug

Almost a smaller version of the beer mug, made of thick heavy glass and used for coffee

Irish Coffee Cup

A uniquely shaped glass with a handle that is used to serve any hot beverage such as Spanish coffee or cocoa.

Handling of Glassware

1. Glassware is highly fragile and most delicate and expensive: hence atmost care has to be taken while handling glass equipments.
2. Glasses are normally stored in a glass pantry and should be placed upside down in single rows on paper-lined shelves, to prevent dust settling in them.

3. Tumblers should not be stacked inside one another as this may result in heavy breakages and accidents.
4. The appearance of the drink mainly depends on the glass and therefore, the glass should be sparkling clean and attractive in shape and style.
5. When glassware is machine or hand washed, each individual item must be polished and dried with a glass cloth made of linen, as water leaves stains on the glasses.
6. Glasses whether clean or dirty have to be handled by the base or stem, since the finger prints left on the glass necessitates polishing.

Chinaware

China is a term used for crockery whether bone china (expensive and fine), earthenware (opaque and cheaper) or vitrified (metallised). Most catering crockery used nowadays tends to be vitrified earthenware, which is very durable and have strengthened. Crockery is also usually given rolled edges to make it more chip resistant.

Chinaware is made of silica, soda ash, and china clay, glazed to give a fine finish. Chinaware can be found in different colours and designs which are always coated with glaze. Chinaware is more resistant to heat than glassware. There are various classification of catering china. They are:

Porcelain

Porcelain is a ceramic material made by heating selected and refined materials, which often includes clay of kaolinite clay, to high temperatures. The raw materials for porcelain, when mixed with water, form a plastic body that can be worked to a required shape before firing in a kiln at temperatures between 1200°C and 1400°C. The toughness, strength, and translucence of porcelain arise mainly from the formation of glass at high temperatures and the mineral mullite within the fired body.

Bone China Bone china is porcelain made of clay mixed with bone ash. This is very fine, hard china that is very expensive. The decorations are to be found under the glaze only. The price of bone china puts it out of reach of the majority of everyday caterers, and only a few of the top class hotels and restaurants would use it. The range of design, pattern and colour is very wide and there is something to suit all occasions and situations.

Earthenware Earthenware may sometimes be as thin as bone china and other porcelains, though it is not translucent and is more easily chipped.

Earthenware is also less strong, less tough, and more porous than stoneware, but its low cost and easier working compensate for these deficiencies. Due to its higher porosity, earthenware must usually be glazed in order to be watertight.

Stoneware

Stoneware is a hard pottery made from siliceous paste, fired at high temperature to vitrify (make glassy) the body. Stoneware is heavier and more opaque than porcelain. The usual color of fired stoneware tends to be grayish, though there may be a wide range of colors, depending on the clay. It has been produced in China since ancient times and is the forerunner of Chinese porcelain.

Chinaware Serving Items

There are wide ranges of chinaware serving items and their sizes vary according to the manufacturer and the design produced. Recent developments in chinaware include the ovenproof ware (dishes, casserole and cocotte dishes), which allow food to be brought straight from the oven to the table. 46

Handling of Chinaware

Whatever quality of china or crockery is used, the most important thing to ensure is that it is washed, rinsed and dried correctly to ensure that no dirt, stains or streaks appear.

1) Chinaware has a high breakage rate and, therefore, needs careful handling.
2) They should be stored on shelves in piles or stakes of approximately two dozen each. Any higher may result in their toppling down.
3) They should be stored at a convenient height for placing on, and removing from the shelves to avoid accidents.
4) Chinaware should be kept covered to prevent dust and germs settling on it.
5) Chipped and cracked items harbor germs and should, therefore, not be used and disposed off carefully.

Tableware

Tableware includes the dishes, glassware, cutlery, and flatware eating utensils (knives, forks, and spoons) used to set a table for eating a meal.

The nature, variety, and number of objects varies from culture to culture, and may vary from meal to meal a s well. Tableware may be categorised as follows:

- *Flatware:* Flatware denotes all forms of spoon and fork. Flatware, especially that used by most people when they eat informally, is usually made of stainless steel.
- *Cutlery*: Cutlery refers to knives and other cutting instruments.
- *Holloware:* Holloware refers to table service items such as sugar bowls, creamers, coffee pots, teapots, soup tureens, hot food covers, water pitchers, platters, butter plates and other metal items excluding flatware and cutlery.

Special Tableware

There is almost an unlimited range of flatwar, cutlery and hollowware in use in the catering industry. Apart from the familiar knife, fork, spoon, vegetable dishes and lids, entrée dishes and lids, soup tureens, teapot, hotwater jugs, sugar basins there are a number of specialist items of equipment available for use with specific dishes. Some common specialist equipments are listed below:

Special Tableware

Siver Tea Tong

The silver tea tongs (called also silver sugar tongs or silver sugar nips) are used for lifting sugar cubes from the sugar bowls and add to tea cups. The basic forms in which they were made are:

- fire tongs, of two arms joined at one end by a pivot
- scissors tongs, of two arms pivoting at the centre, in the form of a pair of scissors (tea tongs or sugar nips)

Ends of tongs may be serrated.

Asparagus Holder

The asparagus holder is an utensil for a diner to hold a single stalk of asparagus. It is made of a single strip of metal, bent in the form of U-shaped tongs, with a small square plate at each end to grip the stalk.

Pastry Slicer

Pastry slicer is used for serving pastries (portion of gâteau)

Pastry Fork

Pastry fork is a small fork designed for eating pastries and other desserts while holding a plate. It is typically designed so that it can be used with the right hand, while the left hand holds the plate. It therefore has the left side widened to be used like a knife to cut the food when pressed down on the plate. Left-handed pastry forks have the right side widened instead. This fork may also be used to lift fruit pieces from the plate.

Oyster Fork

A fork used for picking up shellfish cocktail or oysters. This fork is shaped like a regular fork, but it slightly smaller and the tines are curved outward.

Lobster Pick

This long, narrow utensil is used to pull every shred of meat from the hard-to-reach cavities (such as the legs) of lobsters and crabs. The tip of a lobster pick can either be pointed or in the shape of a tiny, two-prong fork.

Snail Tong and Snail Fork

Small, spring-operated tongs used to hold hot snail shells while extracting the snail. Unlike most tongs, these open by squeezing the handles. When the pressure is released, the tongs snap securely around the snail shell.

Snail Dish

It is a round dish with two ears having six indentations to hold portion of six snails.

Skewers

A long, thin, pointed rod that comes in various sizes. Skewers are made of metal or wood; the former often has a ring at one end. They're most often used to hold meat in place during cooking/ serving, as well as to skewer meat and vegetables to be grilled for shish kebab. The best skewers are square or flat-shaped that hold food securely when moved. Usually made of stainless steel.

Ice-cream Scoop

It is used to remove ice cream from a carton or other container while forming the ice cream into a ball or oval shape. Ice-cream scoops come in several styles and sizes. The simplest is a plain metal scoop- or spade-shaped utensil. Next comes one shaped like a half-globe or oval with a spring-action lever in the handle. When squeezed, the lever moves an arc-shaped blade across the scoop's interior and ejects the ice-cream ball. The nonstick-style scoop has antifreeze sealed inside.

Nutcracker

It is a tool for cracking hard nutshells, usually consisting of two hinged metal arms between which the nut is squeezed.

Stainless Steel

Stainless steel flatware and culery is available in a variety of grades. Use of stainless steels and super stainless steels is expanding in a variety of markets. Stainless steels have higher resistance to oxidation (rust) and corrosion in many natural and man made environments; however, it is important to select the correct type and grade of stainless steel.

Stainless steel is finished by different degrees of polishing: high polish finish, dull polish finish and a light grey matt, non reflective finish, etc.

Stainless steel's resistance to corrosion and staining, low maintenance, relative inexpense and familiar luster make it an ideal base material for tableware. Stainless steel neither tarnishes nor stains. It resists scratching far more than other metals and may, therefore, be said to be more hygienic.

Handling of Tableware

i) Storage of cutlery and flatware is very important. Each items has to be stored in the boxes or drawers lined with baize to prevent the items being scratched

ii) They should be stored in cupboard or room which can be locked.

iii) Cutlery and flatware may be stored in cutlery trollies.

Tables and Chairs

The size and shape of tables depends entirely on the availability of space and the kind of service envisaged. Normally three types of tables are used. They are round, rectangular and square.

The height of the table irrespective of the shape should be 75 cm from the floor level. The diameter of a round table to seat four people should be approximately 92 cm. The size of a square table to seat two people should 76 cm sq and 92 cm square to seat four people. The size of rectangular table to seat four people should be 137 cm x 76 cm. Commercial table tops come in a variety of materials: wood, metal, stone, tile and melamine. Many restaurant table tops are available with edged finishes to prevent scuffs and dents.In some expensive tables, another table top is placed with revolving facility, on top of which the food is placed where th guests can rotate revolving top and serve himself, if he chooses to.

Chairs

Chair are available in various shapes, colours and sizes to suit all occasions. Because of the wide ranges of style, chairs come in varied height and width. However the dimension of chairs should be relative to table dimensions. The average height of the chair should be 92 cm. The seat should be 46 cm from the floor and 23 cm from the top of the table. This would enable guests to sit and eat comfortably, without their legs touching the underside of the table.

Side Station / Dummy Waiter

The side station is also called the dummy waiter or service console. This is a very important piece of furniture in a restaurant. It is used by the service staff for keeping all the service equipment at one place. It is also used as a landing table for the dishes picked up from the kitchen enroute to the table and the dirty dishes from the guest's table to the wash-up area. For the convenience of the service staff, the side station should be strategically located in a restaurant. The side station should be kept clean and presentable as it can be seen by the guests.

The style and design of the side board varies from establishment to establishment. It depends upon:

- The style of service and menu offered.
- The number of waiters working from one sideboard
- The number of tables to be served from one sideboard
- The amount of equipment it is expected to hold.

It is essential that the side board is of minimum size and portable so that it may be moved, if necessary. If the sideboard is too large for its purpose, then it takes up space which could be used to seat more customers. The top should be of heat resistant material which can be easily washed down. After service, the sideboard is either completely emptied out or restocked for the next service.

Trolleys

The various trolleys used in the food and beverage service outlets are:

Gueridon or Flambe Trolley

A gueridon or flambe trolley is a small mobile trolley that can be placed alongside the guest's table. It consists of one or two burners, a gas cylinder and a work and storage space for plates and cooking equipment. Using this trolley, the food is flambed at the guest's table. Only skilled and well rained waiters are allowed to handle this service as there is the risk of spoiling food by overcooking it, and of the flame causing a fire in the premises.

Room Service Trolley

This trolley is known for its versatility. It is used for the service to guests in their rooms. The waiter sets up the meal and covers on the trolley and wheels it into the guest's room. This trolley may also be used as a dining table in the privacy of the guest's room. Beneath the trolley top, provision is made for mounting a hot case to keep the food warm.

Dessert Trolley

This trolley serves as a visual aid to selling desserts. Guests are more likely to order a dessert if they can see what is available, particularly if it is well presented. Some dessert trolleys are refrigerated. Gateaux, pastries, jellies, tarts, pies, flans and souffles can be served from a dessert trolley. This trolley has several shelves and the bottom shelf is reserved for plates, cutlery, linen and other service equipment. A glass or transparent trolley top makes it easy for guests to select a dessert of their choice.

Hors d'oeuvre Trolley

A hors d'oeuvre is the first course of a menu usually consisting of a selection of small items of egg, fish, meat, fruit and vegetables in pungent dressings. This hors d'oeuvre trolley is used to carry variety of appetizers. This trolley is probably the least popular in India, as a majority of guests are not too keen on hors d'oeuvre as a starter. They prefer soups instead. However, this trolley can be used to popularise the special dishes that are introduced in the restaurant from time to time.

Carving Trolley

It is used for carving joints of meat at a guest's table. This trolley is seldom used in India.

Linens are Fabric Goods

Linens are fabric goods, such as tablecloths, napkins and slip cloths. Linen is a material made from the fibers of the flax plant. Originally, many, such as bed sheets and tablecloths, were made of linen. Today, the term "linen" has come to be applied to all related products even though most are made of cotton, various synthetic materials, or blends. The main items of linen normally found in a restaurant are: tablecloths; slipcloths; buffet cloths; trolley and sideboard cloths; and waiter's cloths or service cloths.

Table Cloths

Table linens made from cotton or linen are not only more absorbent but also last longer. The fibers don't pill or pile as easy as with synthetic table linens and they don't become shiny when exposed to an iron's heat. Egyptian cotton and Irish linen are considered the finest materials for table linens because of their long, durable fibers. White is the most popular color for table linens because it's considered formal. Table linens in off white or ivory are also acceptable. A damask (woven) or embroidered pattern is a perfectly acceptable table cloth.

Types of Tables	*Size of Tables*	*Size of Table Cloths*
Square table	76 cm sq 92 cm sq	137 x 137 cm 183 x 183 cm
Rectangular table	136 x 76 cm	183 x 137 cm
Round table	92 cm diameter	184 cm diameter

Table cloths should be large enough to cover the top as well as a portion of the legs of a table without interfering with the guest's comfort while he is seated at the table.The size of the tablecloth varies according to the size of the table it is required to cover.

Slip Cloths or Naperones

These are designed to be laid over the tablecloth to protect it from spillage and give it a longer life. Using a slip cloth reduces the number of tablecloths used and thus reduces the cost of inventory and laundry. Slip cloths may measure 1 metre square approximately.

Napkins or Serviettes

A napkin or serviette is a rectangle cloth or paper used at the table for wiping the mouth while eating. It is usually small and folded. Conventionally, t he napkin is folded and placed to the left of the place setting, outside the outermost fork. In an ambitious restaurant setting, it may be folded into elaborate shapes and displayed on the empty plate. A napkin may also be held together in a bundle (with cutlery) by a napkin ring. Alternatively, paper napkins may be contained with a napkin holder.

Napkins may be of the same colour as tablecloths, or in a colour that blends with the decor of the restaurant. Napkins should be spotlessly clean and well-pressed. The ideal size for a napkin is 56 between 46 to 50 cm sq.

Buffet Cloths

For a buffet table, the minimum size of the tablecloth required is 2 m x 4 m.

Trolley Cloths and Sideboard Cloths

These are usually made from tablecloths well worn and not suitable for use on tables, mended by the housekeeping department and folded to fit a sideboard or trolley.

Waiter's Cloths or Service Cloths

A service cloth is a very important part of service equipment as well as being part of the food server's uniform. It must be kept clean and ironed at all times and only used as a service cloth for certain activities such as:

- Carrying hot plates
- Final polishing of plates
- Wiping small spills
- Brushing crumbs onto a service plate
- Wiping the undersides of the plates before placing plates on the table.

Service cloths are also used by every waiter as protection against heat and to keep uniforms clean.

EQUIPMENT HANDLING

Management invests substantial amount in supplies and equipment. Service staffs are, therefore, expected that these equipment are handled gently and carefully. Staff should be sanitation and safety conscious. Equipment should be handled in the right spot stemmed glass by the stem, tumblers by the base, flatware by the handle. Bowls should never be held by the rim, use appropriate underliners. The thumb should never show on the plate. When setting up cutleries, as well as glasswares, avoid leaving finger marks by using trays or by securing them inside a cloth napkin.

To prevent breakage, be conscious of the rules of equipment handling. Breakages are usually caused by the following factors:

1. *Mechanical Impact* — results from object-to-object collision. This is induced by stacking of glasswares and chinawares, picking of glasses in bouquet, overloading of buspans and trays, putting cutleries inside glasses.
2. *Thermal Shock*—result of sudden change of temperature. This happens when hot water is placed inside a chilled / cold glass and vice versa, abrupt use of glasswares after coming of the dishwashing machines, heating chilled bowl in a microwave.
3. *Improper Handling and Misuse of Equipment*—the equipment for a purpose it was not intended for such as using a glass to scoop ice, using knives for opening cans, etc.
4. *Inattentiveness or Absent-mindedness*—accidents often occur when service personnel are absent-minded or are inattentive in executing services especially when they are carrying breakable equipment.
5. *Environmental Factors* – greasy / wet floor, slippery floor, broken tiles, blind doors.

Measures to Avoid Breakages

- Use trays when serving and bussing.
- Proper system should be followed in stacking and storing equipment.
- Use appropriate door for entry and exit. A separate door for entering and eiting should be installed to prevent collision.
- Use appropriate glass racks. Make sure that the glasses are conviniently, but not tightly inserted in each rack.
- Buss out glasses separately from chinaware.
- Avoid overloading trays and buspans.

Do's and Dont's of Equipment Handling

1. Dump ice out of the glass; preheat the glass before pouring hot water. Don't pour hot drinks in chilled or cold glasses.

2. Stack dishes according to size and kind. Never stack too high.
3. Handle stemmed glasses by the stem and tumblers by the base. Never handle glasses in bouquet.
4. Remove glass / china from buspan one at a time. Don't unload china, glasses at random.
5. Use ice scooper for scooping ice. Never use the glass for scooping ice.
6. Never put cutlery into glasses, put them in appropriate containers.
7. Make sure of an adequate back-up supply of glassware for rush periods.
8. Always be on the lookout for cracked or chipped glassware and remove them.
9. Never allow glass-to-glass contact on overhead racks, keep distant from each other.
10. Never overload the tray / buspan. Load only what it can conveniently accommodate.
11. Never buss glasses in the sink. Buss them directly onto divider racks.
12. Never stack glasses. Use trays and avoid over crowding them to prevent breakage.

Sanitation Standards in Handling Service Equipment

1. Use clean and sanitized glasses, flatware, chinaware and other equipment for service.
2. All service equipment must be wiped dry with clean cloths to avoid watermarks. The cloths used for this purpose must be segregated from other wiping cloths.
3. Bowls should be underlined with appropriate underliner and never to be served with the finger touching the rim.
4. When serving straw serve them with their wrappers or in their respective dispensers.
5. When serving additional utensils or napkin, place them in a small plate to avoid direct contact with hand.
6. The thumb should be kept away from the plate to avoid touching the sauce, meat or dish.
7. When setting up flatware and glasses, avoid leaving finger marks; carry them in trays or with a cloth napkin.

8. Never serve food using cutleries that have fallen on the floor.
9. To avoid contamination, food must be covered when it is not served immediately.

Never serve utensils, cups, glasses or plates that are oily, wet or with fingermarks, spots or lipstick mark.

Bar Special Equipment

Bar Stools

The type of seating you choose for your restaurant or bar must correspond with the length of time you expect your customers to be seated. Fast-food or quick turn-around restaurants will not want to provide seating that encourages lounging and extended stays. Alternatively, a fine dining establishment should make sure they provide comfortable seating. There are different types of bar stools:

Wood Bar Stools and Wood Chairs

Wood furniture provides a clean look that will compliment the existing décor of most any dining space. Wood Bar Stools and wood chairs are sturdy, easy to clean, and require little to no maintenance. Shop our selection of wood bar stools and wood chairs for the best variety of wood furniture styles and finish colours.

Upholstered Wood Bar Stools and Upholstered Wood Chairs

Upholstered wood furniture provides moderate comfort to your customers. Upholstered wood bar stools and upholstered wood chairs allow you to bring more colour into your restaurant or bar since many of our upholstered wood furniture pieces are available in a variety of upholstery colours. Vinyl upholstered furniture is easy to clean and maintain. Shop our wide selection of upholstered wood bar stools and upholstered wood chairs.

Metal Frame Bar Stools and Metal Frame Chairs

Metal frame bar stools and metal frame chairs present a modern look to your restaurant or bar. Metal frame bar stools and metal frame chairs come in a variety of styles and upholstery options.

Lounge Seating

Lounge chairs and lounge bar stools offer deluxe, comfortable seating. Lounge chairs and lounge stools are ideal for restaurants or bars that would like to encourage their customers to stay for longer periods of time. Lounge seating is available in a variety of upholstery colours in plain, tufted and channeled styles. Solid Chrome or Brass accents and bases complete the look of the lounge chairs and lounge bar stools.

Nostalgic 50's Bar Stools and Dining Chairs

Create a feeling of nostalgia in your restaurant or bar with retro, 50's styled bar stools and dining chairs. Heavy duty bar stools reflect the 50's era with Chrome frames and shiny vinyl upholstery. The nostalgic dining chairs feature unique detailing with Chrome frames, tufted upholstered backs and two-toned vinyl upholstery.

Booths

Booth seating is available with wall-mount frames and island frames. Booths are available with wood, laminate or upholstered seats. Laminate and wood booths are easily maintained and ideal for quick-turn around restaurants. Upholstered booths offer comfortable seating to customers that may have a longer wait for their meal to arrive. High-back booths offer a considerable amount of privacy to your customers, which will bring an intimate atmosphere to your restaurant or bar.

Outdoor Furniture

Move your customers outdoors for dinner with outdoor furniture. Choose from a variety of teak outdoor furniture, aluminum outdoor furniture, wicker outdoor furniture and durable resin outdoor furniture. Mosaic tables and mosaic chairs make a colourful addition to your outdoor seating area. Mosaic outdoor furniture features hand-made stained glass table tops and chair seats with powder coated, heat treated wrought iron bases and frames.

Stack Chairs and Folding Chairs

Furniture that allows for stacking or folding is ideal for banquet facilities and multi-purpose rooms. Stack chairs are useful in areas with minimal storage, and are easy to transport. Stack chairs are often referred to as banquet chairs, as they are most commonly used in banquet halls and multi-purpose dining facilities. Folding chairs are a good idea for providing additional seating and are generally cost-effective.

Table Tops and Table Bases

Choose a customised table for your restaurant with mix-and-match table tops and table bases. Choose a table base that will best suit your needs. Standard height table bases measure 28" in height and stand-up height table bases measure up to 42" in height. Once you have chosen a table base choose a table top. Serv-U offers a wide variety of laminated table tops, solid wood table tops, wood edge table tops, metal edge table tops, and aluminum table tops.

Youth Furniture and High Chairs

It is important to provide safe and reliable seating for infants and children that eat in your restaurant. Wood high chairs are sturdy, stackable, and easy to clean. Booster seats are available in a variety of colour choices. It may be wise to purchase the optional safety strap for your booster seats to ensure the booster seat is secured to your dining chairs.

Other Bar Equipments

Back Bar Coolers

Back bar coolers should be placed behind the bar and will typically have 2-3 doors. Back bar coolers can be ordered with a stainless steel countertop or a galvanised top. Back bar coolers are available with solid doors and glass doors. For a multi-purpose unit choose the combination back bar cooler and beer dispenser by True. This unit features a direct draw beer dispenser built in to the back bar refrigerator.

Bar Blenders

Bar blenders allow for higher profits by extending the menu including frozen drinks, ice cream drinks or smoothies. When choosing bar blenders, consider the volume of drinks needed at peak time. High capacity bar blenders can crush a ½ gallon of ice in 3 seconds! Bar blenders containers are available in 32 Oz., 48 Oz., or ½ gallon capacities. Programmable bar blenders and drink stations increase drink consistency and allows operator to complete other tasks. Sound enclosures and in-counter bar blenders reduce the noise from powerful motors.

Bar Sinks

Bar sinks are available in a variety of configurations. Many bar sinks are designed as modular units so you can customise your work space exactly to your specifications. Drop-in bar sinks are great for custom applications. Look for a variety of bar sink units at Serv-U, many bar sink units are available in different depths and widths, to ensure a proper fit with your existing back bar equipment.

Beer Dispenser

Beer dispensers can accommodate one to five different kegs of beer at the same time. Beer dispensers are available in Black vinyl, Woodgrain vinyl and stainless steel. A club top direct draw beer dispenser has a shelf area at the back of the unit, plus sliding lids for quick access to the storage area. A one keg direct draw beer dispenser will hold 1/4 or 1/2 barrel kegs.

Beer Faucets

Choose from Chrome beer faucets, Brass beer faucets, stainless steel beer faucets and Black plastic beer faucets. Quick action stout faucets are perfect for low carbonated ales and stouts. Choose the beer faucet that will work best for your bar or restaurant.

Beer Line Cleaning

Beer line cleaning pumps are designed for use with direct draw and short run beverage systems. Choose from a manual cleaning system or an automatic, heavy duty model designed for larger systems or longer runs. Keep your beer line clean to ensure your customers receive a quality, fresh-tasting product from your bar.

Beer Merchandisers

Beer merchandisers come in a variety of shapes and sizes. Beer merchandisers are great for outdoor use and make transporting large quantities of beer and packaged beverages easy. Choose a beer merchandiser that will accommodate packaged beverages or a 1/4 gallon to 1/2 gallon size keg. Some beer merchandisers will hold multiple kegs, while most will hold one keg.

Beer Pumps

There are several different types of beer pumps available. Choose from a variety of picnic pumps and push pumps. Some beer pumps come with a beer dispensing hose, while other beer pumps have a beer faucet built onto the beer pump.

Beer Taps

Beer taps are available with wing handles and lever handles. Lever handle taps feature a snap-down handle that is safe, fast and easy to use. Wing handle taps operate easily with a quarter turn of the plastic handle.

Beer Towers

Choose from several beer towers for your bar. Beer towers are available with single, double or triple faucets. Many dome draft beer towers are available with up to six faucets, and also feature decorative accents to add flair to your bar.

Bottle Coolers

Choose a frosty brew bottle cooler from Beverage-Air® for high volume and fast pull-down applications. True® bottle coolers include adjustable bin dividers and a built-on bottle opener and cap catcher.

Brass Rail

Quality commercial grade brass railing and polished stainless steel railing are ideal for balcony and stair rails, dance bars, bar rails and guard rails. Solid brass or polished stainless steel bar rails and fittings are sturdy, attractive and extremely durable.

CO_2 Regulators

Single and double gauge CO_2 regulators feature a forged brass body, self-aligning spring plate and relief valve spring. You should monitor the CO_2 regulators to ensure applied operating pressures remain constant (10-12psi/lbs).

Drip Trays

Drip trays are great for catching spills from beer draft towers. Many counter top drip trays feature a threaded drain fitting so you do not need to empty the trays throughout the evening. Counter top dump trays sit on top of the bar and no drain is required, however these dump trays will need to be emptied throughout the evening, as they become full.

Glass Washers

Glass washers are an easy and efficient way to wash and clean bar glassware. Many glass washers feature instant installation and require no plumbing. Glass brushes are an easy solution for bars that do not want to purchase a glass washing machine. Glass brushes feature a sturdy plastic base with rubber suction to firmly hold to the bottom of the sink. Brushes for all glass washers are replaceable.

Ice Caddies

An ice caddy provides a safe method for transporting ice. Many ice caddies feature a sliding lid to help reduce the risk of cross contamination. Choose an ice caddy with casters for easy transportation of ice.

Juicers/Drink Mixers

Choose from manual juicers or electric juicers. Spindle mixers are great for mixing ice cream dinks, smoothies, or any other thick drink. A juicer allows you to make drinks with fresh fruits. Juicers are great for smoothie bars and restaurants serving breakfast and/or brunch items.

Portable Bars

Portable bars are great for banquet halls and rooms, or for taking a party outdoors. All portable bars come with locking casters for ease of mobility from room to room. Portable bars feature storage areas, speed rails and ice bins.

Speed rails

Speed rails accommodate a variety alcohol bottle sizes. Stainless steel speed rails are durable and used in most bars. Speed rails are typically mounted directly to the bar sink.

Wine racks

Countertop wine racks will help you sell more wine by displaying thc product for customers. Choose from different sizes and metal finishes when choosing your wine rack. Each wine rack can accommodate up to six, twenty-one or forty-five wine bottles.

Wine Merchandiser

A wine merchandiser can hold a total wine bottle capacity of 50 bottles. Wine merchandisers include a lighted four-colour "Wine Cellar" sign. The interior floor of the unit can be used to merchandise liter bottles, and the top shelf can be used to merchandise packaged beverages. The specially designed wine bottle shelves allow for proper horizontal storage of wine bottles.

Ashtrays

Restaurants and bars permitting smoking should have plenty of ashtrays on hand to accommodate customers. Choose ashtrays that will be most effective for your restaurant or bar by choosing glass ashtrays, plastic ashtrays, metal ashtrays or disposable ashtrays. It is also a good idea to place smoking receptacles near the entrances and exits of your restaurant and bar so customers may properly extinguish and dispose of all cigarette butts. Many outdoor smoking receptacles will accommodate up to 3,000 extinguished cigarettes and nearly all are weather resistant and flame retardant.

Bar Knives

Bar knives and bar tools are essential for preparing drink garnishes such as lemons, limes, oranges, mint leaves and olives. A forked bar knife is a useful tool that will allow bartenders to safely retrieve condiment items such as cherries or olives from jars and will also cut and slice condiment items. A lemon or lime peeler will easily allow a bartender to peel and zest any type of citrus fruit.

Bar Mats and Shelf Liner

Bar matting improves airflow and moisture drainage when used with wet bar supplies. Interlockable bar matting allows for layout changes and can be trimmed to fit into the existing spaces of your bar. Shelf liner is great for glassware storage or dinnerware storage.

Bar Trays

Smaller round bar trays are ideal for bartenders and servers that need to maneuver through groups of people. Cork lined trays and non skid bar trays are great for transporting beverages and appetizers that could easily spill or slide off the tray. Some bar trays feature a rim or lip around the edge of bar tray to prevent spill from running over the edge of the tray and onto a customer.

Bottle Openers and Corkscrews

While a bottle opener or a corkscrew may seem like a simple purchase, these items will undoubtedly get used very frequently behind almost every bar. Wall mount bottle openers are perfect for behind the bar use, your bartenders and servers will always know where to find a bottle opener. Some varieties of corkscrews and wine bottle openers can also be mounted to a wall or counter for security and extra leverage.

Cocktail Shakers

The cocktail shaker is typically a bartender's most useful tool. Most cocktail shakers are stainless steel 3-piece shakers, and typically include a strainer top and a jigger cap. Many bartenders feel stainless steel cocktail shakers are best, since they chill a drink more quickly than glass cocktail shakers. Vinyl coated cocktail shakers are constructed of stainless steel with a durable coating of vinyl to give the bartender a dry, sure grip.

Drain Trays

Drain trays are available with or without drain fittings. Most drain trays are composed of stainless steel or brass, and feature either a metal grid or a polystyrene grid.

Ice Scoops

Ice scoops are a very useful tool to have behind the bar. Using an ice scoop to fill glasses reduces the risk of cross contamination. Choose an ice scoop that is tapered to facilitate pouring of ice into glasses. A slotted ice scoop will help to separate water from your ice.

Jiggers

A jigger is a dual sided measure cup, and comes in extremely handy behind the bar. Use a jigger when making mixed drinks to ensure you have the proper proportions of each ingredient.

Liquor Pours

Liquor pours are great way to maintain portion control in your bar. Measured pours range in size from 7/8 oz. to 1 1/2 oz. Straight pours will allow an unlimited amount of alcohol to pour from the bottle. Metal liquor pours can dress up your bar with their bright and shiny chrome finish.

Plastic Drinkware and Disposable Drinkware

Polycarbonate drinkware and disposable barware are great for outdoor seating and locations where glass is not permissible. Polycarbonate glassware is durable, shatterproof and dishwasher safe. Disposable barware is made from rigid styrene plastic.

Bar Game Supplies

Pool tables and dartboards are a good source of entertainment for your guests. Cue sticks are available in solid ramin wood, solid hardrock maple, and hardrock maple with a fiberglass coating. Pool table lights add an authentic look to your bar. Choose from plastic shade pool table lights and metal shade pool table lights. Electronic dartboards programmed for 19-30 different dart games are a great alternative to standard dartboards.

Wine Chillers

Wine chillers and wine buckets will keep your customers' wine chilled for the duration of their stay. Double wall wine coolers provide insulation that chills wine at the proper temperature for up to three hours. A genuine marble wine chiller will keep wine cold for 60 minutes. Champagne buckets and wine buckets provide an elegant look, and will typically hold up to two bottles of wine.

Purchasing Food Service Equipment

Purchasing restaurant equipment does not need to be difficult. When purchasing commercial kitchen equipment it is wise to consider the following: safety features, quality, efficiency, any warranty and service plans, the reputation of the manufacturer, and all short- and long-term costs associated with your purchase.

Consider Quality

Many restaurant owners gauge the quality of restaurant equipment by the reputation of the manufacturer. In many instances a well respected brand of restaurant equipment has earned its reputation due to the exceptional value and quality of its products. It is commonly assumed that a name-brand piece of restaurant equipment will outperform that of its un-named competitor. This may not always be the case. Also, purchasing restaurant equipment by an un-named manufacturer may be less expensive.

Consider Cost

A restaurant owner's decision to purchase new restaurant equipment should always be based on more than the initial cost of the unit. The buyer should weigh the total costs by short- and long-term considerations. In most cases new restaurant equipment is more energy efficient to operate than older restaurant equipment. Over time this will allow the restaurant owner to save money on utility costs. The warranty and service plan included with the purchase of a new unit of restaurant equipment may eliminate or reduce maintenance and service costs.

A great way to reduce costly repairs once a warranty or service plan has expired is to practice preventative maintenance and have your restaurant equipment serviced regularly. A new unit of restaurant equipment will include the latest technology and safety features. This will increase the efficiency of your kitchen and bring added safety to your employees.

Consider Your Needs

One way to determine the restaurant equipment needed to effectively and efficiently operate your restaurant is to create a work-flow chart for each item on your menu. Keep track of all restaurant equipment used to make each item on your menu. Be sure to take special notice of the restaurant equipment items used most frequently in the preparation of your menu items. It may be wise to invest more time and money in the purchase of these heavily used commercial cooking equipment units.

Consider the Investment

Most importantly, consider the purchase of your restaurant equipment as an investment. The success of your restaurant relies on your restaurant kitchen's ability to produce a quality product. The quality of your product relies on consistent and positive performance of your restaurant equipment. Experienced restaurant owners know that unreliable restaurant equipment will hurt their bottom line in more ways than one.

References

Albert Pick & Company (Chicago), *Equipment for cafeterias, lunch rooms, restaurants and dining rooms, kitchen equipment,* Chicago: The Company, 1920.

Casado, Matt A. *Food and Beverage Service Manual.* New York: Wiley, 1994.

Chesser, Gerald. *Art and Science of Culinary Preparation: A Culinarian's Manual.* St. Augustine: Educational Institute of the American Culinary, 1992.

Wilkinson, Jule. *Complete Book of Cooking Equipment.* Boston: CBI Pub. Company, 1981.

4

Menu Planning

In a food service establishment, a menu is a presentation of food and beverage offerings. A menu may be a la carte – which guests use to choose from a list of options – or table d'hôte, in which case a pre-established sequence of courses is served.

The first restaurant menus arose roughly one millennium ago, during the Song Dynasty in China - the only region of the world at the time where paper was abundant. At this time, many merchants often congregated in city centers and had little time or energy to eat during the evening. Because of the large variation found in Chinese cuisine from different regions, the restaurants could no longer cater to the local palates, giving rise to the menu.

The word "menu," like much of the terminology of cuisine, is French in origin. It ultimately derives from Latin "minutus," something made small; in French it came to be applied to a detailed list or résumé of any kind. The original menus that offered consumers choices were prepared on a small chalkboard, in French a carte; so foods chosen from a bill of fare are described as "à la carte," "according to the board."

The original European restaurants did not have menus in the modern sense; these table d'hôte establishments served dishes that were chosen by the chef or proprietors, and those who arrived ate what the house was serving that day, as in contemporary banquets or buffets. In Europe, the contemporary menu first appeared in the second half of the eighteenth century. Here, instead of eating what was being served from a common table, restaurants allowed diners to choose from a list of unseen dishes, which were produced to order according to the customer's selection. A table d'hôte establishment charged its customers a fixed price; the menu allowed customers to spend as much or as little money as they chose.

As early as the mid-20th century, some restaurants have relied on "menu specialists" to design and print their menus. Prior to the emergence of digital printing, these niche printing companies printed full-color menus on offset presses. The economics of full-color offset made it impractical to print short press runs. The solution was to print a "menu shell" with everything but the prices. The prices would later be printed on a less costly black-only press. In a typical order, the printer might produce 600 menu shells, then finish and laminate 150 menus with prices. When the restaurant needed to reorder, the printer would add prices and laminate some of the remaining shells.

With the advent of digital presses made by such companies as Canon, Kodak, Ricoh and Xerox, it became practical in the 1990s to print full-color menus affordably in short press runs, sometimes as few at 25 menus. Because of limits on sheet size, typically no greater than 13 x 19 inches (33 x 48 cm), larger laminated menus were impractical for single-location independent restaurants, and more restaurants began using menu covers to hold multiple sheets. The use of covers also makes it possible to update one or more pages of the menu without discarding the entire product.

More recently, the advent of the Xerox iGen3 digital press allows sheet sizes of 14.25 x 22.5 inches (36 x 57 cm), offering the option of larger laminated menus in press runs of as few as 100 copies.

The changing economics of offset printing in the early 21st century made it practical to produce press runs of as few as 300 menus, but some restaurants may want to place far fewer menus into service. Some menu printers continue to use shells. The disadvantage for the restaurant is that it is unable to update anything but prices without creating a new shell.

During the economic crisis in the 1970s, many restaurants found that they were having to incur costs from having to reprint the menu as inflation caused prices to increase. Economists noted this transaction cost, and it has become part of economic theory, under the term "menu costs." As a general economic phenomenon, "menu costs" can be experienced by a range of businesses beyond restaurants; for example, during a period of inflation, any company that prints catalogues or product price lists will have to reprint these items with new price figures. To avoid having to reprint the menus throughout the year as prices changed, some restaurants began to display their menus on chalkboards, with the menu items and prices written in chalk. This way, the restaurant could easily modify the prices without going to the expense of reprinting the paper menus. A similar tactic continued to be used in the 2000s with certain items that are sensitive to changing supply, fuel costs, and so on: the use of the term "market price" or "Please ask server" instead of stating the price. This allows restaurants to modify the price of lobster, fresh fish and other foods subject to rapid changes in cost.

The latest trend in menus is the advent of handheld tablets that hold the menu and the guests can browse through that and look at the photographs of the dishes.

Menu Composing

The main categories within a typical menu in the US are "appetizers," "side orders and a la carte," "entrées," "desserts" and "beverages." Sides and a la carte may include such items as soups, salads and dips. There may be special age-restricted sections for "seniors" or for children, presenting smaller portions at lower prices. Any of these sections may be pulled out as a separate menu, such as desserts and/or beverages, or a wine list. Children's menus may also be presented as placemats with games and puzzles to help keep children entertained.

Menus can provide other useful information to diners. Some menus describe the chef's or proprietor's food philosophy, the chef's resume, or the mission statement of the restaurant. Menus often present a restaurant's policies about ID checks for alcohol, lost items, or gratuities for larger parties. In the United States, county health departments frequently require restaurants to include health warnings about raw or undercooked meat, poultry, eggs and seafood.

As a form of advertising, the prose found on printed menus is famous for the degree of its puffery. Menus frequently emphasize the processes used to prepare foods, call attention to exotic ingredients, and add French or other foreign language expressions to make the dishes appear sophisticated and exotic. Higher-end menus often add adjectives to dishes such as "glazed," "sautéed," "poached," and so on. "Menu language, with its hyphens, quotation marks, and random outbursts of foreign words, serves less to describe food than to manage your expectations"; restaurants are often "plopping in foreign words (80 percent of them French) like "spring mushroom civet," "plin of rabbit," "orange-jaggery gastrique." Brian McGrory quips that, when going to a high-end restaurant, he sometimes feels that he needs "an unabridged dictionary, a Biology 101 textbook, and a pile of Fun With Phonics just to figure out the meaning of gianduja ice cream, hazelnut financiers, yellow watermelon, and bulgur crackers[—] just some of the inscrutable listings from the dessert menu..." Terry Pratchett satirizes this in his novel Hogfather, after a fancy restaurant has its stock of expensive foods replaced with mud and old boots. The resulting menu features such items as Panier de la Pate de Chaussures (Mud mousse in a basket of shoe pastry), Cafe de Terre, and Spaghetti Carbonara (boiled boot laces).

Part of the function of menu prose is to impress customers with the notion that the dishes served at the restaurant require such skill, equipment, and exotic ingredients that the diners could not prepare similar foods at home. In some cases, ordinary foods are made to sound more exciting by replacing everyday terms with their French equivalent. For example, instead of stating that a pork chop has a dollop of applesauce, a high-end restaurant menu might state "Tenderloin of pork avec compôte de pommes." Although the French term "avec compôte de pommes" is an exact translation of "with applesauce," it sounds more exotic – and more worthy of an inflated price tag. Menus may use the French term "concassé" to describe coarsely chopped vegetables or "coulis" to describe a puree of vegetables or fruit. Another example is the French term "au jus," which means that meat is served with its own natural gravy of pan drippings.

In some fast food restaurants, each menu item has a number and patrons are asked to "order by number."

Another phenomenon is the so-called "secret menu" where some fast food restaurants are known for having unofficial and unadvertised selections that customers learn by word of mouth. Fast food restaurants will often prepare variations on items already available, but to have them all on the menu would create clutter. Chipotle Mexican Grill is well known for having a simple five item menu, but some might not know they offer quesadillas and single tacos, despite neither being on the menu board. In-N-Out Burger has a very simple menu of burgers, fries, sodas, and shakes, but has a wide variety of "secret" styles of preparations, the most famous being "Animal Style" burgers and fries. This can also occur in high-end restaurants, which may be willing to prepare certain items which are not listed on the menu (e.g., dishes that have long been favorites of regular clientele). Sometimes restaurants may name foods often ordered by regular clientele after them, for either convenience or prestige.

Types of Menu

Paper Menus

Menus vary in length and detail depending on the type of restaurant. The simplest hand-held menus are printed on a single sheet of paper, though menus with multiple pages or "views" are common. In some cafeteria-style restaurants and chain restaurants, a single-page menu may double as a disposable placemat. To protect a menu from spills and wear, it may be protected by heat-sealed vinyl page protectors, laminating or menu covers. Restaurants weigh their positioning in the marketplace (e.g. fine dining, fast food, informal) in deciding which style of menu to use.

While some restaurants may use a single menu as the sole way of communicating information about menu items to customers, in other cases, the meal menu is supplemented with ancillary menus, such as:

- An appetizer menu (nachos, chips and salsa, vegetables and dip, etc.)
- A wine list
- A liquor and mixed drinks menu
- A beer list
- A dessert menu (which may also include a list of tea and coffee options)

Some restaurants use only text in their menus. In other cases, restaurants include illustrations and photos, either of the dishes or of an element of the culture which is associated with the restaurant. An example of the latter is in cases where a Lebanese kebab restaurant decorates its menu with photos of Lebanese mountains and beaches. Particularly with the ancillary menu types, the menu may be provided in alternative formats, because these menus (other than wine lists) tend to be much shorter than food menus. For example, an appetizer menu or a dessert menu may be displayed on a folded paper table tent, a hard plastic table stand, a flipchart style wooden "table stand," or even, in the case of a pizza restaurant with a limited wine selection, a wine list glued to an empty bottle.

Take-out restaurants often leave paper menus in the lobbies and doorsteps of nearby homes as advertisement. The first to do so may have been New York City's Empire Szechuan chain, founded in 1976. The chain and other restaurants' aggressive menu distribution in the Upper West Side of Manhattan caused the "Menu Wars" of the 1990s, including invasions of Empire Szechuan by the "Menu Vigilantes", the revoking of its cafe license, several lawsuits, and physical attacks on menu distributors.

Menu Board

Some restaurants – typically fast-food restaurants and cafeteria-style establishments – provide their menu in a large poster or display board format up high on the wall or above the service counter. This way, all of the patrons can see all of the choices, and the restaurant does not have to provide printed menus. This large format menu may also be set up outside (see the next section). The simplest large format menu boards have the menu printed or painted on a large flat board. More expensive large format menu boards include boards that have a metal housing, a translucent surface, and a backlight (which facilitates the reading of the menu in low light), and boards that have removable numbers for the prices. This enables the restaurant to change prices without having to have the board reprinted or repainted.

Some restaurants such as cafes and small eateries use a large chalkboard to display the entire menu. The advantage of using a chalkboard is that the menu items and prices can be changed; the downside is that the chalk may be hard to read in lower light or glare, and the restaurant has to have a staff member who has attractive, clear handwriting.

A high-tech successor to the chalkboard menu is the 'write-on wipe-off' illuminated sign, using LED technology. The text appears in a vibrant color against a black background.

Outdoor Menu

Some restaurants provide a copy of their menu outside the restaurant. Fast-food restaurants that have a drive-through or walk-up window will often put the entire menu on a board, lit-up sign, or poster outside, so that patrons can select their meal choices. High-end restaurants may also provide a copy of their menu outside the restaurant, with the pages of the menu placed in a lit-up glass display case; this way, prospective patrons can see if the menu choice is to their liking. As well, some mid-level and high-end restaurants may provide a partial indication of their menu listings–the "specials"–on a chalkboard displayed outside the restaurant. The chalkboard will typically provide a list of seasonal items or dishes that are the specialty of the chef which are only available for a few days.

Digital Displays

With the invention of LCD and Plasma displays, some menus have moved from a static printed model, to one which can change dynamically. By using a flat LCD screen and a computer server, menus can be digitally displayed allowing moving images, animated effects and the ability to edit details and prices.

For fast food restaurants, a benefit is the ability to update prices and menu items as frequently as needed, across an entire chain. Digital menu boards also allow restaurant owners to control the day parting of their menus, converting from a breakfast menu in the late morning. Some platforms support the ability allow local operators to control their own pricing while the design aesthetic is controlled by the corporate entity. Various software tools and hardware developments have been created for the specific purpose of managing a digital menu board system. Digital menu screens can also alternate between displaying the full menu and showing video commercials to promote specific dishes or menu items.

Online Menu

Websites featuring online restaurant menus have been on the Internet for nearly a decade. In recent years, however, more and more restaurants outside of large metropolitan areas have been able to feature their menus online as a result of this trend.

Several restaurant-owned and startup online food ordering websites already included menus on their websites, yet due to the limitations of which restaurants could handle online orders, many restaurants were left invisible to the Internet aside from an address listing. Multiple companies came up with the idea of posting menus online simultaneously, and it is difficult to ascertain who was first. Menus and online food ordering have been available online since at least 1997. Since 1997, hundreds of online restaurant menu web sites have appeared on the Internet. Some sites are city-specific, some list by region, state or province.

Interactive Menu

Interactive Menu is an advanced system that allows customers to self-examine, select and order food and drinks from the restaurant's suggestions. The system can make an individual offer or promotion for every customer of the restaurant, to be adapted to his or her requirements, and even analyze their taste. The presentation of the drinks is visualized through animation and video clips, audio and accompanying advertising. Using this kind of system notifies the customer of the availability or absence of a particular dish, its contents and the way meal is prepared.

Principles of Menu Planning

Menu is one of the important aspects for the success of any foodservice establishment. It infers several interpretations for both the buyers and sellers. Menus are statements of the food and-beverage items provided by a foodservice establishment, primarily based on consumer needs and/or demands and designed to achieve organisational objectives.

Menu can be interpreted as a list of product range that a restaurant offers and the same time it can be a piece of literature or display used to communicate the product range to the customer. "Menus are more than the conventional function of a communications and selling tool. It can be increase restaurant profit". An interesting point is that the battle for pre-eminence menu offered to the consumers is an endless task faced by most foodservice operators.

Menu planning means devising meals that are nutritionally adequate and acceptable to the patrons. There are many factors affect the menu planning process. Menu is the soul of the restaurant. It is one of the important aspects for the success of any foodservice establishment. Menu infers several interpretations for both the buyers and sellers. Menus are statements of the food and-beverage items provided by a foodservice establishment, primarily based on consumer needs and/or demands and designed to achieve organisational objectives.

Menu can be interpreted as a list of product range that a restaurant offers and the same time it can be a piece of literature or display used to communicate the product range to the customer. "Menus are more than the conventional function of a communications and selling tool. It can be increase restaurant profit". An interesting point is that the battle for pre-eminence menu offered to the consumers is an endless task faced by most foodservice operators.

Menu planning means devising meals that are nutritionally adequate and acceptable to the patrons. There are many factors affect the menu planning process.

— Nutritional requirements,

— portion preferences,

— food costs, and

— availability of supplies

Menu-planning principles in foodservice operations are revised when nutrient standards are revised by the triservice nutritional standards regulation.

Seasonal availability of food is important in that menus should be adjusted to take advantage of seasonal changes in the supply of fresh produce. Canned, frozen, or dehydrated fruits, juices, and vegetables supplement the fresh menu items and are comparable in nutritive value.

Limited storage space, especially on small craft deployed on long cruises, prevents the use of many perishable food items. Menus for these activities should plan to use custom foods extensively to take best advantage of available storage space. Menus for such cruises should be planned well in advance to assure balanced stocks that will enable you to prepare nutritious meals. Determining the choice of menu items should include the following considerations:

— The type and capacity of the galley equipment

— The number of personnel to be fed

— The number of workers in the galley

— Avoid menus that require too much last-minute preparation.

Plan a balance between the foods that can be prepared in advance without deteriorating in quality and those that must be prepared just before serving time. Foods that look good and complement each other always have an advantage over those that are less attractive, even though they may be equally well prepared and nutritious. Learn to choose and combine foods in such a way as to achieve variety and harmony, both in appearance and flavor.

Tools of Menu Planning

Developing skill in appraising operating conditions, food acceptance, and food supplies in terms of potential meals is a demanding and responsible task. Balance meals in nourishing and attractive combinations of foods Keep food costs with unjustifiable limitations and prescribed monetary allowances Plan for efficient food supply management and logistics Flexibility and adaptability are essential to the proper planning of meals.

Rarely will you be able to use standard menus. The foods that are written into your ship's menu should vary as operating conditions vary. Even ships of the same type as yours, operating under the same conditions and in the same area, probably could not use exactly the same menus. The ability to adapt menus is a skill you must acquire.

The Food-Preparation Worksheet, is a very important document and should be properly maintained. A food-preparation worksheet should be prepared for each space in which food is prepared. The food-preparation worksheet will prove its worth to you when you use it regularly because it provides much information and guidance. The worksheet helps reveal the strengths and weaknesses of the menu.

When the preparation of the daily menu is plotted on a worksheet, weaknesses and bottlenecks stand out vividly. For example, you may find that all menu items are to be prepared in the same three steam-jacketed kettles or that the three main menu items are to be oven-prepared, each item requiring a different oven temperature. The worksheet helps you plan and organise the work to be performed by your subordinates.

The information written in the Start Preparation, Start Cooking, and Instructions columns will help subordinates plan their work. Careful planning avoids the problem of having too much food prepared ahead of serving time. The worksheet helps you to supervise the work performed by your subordinates.

As a written directive, the worksheet is your way of communicating instructions concerning the preparation of the day's menu to subordinates. You cannot depend on your memory nor can you expect subordinates to depend on their memory. The worksheet helps you to train subordinates who will be responsible for a galley operation in the future.

Discuss the worksheet with your watch captains so that they know exactly how the menu is to be prepared. Point out the supervisory techniques you want them to use in their working relations with the crew. After each meal, meet with your watch captain and key personnel to critique the meal. This is the ideal time to discuss the acceptability of menu items and to record the acceptability on the worksheet. The critique session provides the information essential to promote efficient operations.

If your personnel are accustomed to following a worksheet, give the watch captains the experience of developing one. Let each watch captain prepare the worksheet on a monthly basis, plan the day's work discuss premeal preparation, and hold postmeal critiques. Delegating the development of the worksheet to the watch captain is excellent training if the leading MS is readily available to advise, guide, and monitor discussions and critiques.

Finally, the worksheet serves as a means for establishing control of: (1) issues to the GMs, (2) the quantity of each menu item prepared, (3) the portion size served, and (4) leftover menu items (5) Completed worksheets on file provide the invaluable past history needed for establishing controls. The acceptability of menu items will determine the quantity to break out, quantity to prepare, and any change in portion size.

Customer acceptability of the menu is a major goal of the menu planner. There is no set pattern to indicate what foods the patrons will eat and enjoy. An individual's food tastes may be influenced by many factors, such as likes and dislikes before entering the service, the foods one has learned to eat and enjoy during a service career, and the group of friends one eats with at mealtime. The menu planner should know the customers so that the meals planned will be well accepted.

The following are ways that the menu planner can determine the acceptability of specific foods in the mess. A food acceptance factor is one that expresses the percentage of people who eat a particular dish. To obtain an acceptability factor for individual menu items, divide the number of portions of the item served by the number of patrons in attendance at the meal. An acceptance factor is a valuable index of the popularity of menu items and should be used for this purpose after an item has been tested at several meals.

Acceptance factors for the same menu item may vary from meal to meal. Different combinations of foods on a menu, different weather, or varying appetites may alter the acceptance of an item. A more accurate acceptance factor may result by averaging figures obtained for a particular menu over a period of time. Another way to determine acceptability is to keep a systematic check on plate or tray waste.

This should be recorded on the food-preparation worksheet. Good food acceptance means less plate waste and fewer leftovers to account for in planning future meals. Even popular foods may become monotonous if served too often. The fact that the patrons will take or accept items on the serving line does not prove that these are their preferred foods; they may take it merely because they have no better choice.

Food preferences or attitudes toward foods may be determined by several approaches. One approach is to solicit written opinions from the crew regarding items or classes of foods when you have doubts about their relative popularity. The manner in which the foods are described, the instructions given with the questionnaire, and where and when it is filled out are important factors to consider if you are to obtain good reliable data.

A menu plainer needs to be well informed. Sources of information kept within easy reach will be valuable in planning menus. Previous menu plans on file will give a good indication of what is practical for the preparation facilities and number of personnel served at a particular location.

Cycle Menu System

The cycle menu system is the menu rotation plan recommended for use in GMs. The cycle menu is a series of menus planned to be used consecutively with some variations over a period of time. A cycle menu, rotated with appropriate changes on a quarterly or seasonal basis, is recommended for GMs. They should be reviewed continuously to increase variety and eliminate unpopular dishes.

Cycle meals save time and are easier to analyse thoroughly and to perfect than those written on a weekly basis. Cycle menus also lend themselves to more forecasting of ration costs and requirements for requisitioning and daily food preparation. In some messes, a family night is offered once or twice a month. This affords the family and friends the opportunity to visit the command and enjoy a meal and pleasant conversation.

The principal advantages of a cycle menu are better meals, time savings, improved cost control, and more effective supervision and training. While the cycle menu is in use, the menu planner can refine the menu and make changes-tailoring it to patrons' preferences, available supplies, and incorpo- rating seasonal fruits and vegetables and special events. Breakout quantities can be brought closely in line with actual requirements when menus are repeated.

The cycle period can consist of as many weeks or months as practical. In deciding the most desirable cycle length, the variety and frequency of resupply and the number of duty sections should be taken into consideration as well as the MS watch schedule. Because the accepted cook watch is port and starboard, an odd-numbered day cycle (21 days) allows each watch the opportunity to prepare the entire cycle menu by the time the cycle has repeated two times (42 days).

Control of Rotation

Perfecting the basic menu and introducing variety can be made easier with sample cycle menus available from other sources. Past menus may be used as a guide if they have gained acceptance. Experience gained through actual preparation and service of the menu points out shortcuts, better preparation techniques, proper timing of food preparation, the arrangement of food on the serving line, preferred serving sizes, and the most attractive arrangement of food on the trays.

Supervisors can provide the level of training and supervision required to perfect each meal. If the daily ration control record shows that the cost of the meals in the cycle menu is excessive or is grossly below the allowed ration rate, the menu can be changed to bring costs within acceptable limits. If inventories point out stocks that are either in long or short supply temporary adjustments to the cycle menu can be made to balance stocks.

Seasonal Menu

The menu is seasonal in the sense that plans are altered to include the special foods featured for each season. Foods in season have a higher quality, are usually cheaper, and are better flavored. Menu plans should be made to suit the weather in which you are operating.

Food needs differ, and appetites usually change with variations in temperature. Crisp, cool, fresh finds are appealing to the patron in hot weather. Heavier, heartier foods such as hot soups, stews, and hot cereals are welcomed in cold weather. Fresh fruits and vegetables are at their highest quality and lowest price at seasonal peak. In hot weather, a variety of beverages, including fruit juices, should be available.

The best guides for planning menus and determining loading requirements are accurate records of a ship's own past usage and menu plans or menu summaries of previous extended cruises. Usage data and menus used during extended cruises should be collected to provide a basis for balanced loading for future deployment. Menus not only affect the health and morale of the crew, but also directly affect the endurance of a ship.

Endurance requirements vary among ship types and classes, and the amount of food storage space varies even between ships with identical complements. Proportionately smaller quantities of perishable foods are available on extended cruises, and this calls for increased use of semiperishables, particularly ration-dense foods.

Functions of Menu planning Boards

There are two kinds of menu boards:

— a menu-planning board that actually plans the menu within the foodservice division and

— a menu-review board that functions in an advisory capacity.

A menu-planning board acts on major decisions affecting food supplies, on the selection of food choices commensurate with galley equipment, workload, and other administrative decisions. The menu-planning board should be composed of personnel with foodservice experience.

The menu-review board consists of personnel from all divisions on board. This board can bring in new ideas on menu planning. All commanding officers formulate their own policy as to the number of board members. Menu boards, their requirements and functions.

The commanding officer may grant written permission to the food service officer to make necessary changes in the approved menu. Such authorisation may be furnished in the ship or supply department organisational manual. Under this authority the food service officer may make changes in the menu necessary to meet any emergency that might arise. At the discretion of the commanding officer, a weekly summary of menu changes made and the reasons for the changes are provided to the commanding officer at the time the forthcoming weekly menu is submitted for approval.

Each menu should include a notation at the bottom of the menu stating that "The food service officer is authorised to make changes to this menu when, due to unusual or unforeseen circumstances, it may be necessary to provide substitutions for food items not in stock or to permit timely use of perishable foods." Menu changes should be kept to an absolute minimum and should not be made without advance approval by the food service officer.

Multiple-choice Menus

A selective (multiple-choice) menu includes one or more choices for the crew in each category. One or more choices are recommended under the following circumstances: If a popular entrée or vegetable is to be served, offer an alternative. When a high-calorie, high-fat entrée is to be served, offer an alternative. If savings can be realised by offering a high-cost entrée with a low-cost one, offer a choice. If practical from a production standpoint, a selection of various meal components can be offered, including entrées, vegetables, breads, and beverages.

Menu Drafting

To do the best possible job in menu drafting the Navy menu planner needs a good working atmosphere in which to think. Most meals are planned around main dishes of meat, and other food items are planned to complement main dishes. The menu planner has room for listing each menu item in a meal and has a column for the numbers to eliminate guesswork on the kind of food, the method of preparation, and the essential breakout data.

Use standard abbreviations to achieve coordination between the jack-of-the-dust (or subsistence storeroom storekeeper) and galley personnel; for example, (f) for frozen, (cn) for canned, (dehy) for dehydrated, and (inst) for instant foods. Certain standard menu items, such as coffee, are printed on the draft to facilitate drafting.

Main dishes: Using information from the frequency chart and the spacing pattern, enter the meat, fish, or poultry entrées planned for each day on the menu draft form.

Vegetables: Frequency charts are developed for both potatoes or potato substitutes and vegetables in conjunction with the meat frequency charts so that the items selected will complement the meat, fish, or poultry item planned for each day. Entering the potato or potato substitute and vegetables on the menu draft is the second step in menu planning. Variety of preparation of the entrée items should be introduced on the menu by the selected recipe card.

Salads and Salad Dressing: Hotels offers many varieties of salads and kinds of salad dressings, as well as recipes for relishes. These numerous recipes are a fine foundation for a varied bar of consistently high quality. An array of salads and relishes can be prepared from the excellent variety of fresh, frozen, and canned fruits and vegetables available. When you are selecting salads for the menu, planning is needed to achieve variety and to avoid costly leftovers. Because the salad bar generally offers some variety, there is a temptation to offer the same assortment daily. With good planning, changes from day to day can be achieved.

Breakfast Fruits and Cereals: Steaming hot cooked cereals are a welcome and warming component of a hearty breakfast in cold weather. Warmer climates and higher temperatures tend to swing the popularity pendulum toward dry, ready-to-eat cereals. Offer a choice of fruit and juice each day to make sure a good source of vitamin C is available to the patrons. Either the fruit or the juice should be citrus or tomato. In addition, fruits can be used to introduce variety on the menus; for example, raisins in oatmeal or rice, blueberries in pancakes, and apples in fritters.

Desserts: Desserts should be individualised to each meal just as other menu components, taking into account the patrons' preferences and other factors influencing the menu, such as climate, cooking facilities, and the skills of the personnel. Desserts are classified as light, medium heavy, or heavy. Plan to use the one that goes best with the rest of the meal. If the meal includes hearty salads and creamed vegetables, a light dessert, such as fruit cup or flavored gelatin, is more appropriate than a medium heavy one (puddings or ice cream and cookies) or heavy desserts (cakes and pies).

Balance out the day's dessert by planning alight dessert (chilled pear halves and oatmeal drop cookies) with a heavy dinner at noon and a heavy dessert (spice cake with lemon cream icing) with a light supper. One heavy dessert daily, especially one that must be baked the same day it is to be served, is sufficient for most messes.

To ensure a variety of dessert choices in your menus, make maximum use of mixes, ice cream, prepared pie fillings, gelatin desserts, and other convenience foods. A caution that should be observed, however, in planning desserts is avoiding a repetition of the same flavors. It is easy to miss hidden flavor repetitions when breakfast juices and dinner and supper salads contain fruit. Watch for these duplications in dessert planning.

Breads and Breakfast Pastries: Piping hot yeast rolls and quick breads dress up a meal any day of the year. Hot breads can play an important role in balancing cold meals. When you write a menu, be realistic.

Soups: The soup is one of the last items planned for a lunch or dinner menu. This sequence in menu planning is not based on the relative importance of soup to a menu, but rather on its relation to other menu items. Soups are classified as light, heavy, creamed, and chowder and, as with dessert items, are selected to balance and complement the menu. The number of times a soup is offered each day or each week should be based on the crew's acceptance of soup.

If the acceptance of soup is high and you feel justified in including it on the menu at both lunch and dinner meals, plan to serve a different soup at each of these meals. Make maximum use of dehydrated soups and canned condensed soups in order to offer a variety on the menu. Leftover soups are highly subject to contamination; consequently, they create a health hazard. Fresh soup should be prepared for each meal.

Beverages: The beverage component of menus includes coffee or tea. Milk is very nutritious and deserves a permanent place on the menu. It can be served chilled plain, or flavored, or in hot cocoa as a cold weather beverage. Coffee and tea are not necessary for good health and offering another choice for either beverage is acceptable, such as good quality drinking water.

Iced beverages added to the menu during warm weather are refreshing and provide an enjoyable change from the steady consumption of hot coffee or tea during the winter months. All iced fruit beverages contribute additional vitamins and minerals, as well as energy from the sugar they contain. Avoid overuse of the same juices or fruit beverages on the weekly menus. Milk shake machines and carbonated soda dispensers may be used in the mess also.

Special Meals Menus

Meals have three roles in our life:

1. to support physical health and fitness,
2. to build morale, and
3. to provide an occasion for socialising.
4. Holiday or Special Event Menus

Special meals for holidays or special meal celebrations (in GMs either afloat or ashore) provide opportunities for festivity among the crew.

Creative menus may be planned using foods traditionally associated with the holiday. The meal patterns suggested for breakfast, lunch, and dinner may be changed for holiday or specialty meals to include some extras for the celebration. Well-planned special meals will add interest and enthusiasm among cooks and patrons. They can be as simple or elaborate as time, personnel, and cost permit.

Some GMs may have fancy menus printed for their entire cycle menu or for special events or holidays. The printed menu gives a kind of flavor of its own to special meals. These menus need not be elaborate to be attractive. They can be simply produced using a graphics programme on a computer or you can have them produced professionally through the supply system. Usually if menus are to be printed professionally, they are either going to be used permanently for a cycle menu or for holiday menus repeating from year to year.

Brunch

A brunch is neither breakfast nor lunch. Brunch is something of each of these meals, yet it has its own special identity. The distinguishing features of brunch are time of service and the special-occasion, leisurely atmosphere that can accompany a brunch meal. The brunch meal is usually served between breakfast and lunch time, generally on weekends and holidays. Brunch menus need not be elaborate to be attractive and satisfying.

A number of menu items maybe added to a heavy breakfast meal to make a brunch meal. These may be extra ranging from first course to heavy entées to special types of cakes to complete the meal. Imagination is the major key to successful brunch menus. Select luncheon entrées with staying power that combine easily and appetisingly with breakfast foods. Above all, avoid overtaxing the cooking and serving facilities and personnel by planning menus that, for example, require too much oven space. Cooked-to- order foods are especially appropriate for brunch meals.

Wardroom Mess Menus

As a senior Mess Management Specialist (MS) assigned to a private mess you may hold the position of wardroom supervisor. Because of your knowledge and experience with foodservice and nutrition, the responsibility may rest with you to prepare and submit a nutritionally balanced cycle menu to the mess caterer for review. The mess caterer will then review the menu and submit it to the mess president for approval. The same factors that affect the choice of foods used for the GM menu are used by the menu plainer to plan a private mess menu.

The wardroom menu must also meet nutritional requirements. As with the patrons of a GM, the preferences of wardroom mess members should be surveyed and considered in the menu-planning stage. The wardroom menu also should be limited to the supplies that are available. The menu should not be costly. Also there should be a moderation of high- and low-cost meals to keep the menu within the operating limits of the mess.

Menu Analysis

As menu analysis that determines the success of the menu performance. In broad terms, menu analysis can be defined as a range of techniques and procedures that enable more effective decision making both with respect to marketing and operating the menu. Various tactical solutions to menu analysis have been sought in endless attempts by many restaurant operators to improve menu performance. One of the notable approaches that has gained enormous momentum both from the hospitality literature and educational curriculum is Boston's matrix technique also known as the 'portfolio analysis' or menu engineering'. The "systematic evaluation of a menu's cost and/or sales data for the purpose of identifying opportunities for improved performance".

Although all the menu analysis approaches advocate different tactical solutions for analysing the menu items' performance, they all share the same objective, which to improve (or to provide a solution for) the current menu items performance. Menu analysis is not purely on the "process of analysing costs and sales data in order to manipulate products on the menu [but understand] in-depth customers' need and perceptions". Menu Analysis highlights three main approaches. One of the approaches is "based on intuition and experience rather than detailed quantitative analysis". In hotels, there are alternative approaches to menu analysis that can build revenue and keep repeat customers. The positioning and descriptions of the menu item on the menu can influence its popularity. Creative menu design with the use of tasteful product pictures and the size of the menu are an integral part of menu planners' menu analysis.

There is no definite evidence of what actual/or dominant method(s) of menu analysis are adopted by menu planners in the global foodservice industry. A qualitative approach was undertaken to ascertain chain foodservice attitudes in the menu analysis decision-making. An approach to understanding how menu analysis is conducted by foodservice operators rather than the use of a positivist approach, which is largely based on measurable variables and provable propositions.

Restaurants that have a chain affiliation are known to be more standardised and organised in their overall operations. Mass financial capabilities and diversification of divisions and departments provide huge advantage in making the operations more efficient and effective. Furthermore with the increased numbers of outlets, a need for better menu analysis methodology is surely crucial apart from being competitive in the market.

To a large extent, the variables that needed to be measured were quite complex and subjective because most of the different approaches to menu analysis advocated different criteria and each of them function differently. Some of the menu analysis approaches have incorporated tangible and intangible elements to advocate their menu analysis techniques. Because of this, 'statistical generalisation' or enumerate frequencies' were considered unsuitable, instead 'analytical generalisation' or 'expand and generalise theories' was a more appropriate selection of measurement.

The findings show that the obvious equipment used by the chain operators to analyse the menu performance is the Electronic Point-of-Sale (EPOS). Almost all of these chain companies have an advance computer system, which is linked with the EPOS. Because of this the menu analysis is entirely conducted in the head office and such analysis from the EPOS at the restaurant outlets are no longer applicable. Quantitative data analysis is predominantly the main method to assess the menu mix sales volume popularity) and gross profit profitability/ contribution margin).

The findings imply that once the new menu is launched in the market, the first criterion used to review the menu effectiveness is the menu sales mix reports (quantitative data). Daily sales mix reports are accumulated for a period of one month to produce a monthly sales mix report. Every menu item sales volume and gross profit are analysed and the outcomes of what actions should be done for the menu items are decided in several ways. However, this quantitative data analysis is not the sole determinant to decide what actions should be done to the menu items.

Other criteria such as based on intuition, experience and company's financial policy are also taken into considerations for appropriate alternative approaches. Menu changes are based on strategic decisions rather than simply on analyses of operating performance (and) the addition and removal of a new menu item is often based on competitive and market analysis.

Qualitative analysis approach is indeed equally important as the quantitative data analysis for the chain operators when a menu analysis is conducted, specifically deciding what actions should be done for the menu items. Menu development so that improvement for new and current menu items in term of its value and nutritional acceptances, taste, ingredients and presentation can be enhanced. The analysis of customer trends is obtained in many ways. The findings reveal that market analysis is the common method used to obtain the plausible answers of customer trends.

Analysing the target market disposable income and age population, competitors menu and awareness of current issues in food preferences and acceptances is the main areas of concern in the market analysis. Most of these chain companies have been established for many years therefore, decision on how to analyse, amend and develop the menu items is largely based on previous experiences. Because of this, many of the chain operators analyse their menu items by advertised its on the black board menu, popular radio channels, and relevant magazines.

Customer feedback such as complaints, suggestions and compliments about the menu items are crucial for the success of the menu efficiency. Sometimes low popularity and profitability of menu items may not cause by diminishing of customer demands but poor control of the food production is likely be the culprit. Because of this, mystery shoppers are assigned to analyse the menu performances in term of its quality, presentation, taste, and the waiting period after the order taken. The accumulative of this crucial information is indeed the 'source of aspirations' for the chain operators to act what amendments and developments should be done for the menu items.

Simple Menu Analysis

There are four alternative approaches, which fall under the 'simple menu analysis'.

1. Promotion,
2. Re-position,
3. Retention and
4. Elimination

Any menu items that are categorised 'problem items' will be modified its composition in order to change the items to 'star' or 'prime' category. It is found that the main reasons why the foodservice operators are declined to modify the menu items composition.

Menu Promotion

Promotion is used to analyse further the menu effectiveness because experiences and marketing strategy indicated that lack of awareness from the public eyes may be the caused why the menu items are low in demand. This strategy is adopted because the result of low popularity obtained from the sales analysis may not be necessary due to loss of customer demands. The demand of the menu items is still alive but lack of public attentions can cause the faith of the menu items in jeopardy therefore, every precaution should be observed before the menu items undergo such modifications.

Menu promotion involves both internally and externally. Black board menu and mini table standing menu, which highlights 'problem dishes' only, are the example of internal promotion. On the other hands, using popular radio channels, posters and fliers in busy places such as cinema, hybrid places, etc. is the notable findings in their external promotions.

Menu Repositioning

Changing the presentation and layout of the menu design is quite essential for boosting the menu sales. A matter of fact, this is one of the dominant approaches used to boost the sales of low popularity menu items by placing them at the strategic location known to be in the centre of the menu. Menu items that most want to sell should be placed above the middle on a one-page menu. The analysis carried out on respondents' responses has revealed that placing the items at the wrong position can cause an adverse effect of its demand.

Because of this, the result of the sales analysis to some extent can provoke incorrect decision on what solutions should be taken for the menu items. Additionally, proper choice of words uses to describe the dish ingredients and methods of cooking also played a part for improving the menu popularity.

Menu Retention

Undoubtedly, successful menu performances in term of its popularity and profitability should be retained. There is nothing to do with these menu items except to maintain or/and improve its quality in order to increase the popularity. However, an interesting finding obtained is that any menu items, which are known as 'problem items', are still being retained in the menu. Nonetheless, the composition of these items is subjected to be reviewed and modification is likely to be implemented.

Subsequently, once these three options are finalised and implemented, the menu items will undergo to menu analysis again. In fact, menu effectiveness is an ongoing process mainly because of the changes in customer demands. It is these changes in customer demand, which make the menu items to be reviewed periodically. Needless to say, the ultimate aim is to detect the 'shadow of customer demands' (which either be high or low) before it happened.

Thus, the use of sales analysis to measure the menu effectiveness to correlate with the alternative approaches as to improve the item performance is insufficient. A matter of fact, using market analysis and customer feedback to detect customer trends and correlates with the alternative approaches as to improve the items performance is more convincing than the sales analysis. These findings probably answer the reason why the theoretical menu, which uses hard data to analysis menu item performance as to improve the item popularity and profitability, is problematic.

Menu Elimination

There are several reasons why decision is made to eliminate the menu item. Menu items that are no longer popular properly due to menu fatigue and changes of customer preferences and acceptances such as healthy foods are the real caused why the menu items are eliminated. Limited supplies and escalating in product prices are also found to be the caused for menu items to have been eliminated. An interesting point emerges that decision making to eliminate menu items is predominantly based on qualitative analysis rather than from the sales analysis.

New Menu Items

Decision to introduce new menu items is mainly because of customer demands. The addition of menu items can only be materialised after thorough analysis from market demands. Moreover, current kitchen equipment and personal expertise about the new dishes are also due consideration in the internal analysis. Finally, the new menu items are launched in the market and the process of measuring the menu items effectiveness begins again.

Complex Menu Analysis

There are five alternative approaches, which fall under the 'complex menu analysis'.

1. Presentation,
2. Re-price,
3. Re-costing,
4. Modify recipes and
5. Reposition

These are the notable alternative approaches used by the chain foodservice operators to modify the menu items composition. The finding reveals that most of the chain operators make the decision to modify the menu items based on the actual performance against the predetermined criteria and allow the menu items to be further developed as appropriate. In this case, menu items which fall below acceptable level are bound to be undergone such modifications.

Unfortunately, details of the 'acceptable level' are somehow quite ambiguous. It appears that there is no definite time period when the menu must be changed or modified after the launched of the menu. Regardless of how frequents the menu items are modified, here are the alternative approaches adopted by chain operators as to improve the current menu items performance.

Menu Items Presentation

The main references that are used to decide the modifications of the menu items presentation are mystery shoppers and the customers. Customer feedback such as complaints and suggestions are essential for improving the menu items presentation. An "informal procedure" is likely to have been adopted where such feedback is reported on a random basis based on the recollection of staff experiences.

Unlike the mystery shoppers, there are more formal and standardised, and independently performed by outside foodservice consultant. Depending on this feedback analysis, the presentation of the menu items may be modified either one or combination of these elements: taste, garnishing, saltiness, colour, texture, etc. Nevertheless, the use of chefs artistic expertise in food presentation also plays a part in decision making for menu items presentation.

Menu Re-pricing

Usually, such decision to re-price the menu items is caused by several factors. The finding indicates that inflation is the main caused why chain operators re-price the menu items. Another factor that contributed to menu re-pricing is because of over-pricing the menu items. For example, one of the operators says that over-pricing the menu items could be the main reason why the demand of such items declined and not because of the deterioration of the foods quality or demand.

When the selling price is changed to slightly low than the former one, the popularity of the menu items has increased by 5 percents. In addition, unavoidable factors such increase in distribution costs and liquor tax imposed by the Government also lead to re-pricing the menu items. Of course, other considerations such as company financial policy, food costs and pricing strategies are also contributed to the changing of the selling price.

An obvious finding show that the cause of re-costing menu items is highly correlated with the change of the product specifications. Any changes on products purchase price from the suppliers therefore, leads to the change of the standard specifications. Notably, the standard specifications are designed by the menu planners which than becomes the control tools for menu recipes and portion size. Simply put, any modification on the items' presentation is indirectly caused its recipe specifications to change.

Thus, any changes involve between these factors will lead to menu re-costing. Apart for that, the change of the item portion size also leads to menu re-costing. Above all, many chain operators have allocated a budgeted food costs by the finance department for every chain's outlet for cost control purposes. Hence, any chains' outlets that are found to have been exceeding the budgeted food costs that outlets' menu items cost will be reviewed and menu re-costing is subsequently followed.

Recipes Modification

Recipe modification is basically linked with the menu re-costing.

Menu Re-positioning

Menu items that involve several modifications from its name, recipe, selling price and presentation. After the menu items undergo several modifications (depending on how many menu items are modified) new menu design is developed with high probability of changing the menu layout and general presentation of the menu card, since the former menu card is no longer applicable with the modifications being made. However, if only a small proportion of the menu items undergone such modifications than the menu items may go for promotion or repositioning.

Menu and Cost Control

The menu is the foundation for the control process in a food and beverage operation. The menu planning control point begins the control process. Control points are basic operating activities that must be performed in any food service establishment. It also depicts the movement of servers from the kitchen to the dining room and the flow of food products from service staff to guests. (It is sometimes helpful to think of serving [moving the product from production staff to service staff) and service [moving products from service staff to guests] as separate tasks.

Beginning with menu planning, each control point plays a crucial role in determining the success or failure of a food and beverage operation. Each control point is a miniature system with its own structure and functions. Each basic operating activity has specific objectives, guidelines, standards, and internal processes that contribute to the success of the operation and the ultimate goal: guest satisfaction.

When a food and beverage operation is seen as a system of control points, the control activities associated with each function are easier to identify and carry out on a daily basis. This systems approach permits the manager to establish an audit trail of control activities. In short, the manager becomes proactive instead of reactive; that is, the manager takes time for short and long range planning in the hope of controlling future events, rather than waiting for crises to develop and then taking a "fire fighting" approach.

The process of planning a menu never ends; the final menu is never achieved. Rather, the process is ongoing, dynamic, and based on the expectations of the operation's present and potential guests-its target markets. From creating an image to communicating a plan for satisfying the guests, influencing the guests' purchase decisions, merchandising the correct products, and more, the menu has a continuous impact on all aspects of an operation. A properly planned and well-designed menu stimulates revenue and increases the guest check average, because whenever a menu is presented to a guest, a sales transaction begins. And the menu not only creates but also reflects the operation's image.

The image may be elegant, businesslike, fun, ethnic, or trendy, depending on what the target market(s) desire. The menu has an impact on every aspect of a food and beverage manager's job as well as the operation itself. The following sections identify some of the more important areas of a food service operation that are directly affected by the menu.

Product control procedures: The food and beverage products must be controlled. If an operation needs shrimp to produce a menu item, shrimp will need to be purchased, received, stored, issued, prepared, cooked, and served.

Cost control procedures: Careful cost, control procedures must be followed as more expensive products are served, as service styles dictated by the menu become more complex, and as guests desire a "dining experience," not just a " meal."

Production requirements: Food items required by the menu must be produced consistently. Product quality, staff productivity and skills, timing and scheduling, and other kitchen (back- or heart-of-the-house) functions are all dictated by the menu.

Nutritional content of meals: Non-commercial food service programmes and, increasingly, commercial food service operations are concerned about the nutritional content of food served to consumers. The menu can have an impact on the health and well-being of those to whom it is offered.

Equipment needs: Equipment must be available to prepare products required by the menu. The menu must be balanced based on available equipment resources so that no one station is overloaded or underutilised.

Sanitation management. Since the menu sets the stage for the remaining control points, management must consider menu items in light of possible sanitation hazards. Once the potential hazards are identified, the risks can be reduced.

Layout and space requirements. There must be adequate facilities for the staff and equipment required to produce items listed on the menu. The layout and design of facilities establish the physical space within which food production and service take place. The physical facilities must be adequate for the purchasing, receiving, storing, issuing, production, and serving of every item on the menu.

Staffing needs. Employees must be available to produce and serve all items required by the menu. As a menu becomes more complex, greater demands may be placed upon the staff. Staffing needs are also influenced by the degree to which the menu uses convenience food items (food items the operation purchases that require very little preparation).

Service requirements. The food and beverage manager must carefully plan how products will be served to the guest. The menu affects the skill levels required for service personnel along with equipment, inventory, and facilities needed in the front of the house.

Revenue control procedures. For example, when a simple menu is served in a fast-food operation, the potential for revenue control problems is not as great as the problem potential in a table service restaurant offering an elaborate menu.

Marketing Implications of the Menu

The menu is not only an important control tool, it is also a sales, advertising, merchandising, and marketing tool. In this respect, the menu addresses both control and marketing-related concerns and blends them into a workable system.Because it lists the items an operation is offering for sale, a menu, in effect, communicates a property's food and beverage marketing plans. In developing its marketing plans, a property needs to assess the products, service, ambience (theme and atmosphere), and perceived value that its target market(s) expect. Items selected for inclusion in the menu should be based on the needs and desires of the operation's target markets. In carrying out its marketing plans, the food and beverage operation must strive to meet or exceed the expectations of its target markets.

Management must never forget the marketing implications of the menu planning process. Notice that the most important and numerous concerns involve the guest and the quality of menu items. These are also the most complex concerns. Others include cost, availability, and production/operation concerns. In addition, menu planners should study the competition and the types of menu items offered by both direct and indirect competitors in the area. It is especially necessary to consider items offered by competitors who are trying to attract the same target market(s).

Theme and Atmosphere

The complexity of menu planning in commercial properties depends upon the ambience of the food and beverage operation. Menu planning for table service restaurants is different from menu planning for banquet or buffet service operations. Ambience, the guests check average, and marketing concerns are prime examples of these differences.

Many food and beverage operations have a specific theme and atmosphere. French, Italian, and Chinese restaurants are examples of operations with ethnic themes. Others feature the cuisine of the American Southwest (for example, chilire-lenos, tortillas, enchiladas) or Cajun cuisine (for example, jambalaya, gumbo, blackened redfish). Still others create a healthy ambience by capitalising on an atmosphere and theme built on open, airy, plant-filled facilities that serve high quality, light, fresh foods. In any case, menu items offered must be compatible with the theme and atmosphere of the operation.

In the past, food service managers often attempted to diversify their menus by adding many new menu items. Since most items were made from scratch, the number and variety of raw ingredients increased correspondingly. Another strategy, called" rationalisation," limits the menu to those items that best enhance the operation's image. Its objective is simplification for the sake of operational efficiency. An operation can offer several menu items that use the same raw ingredients. This cross-utilisation enables an operation to prepare and serve many menu selections with a limited number of raw ingredients.

When the menu is carefully planned to ensure a balance of menu selections in each category, the results of these new strategies can be a streamlining of the purchasing, receiving, storing, issuing, production, and serving control points. Today, as in the past, food service managers are searching for new menu item alternatives. The increasing number of highquality convenience foods has made it easier to offer new items without having to buy additional raw ingredients or elaborate equipment. Highquality convenience products can be purchased in semi-prepared or fully prepared forms. Because they have built-in labour, they also reduce inhouse labour requirements. Of course, convenience food products usually have a higher AP (as purchased) price than the raw ingredients from which they are made.

It is always best to base initial menu plans on the needs and desires of the target market(s). However, several other factors may influence the menu selection. Among these factors are the recommended storage conditions; personnel skill levels; the product's availability and seasonality; the stability of quality and price levels; and the operation's ability to purchase, produce, and serve the menu items in a safe, sanitary, and cost-effective way.

Menu Building

Entrees are typically selected first in the menu planning process. It is important to consider not only the types of entrees, but also their costs, preparation methods, and compatibility with theme and atmosphere. A basic decision in planning the entree base concerns the number of entrees to offer. How many menu items should the operation provide? Some managers feel they should have something for everyone and, therefore, provide a wide range of entrees. This approach creates a number of problems that require careful planning and control to resolve.

The variety of entrees also affects the types and quantities of ingredients (each with its own standard purchase specifications) that must be received, stored, issued, produced, and served. A corresponding amount of preparation equipment and number of skilled personnel must also be available, and production/ service problems are more likely to occur. In summary, control is more complex.

The reverse approach of making available only a limited number of entrees reduces these types of problems considerably. In the United States there are many specialty/theme restaurants that offer relatively few entrees. By focusing on a specific segment of the market, this type of operation not only simplifies marketing techniques, but also minimizes many inhouse production, serving and control problems.

After selecting entrees, menu planners must choose menu items to complement the entrees. A common procedure is to plan appetizers and/or soups, followed by high-starch items and/or vegetables (if not part of the entree), then accompanying salads, and, finally, other menu components such as breads, desserts, and beverages. Trends in entree consumption affect the other items added to the menu.

Dining Trends

One dining trend compatible with many lifestyles is "grazing." Grazers are unlikely to select a full meal, but rather choose appetizers, salads, and desserts to complete their menu selections. Grazers are more likely to choose smaller portions of more menu items than to select a larger portion single entree. Therefore, menus featuring a wide selection of appetizers, salads, and desserts are popular with grazers. Menus are being designed with interchangeable courses, sometimes referred to as "modular cuisine."

The grazing trend is expected to continue and grow as guests change their eating habits and focus on the perceived high value of making multiple menu selections to "build their own" meals. The grazing trend seems to be particularly popular with the health- and fitness-conscious baby boomers, whose lifestyles reflect their desire for variety.

If a food and beverage operation's business is transient and the clientele changes frequently, the menu may be static (remain the same). Generally, menus that change-dynamic menus-are preferable to static menus. However, menu variability depends on the seasonal availability of raw ingredients at reasonable costs, the number and types of courses offered, the potential for using leftovers and local ingredients, the preferences of the guests, the operation's image, and the desires of the target markets.

When the business is highly repetitive and involves regular guests such as business people and others who reside in the local area, there is a greater need for daily specials that regularly change. Often, daily specials feature local or regional fresh ingredients and permit the menu planner to take advantage of reduced costs and increased availability to add interest to a menu. A trend today in daily specials is to announce their availability on attractive, eye-catching iridescent or colorfully lighted menu boards and suggestively merchandise them to guests.

Menu Design

The design of the menu can influence the guest's purchase decisions, stimulate sales of additional or preferable menu items, and increase the guest check average. Guests are influenced by visual cues provided by the menu. Readability, artwork, type styles, physical design, and layout play an important role in merchandising the food and beverage products that are profitable to the operation and satisfying to the guests. Menu items featured in these positions often draw the reader's attention because of their location. Of course, other devices such as art, pictures, and graphics can be used to draw the reader's attention elsewhere.

Menu Changes

Because conditions change, a food service operation's menu must also change. Menu changes are influenced by both external and internal factors.

External factors

External factors include consumer demands, economic conditions, the competition, supply levels, and industry trends. Consumer demands are perhaps the most important factor to consider in changing a menu. Management should first decide which potential markets it wants to attract with the modified menu. Then the proposed menu change must be evaluated in light of the negative and positive effects it may have on current guests.

Economic conditions include the cost of ingredients and the potential profitability of new menu items. Menu items offered by the competition may dictate choices to be made available. For example, a hotel food service located next to a restaurant offering the "best Chinese food in town" may elect not to serve Chinese cuisine. Supply levels relate the price to the quality and quantity of the proposed menu items. Supply levels are highly variable for some seasonal raw ingredients such as fresh fruits and vegetables. Industry trends provide general information about how the industry is responding to new demands. At present, an overall trend in many areas relates to a more sophisticated guest who is searching for an increasingly higher price-value relationship and who will pay more to receive more.

Internal factors

Internal factors that may result in a proposed menu change include the facility's meal pattern, concept and theme, operational system, and menu mix. The typical meal pattern is breakfast, lunch, and dinner. Management must decide if existing meal periods should be continued or altered. Expectations of guests have a direct influence on this decision. Any change must fit with the establishment's concept and theme. A restaurant that is known as the best steakhouse in the city may do itself a disservice by adding an extensive variety of fresh fish and shellfish to the menu. An establishment's image may also rule out certain foods that do not blend with its theme and decor. For example, even though ethnic foods are growing in popularity, a hotel restaurant may find it difficult to fit ethnic foods into its projected image.

Menu changes are also modified by the establishment's operational system. For example, if extensive new equipment purchases are crucial to the successful production and service of the menu item, the change may be too costly. Also, the change may raise both food and labour costs to unacceptable levels. Or, in some cases, the skill levels of production and service personnel may not be adequate to successfully produce and present the new menu item. The operation's existing menu has a certain overall combination or mix of items. This menu mix will be affected by any change in individual items. All of these factors should be evaluated before menu changes are finalised and implemented.

CALCULATING MENU SELLING PRICES

Commercial food service operations, as well as many institutional facilities, must establish appropriate selling prices for menu items. Objective pricing methods ensure that the property's profit requirements, as well as the value guests attach to the entire dining experience (including service, cleanliness, and ambience), are incorporated into the selling price. Pricing approaches examined are:

Subjective Pricing Methods

Although prices determine to a large extent whether financial goals of the operation are met, many managers use very subjective pricing methods. These methods establish prices, but generally fail to relate them to profit requirements or even costs. When the subject of pricing methods comes up, many managers speak about the" art" of pricing and suggest that intuition and special knowledge about guests' ability to pay are the most important considerations. Consider the following pricing methods and notice that each is based simply upon the manager's assumptions or guesses about what prices should be.

Reasonable Price Method

This method uses a price that the food service manager thinks will represent a value to the guest. The manager presumes to know-from the guest's perspective-what charge is fair and equitable. In other words, the manager asks, "If I were a guest, what price would I pay for the item being served?" The manager's best guess in answering this question becomes the product's selling price.

Highest Price Method

Using this plan, a manager sets the highest price that he or she thinks guests are willing to pay. The concept of value is stretched to the maximum and is then "backed off" to provide a margin of error in the manager's estimate.

Loss Leader Method

With this plan, an unusually low price is set for an item (or items). The manager assumes that guests will be attracted to the property to purchase the lowpriced items and that they will then select other items while they are there. Beverage or food prices on some items are set low to bring guests into the property, but purchases of other items are necessary for the operation to meet profit requirements. This pricing method is sometimes used as an " early bird" or senior citizen discount to attract specific segments of the market.

Intuitive Price Method

When prices are set by intuition alone, the manager takes little more than a wild guess about the selling price. Closely related to this approach is a trial-and-error pricing plan-if one price doesn't work, another is tested. The intuitive price method differs from the reasonable price method in that there is less effort to determine what represents value from the guests' perspective.

These pricing methods are based on assumptions, hunches, and guesses. Such methods are generally ineffective because they do not consider profit requirements and the product costs necessary to put the item on the table.

These subjective pricing methods may be common in the food service industry simply because they have been used in the past, because the manager setting prices has no information about product costs or profit requirements to work with, and/or because the manager is not familiar with more objective methods. In today's market, with increased consumer demands for value in dining, and with higher purchase prices for products needed by the property, these plans seldom work.

Simple Mark-Up By Multiplier Pricing Methods

Some pricing methods use a mark-up by a multiplier based upon food costs for menu items. The methods are designed to cover all costs and to yield the desired profit. The following sections examine ingredients mark-up pricing, prime-ingredient mark-up pricing, and mark-up with accompaniment costs. Advantages and disadvantages of these methods are also discussed.

Ingredients Mark-Up Method

The ingredients mark-up pricing method attempts to consider all product costs: food costs when pricing food items, and beverage costs when pricing beverages. The three steps to pricing with this method are as follows:

— Determine the ingredients' costs.

— Determine the multiplier to use in marking up the ingredients' costs.

— Establish a base selling price by multiplying the ingredients' costs by the multiplier to calculate a final selling price.

A base selling price is not necessarily the final selling price. The simple output from formulas may not be an appropriate final selling price. Rather, a base selling price is considered a starting point from which other factors must be assessed and the price adjusted accordingly.

Prime-Ingredient Mark-Up Method

The prime-ingredient mark-up pricing method differs from the ingredients mark-up method in that only the cost of the prime ingredient is marked up. In addition, the multiplier used must be greater than the multiplier used when considering the total cost of all ingredients. Using the same oyster platter example, assume the prime ingredient cost is \$2.65. If a multiplier of 5.02 is used, the oyster platter is priced at \$13.30. The price is calculated as follows:

Base Selling Price = Prime Ingredient's Cost x Multiplier \$13.30 = \$2.65 x 5.02\$

If the cost of the oysters in this example increases to \$2.75 for the dinner portion, the new price would be \$13.81 (\$2.75 x 5.02). The prime-ingredient approach assumes that the costs of all ingredients change in proportion to the prime ingredient. That is, when the prime ingredient's cost increases 10 percent, then other ingredients' costs are assumed to increase also by 10 percent.

Mark-Up with Accompaniment Costs

Using the mark-up with accompaniment costs pricing method, managers determine ingredient costs based only upon entree items and then add a standard accompaniment or "plate" cost to this amount before multiplying by a multiplier. This plate cost is an average cost for all non-entree and other relatively inexpensive items including salad, vegetables, bread, butter, and nonalcoholic beverages.

Determining the Multiplier

The mark-up pricing methods just discussed are simple to use and, for that reason, are commonly used in the food service industry. A significant disadvantage, however, involves determining the multiplier. How does a manager decide this? For many managers, it is a subjective decision based primarily upon experience and "rule of thumb" (such as the traditional 40 percent food cost). Should managers use last year's average food cost percentage? Should they use a statistic supplied by a national, state, or other food service association or consulting firm? It is, of course, possible to use a multiplier based upon the planned food and other costs from the operating budget. If, on the average, menu items are priced to yield the food cost percentage dictated by the budget, planners have developed a simple foundation for generating revenue sufficient to cover food costs and to yield a contribution margin (food revenue minus food costs) sufficient for other expenses and profit requirements.

The little time required to generate and use this multiplier based on the operating budget may make it especially cost effective for many small-volume operations. However, the impact of sales mix cannot be overlooked. If, for example, increased unit sales of a higher food cost percentage item replace sales of its counter parts with lower food cost percentages, the average food cost percentage can be made according to budget-but with undesirable financial results. There are other potential disadvantages of using simple multiplier pricing methods.

For example, these pricing methods do not reflect higher or lower labour, energy, or other costs associated with production of specific menu items. Rather, they either assume that all operating costs relate in some direct way to food costs or that these cost differences can be ignored. These assumptions may not be warranted as one considers the extensive amount of labour required to prepare some items relative to others.

The mark-up pricing methods using a multiplier also assume that all food costs associated with producing a menu item are known. In fact, many other costs may be excluded from the cost of ingredients used as the base for the multiplier. For example, operators not adjusting cost of goods sold by values of transfers to and from the food department would ignore these costs.

Contribution Margin Pricing Method

The term contribution margin refers to the amount left after a menu item's food cost is subtracted from its selling price. The contribution margin is the amount that the sale of a menu item" contributes" to pay for all non-food costs allocated to the food service operation and to help with profit requirements. With a contribution margin pricing method, managers can set base selling prices for menu items by following two steps:

— Determine the average contribution margin required per guest by dividing all non-food costs plus required profit by the number of expected guests.

— Determine the base-selling price for a menu item by adding the average contribution margin required per guest to the item's standard food cost.

Ratio Pricing Method

The ratio pricing method determines the relationship between food costs and all on-food costs plus profit requirements and uses this ratio to develop base selling prices for menu items. The three steps to ratio pricing are as follows:

— Determine the ratio of food costs to all non-food costs plus required profit by dividing all non-food costs plus profit by food costs.

— Calculate the amount of non-food costs plus profit required for a menu item by multiplying the standard food cost of the menu item.

— Determine the base selling price of a menu item.

The ratio method of menu pricing is simple to use and can be based on operating budget requirements. However, it does have several disadvantages. In an operation offering both food and beverages, it is necessary to separate non-food costs and profit requirements between the two revenue centers. Also, under this pricing method, each meal assumes an equal share of non-food costs and profit. The ratio pricing method does not compensate for higher labour costs associated with the preparation of laborintensive menu items.

Simple Prime Costs Method

The term prime costs refers to the most significant costs in a food service operation: product (food and beverage) and labour. A simple prime costs pricing method involves assessing the labour costs for the food service operation and factoring these costs into the pricing equation. The three steps to simple prime costs pricing are as follows:

— Determine the labour cost per guest by dividing labour costs by the number of expected guests.

— Determine the prime costs per guest by adding the labour cost per guest to the menu item's food cost.

— Determine the menu item's base selling price by dividing the prime costs per guest by the desired prime costs percentage.

The food cost for the menu item is the standard cost derived by costing the item's standard recipe. Labour costs and estimated guests are obtained from the approved operating budget. The desired prime costs percentage combines projected food and labour cost percentages, also from the operating budget.

The food service manager would then adjust this base selling price in relation to other factors, such as the operation's target markets and the competition. Advantages of this method are its focus on both food and labour costs and the fact that it is easy to use. An obvious disadvantage is the need to assign an equal labour cost to each menu item, even though the actual labour costs for menu items may vary greatly. The specific prime costs pricing method attempts to overcome this problem.

Specific Prime Costs Method

With the specific prime costs pricing method the food service manager develops multipliers for menu items so that the base selling prices for the items cover their food costs and their fair share of labour costs. Items with extensive preparation have higher labour costs and should have higher mark-ups. Conversely, items not requiring extensive preparation have lower labour costs that can be reflected in a lower mark-up.

The manager first divides all menu items into two categories: those that do and those that do not involve extensive preparation labour. The definition of extensive preparation labour is left to the manager to determine. For example, perhaps stew made from scratch is considered laborintensive to prepare, while a steak that only has to be broiled is considered non-laborintensive. Typically, all items are assumed to require approximately the same amount of labour for service and cleanup; these labour costs are shared by both categories of menu items.

Next, the manager allocates appropriate percentages of total food costs and labour costs to each category of menu items. Let's assume that the manager's analysis of menu items sold during a recent period showed that:

— 60 percent of the total food cost is expended for items requiring extensive preparation.

— 40 percent of total food cost is expended for items requiring little preparation.
— 55 percent of all labour costs is incurred for preparation of all menu items.
— 45 percent of all labour costs is incurred for service, cleanup, and other nonpreparation activities.

While the specific prime costs pricing method establishes base selling prices for the items to cover their fair share of labour costs, there are several disadvantages to this pricing method. Significant time may be spent in classifying menu items into extensive-preparation and non-extensive-preparation categories. Time will also be spent performing the necessary calculations. Also, this pricing method forces managers to assume that the relationships among all other operating costs vary in the same proportion as food costs. While this is often a reasonable assumption, there may be costs, such as higher energy costs, associated with preparing some items that reduce the accuracy of this method.

Important Pricing Considerations

The concept of value (price relative to quality) is always important. Guests pay for more than just the product (food and beverage) when they visit the operation. Quality of service, cleanliness of the facility, and atmosphere are also part of the dining experience and should, even if subjectively, be factored into the selling price decision. The basic law of supply and demand is another factor to be considered. Ultimately, the price that can be charged is established by the guests themselves as they decide whether to return to the property.

Volume concerns must also be considered. As fewer guests are served, overhead charges per guest increase; selling prices must be higher. The reverse is also true: more guests may allow the manager to reduce overhead costs in the pricing decision. The price charged by the competition for a similar product is another concern. The more an operation can differentiate its products from those of the competition, the more freedom operation has in setting a selling price.

For example, perhaps two properties offer a similar steak dinner. While the price charged for the steak is important, there are other factors that may influence people to visit one property or the other. Perhaps one property provides entertainment, while the other offers an attractive atmosphere. Emphasising the differences between the property's own products and services and those offered by other businesses is one way to remain competitive.

One technique that can be used to attract guests from competitors is lowering menu prices. This may succeed in bringing more people into an operation, but only if the lower priced items are considered by guests as substitutes for what the competition offers. If there are no significant differences between what one operation offers and what the competition offers, then guests may see price as the determining factor in selecting one property over the others. However, if there are non-price-related differences that are important to guests (such as atmosphere, entertainment, etc.) this technique may not work.

Raising prices is also a way of responding to pressures from competition. With higher prices, fewer menu items will need be sold for the operation to meet profit requirements. However, raising a menu item's selling price may be effective only the increased revenue from the price increase makes up for the revenue lost as demand falls off and current guests begin to buy other menu items as substitutes. In fact, in some cases, more effective strategy for increasing total revenue may be lowering a menu item's selling price. Lowering prices may increase the volume of unit sales, and this increase may produce an increase in total revenue.

Menu Evaluation

You know the menu is a most important tool influencing the success or failure of food and beverage operation. The process of menu engineering is an increasingly popular approach to this problem of menu evaluation.

What is a "good" menu item? There are two measures of how good a menu item is: its popularity and its profitability. A popular menu item is ordered frequently by guests. A profitable menu item generates a high contribution margin. Menu items can be evaluated in terms of both their popularity and profitability. Basically, the menu engineering process uses information readily available to the food and beverage manager to classify menu items into four types:

— Stars-items that are popular and profitable
— Plowhorses-items that are not profitable but popular

— Puzzles-items that are profitable but not popular

— Dogs-items that are neither profitable nor popular

To classify each menu item into one of the four basic categories, managers must develop a practical way to define and measure the relative profitability and popularity of each menu item. This can be accomplished by using information about standard food costs and frequency of unit sales.

Some managers assume that the lower a menu item's food cost percentage, the more profitable the sale of the item is to the operation. In other words, the lower the percentage of revenue needed to pay for the food needed for the menu item, the larger the percentage of revenue available for all other expenses and profit. While this theory sounds good, it can be easily disproved.

Information about frequency of unit sales for each menu item can be gathered by tallying the number of each item sold during some specified time period (such as two weeks). This information can be abstracted from guest checks or, more frequently, by analysis of unit sales information from the electronic register or production records indicating leftovers, if applicable. Popular items are those with a relatively high menu mix percentage. Accordingly, "star" menu items are those with relatively high contribution margins and high menu mix percentages, while items classified as "dogs" score relatively low on both measures.

In performing a menu engineering analysis, it is not enough to consider menu items individually. Each item's contribution margin and menu mix percentage will provide measures for the item's levels of profitability and popularity, but the problem is to evaluate how high or low these levels are in comparison with all other menu items.

Profitability

The basis for measuring the degree of profitability of each menu item is the average contribution margin. A "high" contribution margin for an individual menu item would be one that is equal to or greater than the average contribution margin for all menu items. The concept of the menu's average contribution margin provides managers with a precise measure of each menu item's profitability, and it is easily calculated from readily available information. Recall that the contribution margin of a menu item is calculated by subtracting its food cost from its selling price.

Since the manager knows the costs incurred and the revenue generated for each individual menu item, the total menu costs and the total menu revenues generated can be determined by simply summing the figures for each menu item. The total contribution margin for all menu items is calculated by subtracting total menu costs from total menu revenues. Finally, the average contribution margin is calculated by dividing the total menu contribution margin by the total number of menu items sold during the specified time period in which unit sales data were collected. Individual contribution margins for each menu item can now be compared to the average contribution margin for all menu items to assess each item's level of profitability. A profitable menu item is one whose individual contribution margin equals or exceeds the average contribution margin.

Degree of Popularity

The basis for measuring the degree of popularity of each menu item is called the popularity index. This index is based upon the notion of "expected popularity." For the purpose of analysis, each menu item is assumed to be equally popular. This means that each item is "expected" to contribute an equal share of total menu unit sales. Therefore, the expected popularity of each menu item is calculated by simply dividing 100 percent (i.e., total unit sales) by the number of items on the menu.

Improving the Menu

The benefits of menu engineering can only accrue if information gained from the menu engineering analysis is used to improve the menu. What can a food and beverage manager do with this knowledge about the various food item classifications?

Managing plowhorses

First, let's consider plowhorses. Guests like these items, but, unfortunately, plowhorses do not contribute their fair share of contribution margin. Possible strategies for managing a plowhorse menu item include:

— *Increase prices carefully*. Perhaps the item is popular because it represents a great value to guests. If prices could be increased, the item may still represent a good value, may remain popular, and may generate a higher contribution margin. This alternative may be most effective when the item is unique to the property and cannot be obtained elsewhere.

— *Test for demand.* If there is no strong resistance to price increases, it may be useful to complement an increased price with other strategies such as repackaging the item or repositioning it on the menu. These other strategies may be designed to maintain or increase the item's popularity while generating a higher contribution margin through the increase in selling price. If prices are to be increased, this should probably be done in several stages rather than all at once.

— *Relocate the item to a lower profile on the menu.* Depending upon the menu layout, certain areas of a menu represent a better location than others. A plowhorse can be relocated to a less desirable area of the menu. Since the item is popular, some guests will search it out. Others will be drawn to higher profile areas of the menu that list more profitable items the property wishes to sell.

— *Shift demand to more desirable items.* Menu engineering allows the manager to determine which items to sell-those high in popularity and high in contribution margin.

— *Combine with lower cost products.* The contribution margin of a plowhorse can be increased if lower cost meal accompaniments are offered with the entree. Perhaps, for example, higher priced vegetables and dessert accompaniments can be replaced with other, less expensive items without reducing the item's popularity. If this can be done, the contribution margin will increase.

— *Assess the direct labour factor.* The food and beverage manager should know if there is a significant amount of direct labour required to produce the plowhorse item. If an item with a low contribution margin does not have a significant amount of direct labour involved in production (a convenience food product, for example), the manager may be able to justify the lower contribution margin since fewer revenue dollars will be required to compensate for labour cost.

— *Consider portion reduction.* If the portion size is reduced, the product cost will be decreased and the contribution margin will increase. This alternative must be viewed with caution, of course, since the guest's perception of value may decrease when the portion size is reduced.

Managing puzzles

Puzzles are items that are high in: contribution margin but low in popularity-items the food and beverage manager desires to sell since their contribution margins relatively high. The challenge is to find ways to increase the number of guests ordering these items. Alternatives include:

— *Shift demand to these items.* Techniques include repositioning the items to more visible areas of the menu, renaming them, using suggestive selling techniques, developing advertising campaigns, using table tents, using buttons and badges on server uniforms, highlighting items on menu boards at the entrance to the dining area, and other strategies to increase the item's popularity.

— *Consider a price decrease.* Perhaps an item is low in popularity because it does not represent a value to guests. If this is the case, the selling price might be decreased with the contribution margin still remaining higher than average. This could lead to increased popularity, since a reduced selling price would represent a greater value to the guest.

— *Add value to the item.* Offering a larger portion size, adding more expensive meal accompaniments or garnishes, and using higher quality ingredients are among the ways that value can be increased. These techniques may lead to increased popularity and to a contribution margin that is lower, but still higher than the average generated by the menu.

Managing stars

Stars are items that are high in contribution margin and high in popularity. The best advice for managing stars includes:

— Maintain rigid specifications. Do not attempt to alter the quality of the product being served.

— Place in a highly visible location on the menu. Stars are items that the food and beverage operator wants to sell. Therefore, make sure guests are aware of their availability.

— Test for selling price inelasticity. Perhaps the star is popular because it is a significant value to the guest. Or, perhaps the star is not available in its existing form elsewhere in the, marketplace. These might be two instances in which the price could be increased without a decrease in popularity.

— Use suggestive selling techniques. Some of the techniques for shifting demand to puzzles might also be useful for stars.

Managing dogs

Dogs (items that are low in contribution margin find low in popularity) are obvious candidates for removal from the menu. After all, they do not contribute their fair share of contribution margin and they are not popular. Alternatively, the selling price could be increased, since this would at least generate a higher contribution margin. When ail dogll requires a significant amount of direct labour, does not permit sufficient use of leftovers, and has a relatively short storage life, the reasons for removing the item from the menu become more compelling.

The manager, guests, employees, and others may offer their opinions about the revisions. They may subjectively assess the menu's "worth" and offer their views about its improvements over earlier versions. By contrast, menu engineering can be used to evaluate menu revisions in an objective manner. For example, if the popularity of an individual menu remains stable (or increases) while its contribution margin increases, the revised menu is a good one.

References

Hoke, Ann, *Restaurant menu planning,* New York, London: Harper & brothers, 1940.

Anderson, *Kenneth. International Menu Speller.* New York: Wiley, 1993.

Scanlon, Nancy Loman. *Marketing by Menu.* New York: John Wiley, 1999.

Wigger, G. Eugene. *Themes, Dreams, and Schemes: Banquet Menu Ideas, Concepts, and Thematic Experiences.* New York: John Wiley, 1997.

5

Catering Operations

Hospitality is probably the most diverse but specialized industry in the world. It is certainly one of the largest, employing millions of people in a bewildering array of jobs around the globe. Sectors range from the glamourous five-star resort to the less fashionable, but arguably more specialised, institutional areas such as hospitals , industrial outfits, schools and colleges. Yet of these many different sectors, catering has to be the most challenging. Whatever the size of the catering operation, the variety of opportunities available is endless.

The food service industry (or catering industry) encompasses those places, institutions and companies that provide meals eaten away from home. This industry includes restaurants, schools and hospital cafeterias, catering operations, and many other formats, including 'on-premises' and 'off-premises' caterings.

Food is the sustainer of life regardless of whether they belong to animal kingdom or plant kingdom. All living beings consume food as they come in nature. Subsequently they may convert the raw natural food into usable form on their own. This transformation never involves the art and science of coking, which is a speciality of human beings alone.

Importance of food for the human beings is amply, accurately and appropriately stated in the following age old sayings: "hungry man is an angry man" and "even the army marches on stomach" where stomach implies food Employment of largest number of people in the world in general terms (at home) and in commercial terms (catering) is in food preparation and servicing. Roughly half the world population (women) is actively engaged in the art and science of food production and then alone comes reproduction.

Food production, simply stated, is the transformation of raw food material into palatable, appetizing and easily palatable tasty food. Unlike all other living organisms, man has to "buy" food by paying money. Where does the money come from? It comes only from industries. Any industry in the world has the primary objective of making money. Money so generated by the industrial activity is shared between the employer and the employee, however disproportionate it may be. Money so shared is used to take care of the three important objectives: food, clothing and residence. Whatever left after meeting these primary objectives may go towards acquiring wealth.

As clearly stated above, food is the very basis of existence or survival. To buy food, man needs money. The money comes or must come from industries, all of which have the primary objective of making money and share with those who help generate it. Since the raw food needs to be transformed into palatable food fit for consumption which is achieved, as already stated, through general cooking (household) or commercial cooking (catering). Therefore, there is no industry in the world which is not directly or indirectly, one way or the other, related to the food (catering) industry. Commercial food industry or the catering industry is the only industry that provides food, at a price, away from home. Various types of catering services available would include general or speciality services such as transport catering, welfare catering, industrial catering, etc.

Catering is a multifaceted segment of the food service industry. There is a niche for all types of catering businesses within the segment of catering. The food service industry is divided into three general classifications: commercial segment, noncommercial segment, and military segment. Catering management may be defined as the task of planning, organizing, controlling a n d executing. Each activity influences the preparation and delivery of food, beverage, and related services at a competitive, yet profitable price. These activities work together to meet and exceed the customer's perception of value for his money.

Catering management is executed in many diverse ways within each of the four segments. The first, commercial segment, traditionally considered the profit generating operation, includes the independent caterer, the restaurant caterer, and the home-based caterer. In addition, hotel / motel and private club catering operations are also found in this category.

The non-commercial segment, or the 'not-for-profit' operations, consists of the following types of catering activities: business / industry accounts, school, college and university catering, health care facilities, recreational food service catering, social organizations and transportation food service catering. The military segment encompasses all catering activities involved in association with the armed forces and / or diplomatic events.

Types of Catering

There are two main types of catering on-premises and off-premises catering that may be a concern to a large and small caterer. On-premise catering for any function - banquet, reception, or event - that is held on the physical premises of the establishment or facility that is organizing / sponsoring the function. On-premise catering differs from off-premise catering, whereby the function takes place in a remote location, such as a client's home, a park, an art gallery, or even a parking lot, and the staff, food, and decor must be transported to that location. Off-premise catering often involves producing food at a central kitchen, with delivery to and service provided at the client's location. Part or all of the production of food may be executed or finished at the location of the event.

Catering can also be classified as social catering and corporate (or business) catering. Social catering includes such events as weddings, bar and mitzwahs, high school reunions, birthday parties, and charity events. Business catering includes such events as association conventions and meetings, civic meetings, corporate sales or stockholder meetings, recognition banquets, product launches, educational training sessions, seller-buyer meets, service awards banquets, and entertaining in hospitality suites.

On-Premise Catering

All of the required functions and services that the caterers execute are done exclusively at their own facility. For instance, a caterer within a hotel or banquet hall will prepare and cater all of the requirements without taking any service or food outside the facility. Many restaurants have specialized rooms on-premise to cater to the private-party niche. A restaurant may have a layout strategically designed with three separate dining rooms attached to a centralized commercial food production kitchen. These separate dining rooms are available at the same time to support the restaurant's operation and for reservation and overflow seating. In addition, any of the three dining rooms may be contracted out for private-event celebrations a n d m a y require their own specialized service and menu options. Other examples of on-premise catering include hospital catering, school, University/ college catering.

Off-Premise Catering

production facility is a freestanding commissary, which is a kitchen facility used exclusively for the preparation of foods to be served at other locations. Other examples of production facilities include, but are not limited to, hotel, restaurant, and club kitchens. In most cases there is no existing kitchen facility at the location where the food is served. Caterers provide single-event foodservice, but not all caterers are created equal. They generally fall into one of three categories:

1. *Party Food Caterers*: Party food caterers supply only the food for an event. They drop off cold foods and leave any last-minute preparation, plus service and cleanup, to others.
2. *Hot Buffet Caterers:* Hot buffet caterers provide hot foods that are delivered from their commissaries in insulated containers. They sometimes provide serving personnel at an additional charge.
3. *Full-Service Caterers*: Full-service caterers not only provide food, but frequently cook it to order on-site. They also provide service personnel at the event, plus all the necessary food-related equipment— china, glassware, flatware, cutleries, tables and chairs, tents, and so forth. They can arrange for other services, like décor and music, as well. In short, a full-service caterer can plan and execute an entire event, not just the food for it.

Catering Establishments

Various catering establishments are categorised by the nature of the demands they meet. The following are some of the catering establishements.

Restaurant

A restaurant is an establishment that serves the customers with prepared food and beverages to order, to be consumed on the premises. The term covers a multiplicity of venues and a diversity of styles of cuisine. Restaurants are sometimes also a feature of a larger complex, typically a hotel, where the dining amenities are provided for the convenience of the residents and for the hotel to maximize their potential revenue. Such restaurants are often open to non-residents also.

Transport Catering

The provision of food and beverages to passengers, before, during and after a journey on trains, aircraft and ships and in buses or private vehicles is termed as transport catering. These services may also be utilised by the general public, who are in the vicinity of a transport catering unit. The major forms of modern day transport catering are airline-catering, railways catering, ship catering and surface catering in coaches or buses which operate on long distance routes.

Airline Catering

Catering to airline passengers on board the air craft, as well as at restaurants situated at airport terminals is termed as airline catering. Modern airports have a variety of food and beverage outlets to cater to the increasing number of air passengers. Catering to passengers *en route* is normally contracted out to a flight catering unit of a reputed hotel or to a catering contractor or to the catering unit operated by the airline itself as an independent entity.

Railway Catering

Catering to railway passengers both during the journey as well as during halts at different railway stations is called railway catering. Travelling by train for long distances can be very tiring; hence a constant supply of a variety of refreshment choices helps to make the journey less tedious. On-board meal services are also provided on long distance trains.

Ship Catering

Ship catering is catering to cargo crew and passenger ship passengers. Ships have kitchens and restaurants on board. The quality of service and facilities offered depends on the class of the ship and the price the passengers are willing to pay. There are cruises to suit every pocket. They range from room service and cocktail bars to speciality dining restaurants.

Surface Catering

Catering to passengers traveling by surface transport such as buses and private vehicles is called surface catering. These eating establishments are normally located around a bus terminus or on highways. They may be either government run restaurants, orprivately owned establishments. Of late there has been a growing popularity of Punjabi style eateries called dhabas on the highways.

Outdoor Catering

This catering includes the provision of food and drink away from home base and suppliers. The venue is left to the peoples' choice. Hotels, restaurants and catering contractors meet this growing demand. The type of food and set up depends entirely on the price agreed upon. Outdoor catering includes catering for functions such as marriages, parties and conventions.

Retail Store Catering

Some retail stores, apart from carrying on their primary activity of retailing their own wares, provide catering as an additional facility. This type of catering evolved when large departmental stores wished to provide food and beverages to their customers as a part of their retailing concept. It is inconvenient and time consuming for customers to take a break from shopping, to have some refreshments at a different location. Thus arouse the need for some sort of a dining facility in the retail store itself. This style of catering is becoming more popular and varied nowadays.

Club Catering

Club catering refers to the provision of food and beverages to a restricted member clientele. Some examples of clubs for people with similar interests are turf clubs, golf clubs, cricket clubs etc. The service and food in these clubs tend to be of a fairly good standard and are economically priced.Night clubs are usually situated in large cities that have an affluent urban population. They offer entertainment with good food and expensive drinks.

Welfare Catering

The provision of food and beverages to people to fulfil a social obligation, determined by a recognised authority, is known as welfare catering. This grew out of the welfare state concept, prevalent in western countries. It includes catering in hospitals, schools, colleges, the armed forces and prisons.

Industrial Catering

The provision of food and beverages to 'people at work,' in industries and factories at highly subsidised rates is called industrial catering. It is based on the assumption that better fed employees at concessional rates are happy and more productive. Catering for a large workforce may be undertaken by the management itself, or may be contracted out to professional caterers. Depending on the choice of the menu suggested by the management, catering contractors undertake to feed the workforce for a fixed period of time at a predetermined price.

Leisure-Linked Catering

This type of catering refers to the provision of food and beverages to people engaged in 'rest and recreation' activities. This includes sale of food and beverages through different stalls and kiosks at exhibitions, theme parks, galleries and theatres. The increase in the availability of leisure time and a large disposable income for leisure activities has made it a very profitable form of catering.

Management of On-premise catering

On-premise catering is catering for any function-banquet, reception, or event-that is held on the physical premises of the establishment or facility that is producing the function. On-premise catering differs from off-premise catering, whereby the function takes place in a re-mote location, such as a client's home, a park, an art gallery, or even a parking lot, and the staff, food, and decor must be transported to that location. Off-premise catering often involves producing food at a central kitchen, with delivery to and service provided at the client's location. Part or all of the production of food may be executed or finished at the event location.

At times, off-premise caterers must rely on generators for electricity, truck in potable water, devise a trash system, and otherwise "rough it." Although some hotels and restaurants offer off-premise catering, most do not "cater-out." A few of them, however, have entered the off premise catering market and are capable of providing offsite production and service. Exact statistics are not kept for these two functions, but it is estimated that on-premise catering accounts for about two thirds of all catering sales in the United States, with off-premise cater-ing accounting for the remaining third.

Catering, both on-premise and off-premise, is one of the fastest growing segments of the U.S. foodservice industry and has enjoyed success and expansion over the years. The National Restaurant Association (NRA) notes that catering and takeout sales will generate considerable growth in U.S. foodservice sales throughout the foreseeable future. Every day thousands of business and social groups get together for their members to enjoy each other's company and the variety of refreshments that are usually found at these gatherings. Groups generally prefer professionally prepared and served food and beverages. This allows hosts to concentrate on their personal, social, and business activities, simultaneously enjoying the events. And, as a bonus, they can leave the cleanup to someone else.

On-premise caterers-such as hotels, convention centers, and restaurants-usually have the advantage of offering many services under one roof. They can also provide sufficient space to house an entire event and plenty of parking. In general, each catered event has one host and one bill. Many localities have independent banquet halls, civic auditoriums, stadiums, arenas, ethnic social clubs, fraternal organizations, women's clubs, private city or country clubs, athletic clubs, hospitals, universities, libraries, executive dining rooms in office buildings or corporate headquarters, churches, recreation rooms in large apartment or condominium complexes, parks, museums, aquariums, and restaurants with banquet rooms. Some of these facilities are often more competitive than hotels, as they have more flexible price structures because of their lower overhead expenses. Some are public facilities and are tax-exempt.

A number of these facilities provide their own catering in-house, others are leased to and operated by contract foodservice companies that have exclusive contracts. Still others will rent their facilities to off-premise caterers. Another recent competitor for catering business has been the proliferation of takeout services. Some supermarkets and department stores have developed gourmet takeout, deli, and bakery facilities, and many can produce beautiful, reasonably priced buffet platters. More and more restaurants are heavily engaged in takeout business, particularly around the holidays.

However, if not properly monitored, a "cater-out" can disrupt the normal work flow and efficiency of a restaurant, damage morale, and skew ordering and purchasing routines. Off-premise functions can be a significant source of additional sales revenue and profits for those hotels and restaurants that have the necessary equipment and personnel to handle large off-site catered affairs. However, unless the facility is set up to do this correctly, the work can be too distracting and the added expense may wipe out any incremental profits. For example, transporting perishable food requires proper trucking for food safety. A refrigerated truck or a great amount of ice must be used to maintain safe temperatures.

Staffing is also an issue. Hotel servers are accustomed to a division of labor and often are not pleased when they are asked to perform tasks off-site that are not required when they are working within the facility. In a hotel, servers do not set up equipment or do the cleaning, hauling, and other duties that are required at an off-premise site. There may also be union implications if job descriptions are violated.

Catering can also be classified as social catering and corporate (or business) catering. Social catering includes such events as weddings, bar and bat mitzvahs, high school reunions, birthday parties, and charity events. Business catering includes such events as association conventions and meetings, civic meetings, corporate sales or stockholder meetings, recognition banquets, product launches, educational training sessions, seller-buyer entertaining, service awards banquets, and entertaining in hospitality suites. The estimated 75 percent of all catering sales generated by business catering is due to the sheer volume of people served daily at meetings in hotels and convention centers, where meals for thousands are produced regularly.

The hotel caterer is only one of many types of caterers that seek to satisfy the public's catering needs. A hotel usually has the advantage in this competitive field because it can normally offer many services under one roof as well as sufficient space to house an entire event, thereby enticing the customer with a one-stop-shopping opportunity. An up-scale hotel often provides a more glamorous and exciting location.

The hotel must realize, however, that other caterers abound in the industry, and even though they may be much smaller and unable to offer a smorgasbord of choices, they nevertheless eagerly court many of the same customers sought by hotel caterers. For instance, in some parts of the country there are independent banquet halls, convention facilities, and conference centers. Some of these properties are able to compete with hotels for the same customers because they have more flexible price structures owing to lower overhead expenses.

A hotel may have the advantage in some instances: If a client is able to buy out the entire facility, the hotel can offer a generous price reduction because of the sleeping room revenue derived from the group. Some restaurant operations have attached banquet rooms that can be used for several types of catered events. It is expensive to maintain a room that may be empty three or four nights per week, so the banquet room is often used as overflow restaurant dining space on busy nights.

A restaurant can book many small functions if it takes time to court this business. However, before going after this business, the catering executive must be careful to avoid those catered events that cannot be charged enough to cover all variable and fixed overhead costs associated with opening a function room. For instance, a restaurant that uses a section of its regular dining room to house a catered event will not incur significantly greater heating and cooling expenses; the dining room must be heated or cooled regardless of the number of guests expected.

A hotel, however, must consider the feasibility of opening a function room; if the room is opened, incremental heating and cooling expenses will be incurred, whereas if the room remains closed, these expenses are avoidable. In some cases, although a particular group may turn a profit for the average restaurant, a hotel property may be less fortunate. Private clubs do a great deal of catering for their members. Country clubs concentrate on social events, such as weddings and dances. City clubs specialize in business catering, such as for corporate meetings, board luncheons, and civic events. Resorts often have outdoor functions at remote locations on the property.

Profitoriented hospitals do a good amount of catering business for medical meetings and staff functions. In most cases, they compete directly with hotels for these functions. There are several types of tax-exempt organizations that offer catering services to anyone willing to pay for them. For instance, universities, colleges, hospitals, libraries, churches, museums, and military clubs vigorously compete for catering events because they help subsidize their major nonprofit activities.

Many taxpaying catering businesses are especially unhappy with these so-called nonprofit competitors; however, nonprofit groups consistently fight any type of government restraints on these activities. Contract foodservice companies operate many facilities that are capable of supporting catering events. For instance, many of these firms operate foodservices in large office buildings, where executive dining rooms can be used to house special parties and meetings.

Some contract foodservice companies are also capable of handling off-premise catering functions. Most convention centers are public institutions that use in-house contract services typically operated by national catering companies. Privately owned companies function as an internal catering department and enjoy all of the amenities and unique environments offered by the facility. They tend to focus on conventions and trade shows and often have the opportunity to cater megaevents because of the large amount of exhibit space, as well as attached areas, available.

Some mobile caterers, with the proper equipment, provide complete meal production and service on location. For instance, a few companies specialize in feeding forest fire fighters, disaster relief workers, movie and television production crews in the field, people taking extended camping trips or fishing/rafting excursions, construction site workers, or other such groups.

Normal Management Functions

The person in charge of the catering department must perform the normal management functions. He or she has the following responsibilities:

— *Planning:* The catering department must accomplish both financial and nonfinancial objectives. To do so, it must develop appropriate marketing, production, and service procedures. It must also ensure that the department's operating budgets and action plans are consistent with the facility's overall company objectives.

— *Organizing*: The catering department must organize the human and other resources needed to follow the plan. Staff members must be recruited and trained. Work schedules must be prepared. And performance evaluations must be administered.

— *Directing*: Employee supervision is an integral part of every supervisor's job. The supervisory style will emanate from top management. The catering department's supervisory procedures must be consistent with company policies.

— *Controlling*: The catering department manager must ensure that actual performance corresponds with planned performance. Effective financial controls ensure that actual profit and loss statements are consistent with pro forma budgets, and effective quality controls ensure that production and service meet company standards.

Catering departments have a variety of objectives. The weight and priority given to each will depend on company off-premise cateringpolicy. The following are among the most common objectives:

— *Earn a fair profit on assets invested in the catering business.*

— *Generate sufficient catering sales volume, enough to defray all expenses and leave a fair profit.* Caterers must be careful not to generate a lot of business that will not pay for itself. They must practice selective sales strategies in order to maximize profits. Usually, the only time a catering executive should consider booking a marginally profitable event is if it is a party designed to show off the catering facilities, such as a charity event. It may also be contemplated if the property wants to host VIPs who may indirectly generate future catering revenues, or during the slow season, to keep staff employed.

— *Deliver customer satisfaction.* Meeting this objective will lead to repeat patronage as well as positive referrals. All foodservice operations, including the catering segment, thrive on repeat patronage.

— *Provide consistent quality and service.* Customers are happy when the actual quality and service received parallel those that were promised. Punctuality and consistency are hallmarks of a well-run catering department.

— *Convey a particular image.* Caterers often want to be known as specializing in certain types of products and services, such as weddings or unusual themed events. They strive to be unique because they want customers to think of them whenever a specific atmosphere or ambiance is required. Catering is often a facility's most visible characteristic on the local and national levels. It alone has the greatest potential to become a facility's "signature"-its major claim to fame.

— *Develop a reputation for dependability.* Regardless of the pressure that any event places on the staff, catering departments want clients to have confidence that their needs will be met. The catering department must adequately fill the role of liaison between clients and all of the property's services.

— *Develop a reputation for flexibility.* To be dependable, the caterer must be flexible. The catering department must be able to react on a moment's notice. Clients will remember fondly the facility that bailed them out at the last minute.

— *Stay on budget*. To meet this objective, the caterer must be on guard against adding "surprise" charges that go over budget.

Catering departments are organized according to the needs of the particular facility. For example, a hotel's primary profit center is its sleeping rooms division, with the catering department usually being the second most profitable department. Consequently, all hotel departments are generally organized and administered to maximize the sales and profits of sleeping rooms and catered functions. There are two general types of catering department organizations. In one form, the department is organized in such a way that all catering personnel are under the supervision of the property's food and beverage director.

The food and beverage director is responsible for the kitchens, restaurant outlets, and banquet operations, as well as for client solicitation and service. Within this structure, catering must secure the right to sell function space from the sales department, which controls meeting space. Sales managers are often reluctant to call their clients and ask them to release space they are holding as part of a meeting they have booked. Meetings are often booked years in advance, and savvy meeting planners, not knowing all of their space needs that far ahead, will institute a "hold all space" clause in their contracts.

In such an organizational structure, convention service managers are primarily responsible for room setup, but not for food or beverages. Alternatively, the catering department may be organized so that catering personnel are under the supervision of the sales and marketing director, with other employees, especially banquet servers, still reporting to the food and beverage director. In this situation there is generally a director of catering and convention services, who must work closely with the director of sales and marketing as well as with the food and beverage director.

Within this structure, catering managers and convention service are in the same department, both taking care of the food, beverage, and room setup needs of clients. The convention service managers do not sell the event, but take over client business booked by sales and marketing. They handle the planning and logistics of any meals or receptions and develop the appropriate service procedures needed to plan and implement successful and profitable catered events.

Catering managers then sell shortterm food and beverage events to the local market or to functions without sleeping rooms, such as weddings, local banquets, and the like. With the revenue of catering being the responsibility of the marketing director, rather than the food and beverage director, sales managers are more likely to call clients to have rooms released for local banquets. In the second type of organizational pattern, the sales and marketing and food and beverage directors split the workload and coordinate catering sales and service.

In other facilities, the catering department handles all food and beverage service, and convention services personnel take care of all nonfood logistics, such as function room setups and teardowns, sleeping room arrangements, and so forth. There are advantages and disadvantages with each organizational form. The major advantages associated with the organizational forms are as follows:

— *Increased efficiency*: Clients work with one designated person who has authority to oversee the event from inception to completion. Last-minute requests and changes can be implemented quickly.

— *Isolated responsibility*: Responsibility is assigned to one person. Management and clients know exactly whom to contact if questions arise. This is a very critical position, in that the contact person is responsible for translating a client's needs and wishes into reality.

— *Job enrichment*: A person in charge of an event enjoys more variety than does a person involved with only one or two aspects.

— *Repeat patronage:* When clients deal with one person, there are additional opportunities to solicit repeat patronage and referrals.

— *Improved communications*: Because there are fewer persons on the communications chain, ambiguities and misinterpretations should be minimal.

The following are the major disadvantages of the organizational forms:

— *Excessive workload*: One person may not have enough hours in the day to perform all the necessary tasks.

— *Too many bosses*: The food and beverage department cannot be totally isolated; it must interact to some degree with the sales and marketing department. Unfortunately, this overlap may violate established chain-of-command policies unless the relationships are spelled out clearly.

— *Lack of specialization*: It is difficult to train one person to be expert in so many areas. However, if the catering manager is only the information point of exchange between clients and all other facility services, this potential problem can be minimized.

— *Excessive delegation*: If one person is not expert in all areas, the odds are that he or she will delegate responsibility freely. This can defeat the positive aspects of including all tasks under one person's direction. It also can confuse catering staff members.

As a general rule, catering department organization will be influenced by the support of upper management and

(1) the size of the facility,

(2) the types of functions catered,

(3) corporate policy, and

(4) the overall level of service offered by the facility.

Catering typically handles all food and beverage requirements, and convention service handles all nonfood arrangements.

Qualifications of Job candidates

A job specification contains the qualities sought in a job candidate. Before hiring a catering department employee, a manager generally looks for at least five major qualities:

Technical Skills

Ideally, catering employees will have knowledge and skills in food and beverage preparation and service. At the very least, they must have an aptitude to learn and become familiar with the items on your menus and your services so that they can respond adequately to client inquiries. It is required that most, if not all, catering employees have excellent sales skills. For some job positions, the primary qualification is the ability to sell. For instance, a sales representative's major asset is his or her ability to sell. However, even those employees primarily involved with guest service should have the ability to up$ell clients. They should be able to encourage clients to purchase additional, or higher quality, products and services, thereby increasing catering profits.

Communications skills are absolutely essential for catering staff members. Each function is a unique undertaking. There is no standard pattern or event template. Consequently, open and intelligible communications are critical to the success of a catered event. It is important for staff to be sufficiently articulate to communicate effectively with the host, the guests, and other staff members.

Conceptual Skills

As much as possible, catering department employees must be able to view the entire catering function and not see things exclusively from the perspective of their particular jobs. For instance, a banquet chef must appreciate the ceremonies involved with a wedding function and not ignore them when preparing and coordinating food courses.

Catering staff members must be able to take a client's "vision" of the function (including needs, wishes, purpose of the function, and budgetary constraints) and develop an event (through negotiations) consistent with this vision that can be delivered effectively and efficiently by the catering department. The planned catered event must meet the client's requirements.

Interpersonal Skills

Customer-contact skills are extremely important in the hospitality industry. Getting along with people, and satisfying them while simultaneously making a profit, is a challenge that must be met and overcome by all catering staff members. Unlike technical and conceptual skills, these skills generally cannot be taught-they are inherent. As Ellsworth Statler, founder of Statler Hotels, said once in the late 1800s, "Hire only good-natured people."

Other characteristics that managers look for in job candidates depend on the type of position and company policies. For instance, if the facility has a promotion-from-within policy, a manager will seek a job candidate who has the ability and desire to advance and grow with the company.

Policies of Catering Department

The facility must establish policies to guide the catering department's relations with clients. Typical policies include the following considerations.

— *Food and beverage prices*: It is a good idea to note that any listed prices are subject to change; in other words, the caterer should not assume responsibility if potential clients are viewing outdated menus. Caterers usually note that published menu prices are subject to change unless firm price guarantees are negotiated and included in a catering contract. If competitive bids are being prepared, all prices must be computed according to standard compan

— *Gratuities or service charges.* These are automatic charges added to the catering prices. Most properties add a 15 to 19 percent gratuity to the bill. You cannot assume that all clients are aware of these traditional charges: They must be informed about them up front.

— *Tips.* These are voluntary gifts. Some clients will want to tip some or all employees if they receive exceptional service. If you have a no-tipping policy, however, clients must know about it. Most government-owned facilities do not allow tipping.

— *Deposits.* The deposit procedures must be spelled out clearly. Clients must be informed of the amount that must be paid, when it must be tendered, and how it will be applied to the final billing.

— *Refunds.* Although no one likes to broach a negative subject, it is important to detail your refund policies and procedures in advance.

— *Guarantees.* A client must usually give a firm guarantee (guest count) two or three days in advance of the event. The facility will prepare food for that number of guests, plus a stipulated percentage over the guarantee to accommodate any guests who decide to attend at the last minute. For instance, most facilities will agree to handle the guaranteed number of guests and to overset about 3 to 5 percent, up to a maximum number-for example, 5 percent over or up to 100 persons maximum.

If the function is very large, a facility generally uses a sliding scale guarantee. For instance, although it may agree to a 5 percent overset for parties up to 500 persons, it may agree to accommodate only a 3 percent overage for parties in excess of 500.

Negotiating guarantees is a very tricky undertaking. The wise catering executive ensures that clients understand clearly the facility's position. Guarantees, as well as deposits, refund policies, miscellaneous charges, menu prices, and so forth, should always be spelled out very clearly in the catering contract. Some caterers require a client to initial each line item to indicate understanding.

Minimum purchase policy requires a client to purchase a minimum amount of catering services if he or she wants to book one or more events. For example, some big hotels in Las Vegas will not allow a convention to block out meeting room space unless there is a corresponding minimum amount of food and beverage business guaranteed. This food and beverage minimum is based on a set amount per guest room night.

Setup charges. If they are not included in the food and beverage menu prices, clients must be told in advance about these extra charges. A large function does not ordinarily incur additional setup charges; however, small groups may be subject to them. Extra charges can accrue if a room needs a fast turnover and extra labor must be called in to accomplish the job.

Most facilities will charge clients rent for the use of function rooms if they are used for meetings and other events that do not include significant food and beverage sales. For instance, there may be a charge for a room if the event does not generate at least $35 per person for food and/or beverage. The rental rate is usually calculated to cover the fixed overhead and provide a fair profit for the caterer. Some facilities have a sliding scale, with the charge depending on the dollar amount being generated.

Other extra charges. Depending on the size of the function, a facility may add on extra charges for bartenders, cashiers, valet parking, coat-checking facilities, and directional displays. If clients require additional labor because their functions are scheduled to last longer than normal, they will usually be assessed a service charge to cover the extra payroll cost (sometimes calculated as man-hour overtime).

Clients who have established credit ratings are usually allowed to put up a minimum deposit and pay the remaining balance within an allotted time, generally 30 days. Clients without credit approval usually must put up a large deposit and pay the remaining balance at least 2 days prior to the event or immediately after the function ends. Clients who are somewhere between having an established credit rating and no credit rating normally must provide a deposit and pay the remaining balance at the end of the catered event.

Outside food and beverage. Most, if not all, facilities will not allow clients to bring in their own food and beverage supplies. In most situations, the facility's liquor license, liability insurance, health permit, and/or business license forbids the use of personal products.

If the law and the facility allow clients to bring in their own products, there is usually a charge for setup service. For instance, if a client is allowed to bring in his or her own liquor, there may be a standard, one-time corkage fee for the service, or the facility may charge a standard fee for each drink prepared and served.

The facility must ensure that clients realize that the pertinent liquor laws will not be suspended during their catered events. For instance, wedding hosts may not see anything wrong with serving wine to an underage guest at a private party. However, the law does not make this distinction. The same is true for service to visibly intoxicated guests; they cannot legally be served by the banquet staff. If clients request self-service bars, some caterers will require them to sign a waiver of liquor liability so that they are not held responsible for the actions of the guests.

This type of waiver is necessary because, in the case of self-service, the facility does not have bartenders and cocktail servers onsite to monitor underage drinking and service to visibly intoxicated guests. Because of this potential liability, many caterers do not permit self-service bars.

Many clients need to use their own signs, displays, decorations, and/ or demonstrations at booked events. The facility usually reserves the right to approve these items and to control their placement and location. If clients are allowed to have displays, the facility usually expects the clients to be responsible for any damage done and any extraordinary cleanup that may result.

The removal of confetti, rice, and birdseed can pose a challenge. Similar restrictions may apply to other materials, such as paper products, decorations, and equipment. Tape and tacks can damage walls, and some items can be fire hazards.

Responsibility for loss and/or damage. Personal property brought into the facility by guests are not usually covered by the facility's insurance policies. Consequently, clients and their guests must be informed of this policy, and agree to it, before receiving permission to use their own property.

A facility usually expects clients to agree to in-demnify it against any claims, losses, and/or damages, except those due solely to the negligence and/or willful misconduct of the facility staff. The facility also wants protection from claims made by outside service contractors, such as florists, decorators, or audiovisual (AV) firms engaged by clients. Furthermore, clients are expected to stipulate that by paying the final bill, they agree that there are no disputes with the products and services received.

There are times when a facility will be unable to perform through no fault of its own. For instance, bad weather, a strike, a labor dispute, or another circumstance may hamper the facility's ability to service its clients. Consequently, clients must agree to hold harmless the facility under uncontrollable conditions of this type.

A policy regarding substitutions is similar to the policy on uncontrollable acts. Occasionally, supply problems may force a caterer to substitute menu products, or it may be necessary to move a function from one meeting room to another. For instance, an out-door event may have to be moved indoors at the last minute because of inclement weather. Or a contractor's strike may force the facility to substitute other space of comparable size and quality. Although few of us want to think about these potential problems, clients must be advised in advance that they could occur. Always provide proper advance communication with clients so surprises do not anger them.

A facility may require a client to provide additional security for his or her event. For instance, a meeting of diamond dealers would be expected to schedule a great deal of personal security that is provided by or approved by the facility. Alternatively, the facility may reserve the right to hire additional security guards and bill the event host. If you outsource valet parking, always check references to ensure the security of your patron's automobiles.

Some functions may need to be approved and/or licensed by the local government licensing agency. For instance, a function that has a cover charge may need a temporary admission license. The facility should reserve the right to refuse service to any client who does not hold the appropriate licenses and permits prior to the event.

Roles and Responsibilities of a Waiter

A successful restaurant is one which the guests are anxious to visit again, a place where they feel as comfortable as in their own homes. This pleasant atmosphere is produced by courtesy; good well-cooked food; advice in selecting from the available dishes; a knowledge of how they are prepared; and quiet, efficient, but unostentatious, service. It is by these amenities that both buyer and seller are satisfied and goodwill of the business increased. At the end of the visit the customer is made to feel that he got his money's worth in terms of both quality food and courteous service.

Good waiters are necessary to the success and development of the hotel and catering industry. Waiters play an important part as, in effect, an efficient salesman of food, one who assists materially in merchandising and its accompanying services. Waiter is in direct contact with the guests and therefore much of catering establishment's success depends on the skills, interest and personable qualities of the waiter. The waiters are prompted to develop tact and initiative and by keeping their brains active and reveal their personality.

The English writer, Wilfred Gowers-Round, wrote a number of 'Rules for Waiters' that he called a 'Manifesto.'

- A waiter's job is to serve and never to impose himself.
- The goal of waiting is inconspicuous but pleasing service.
- Waiters must be clean and smart and should never wear cologne.
- Under no circumstances should a waiter ever touch a diner.
- Wine glasses should never be filled too full.
- Unasked for advice should never be offered.
- If diners are content to pour the wine themselves, let them.
- Unless asked, no plates should be removed until all have been finished.
- Women diners should be afforded respect equal to men.
- While attending to the customer, the waiter should make sure the diner's coffee cup / water goblet, bread basket, butter, sugar, cream and clean ashray are kept full at all times.
- The bill should be placed on the table without ceremony.
- If the diner so desires, the waiter should carry the money to the cash counter, pay the bill and return the balace to the diner.

Waiting staff, wait staff, or waitstaff are those who work at a restaurant or a bar attending customers - supplying them with food and drink as requested promptly and pleasantly. The waiter is popularly known as a Steward or Commis-de-Rang. A female who "waits" on tables is often called a waitress. The gender-neutral server and collective waitstaff can also be used. Some people prefer to use gender-neutral language, using waiter indiscriminately for males and females, waitperson, server, or waitron.

Duties of Waiting Staff

The duties of waiting staff include preparing tables (table setting) for a meal, taking customers' orders, serving drinks and food, and cleaning up before, during and after servings in a restaurant. He must have knowledge of proper rules of etiquette in order to furnish working service in either a formal or informal sitting. Other task of a waiter includes:

1. Reports to Senior Captain / Captain to receive necessary instruction for the shift and for any menu changes.
2. Has to attend briefings conducted by senior captain.
3. Sets the assigned tables and ensures that the services area too is well-stocked with linen, silver, glassware, china etc. Sets up any special displays that be used for the meal period.
4. Greets guests and sometimes assists the host/ hostess in seating guest. Fills water glasses, serves butter, cocktails, answers questions about menu items and makes suggestions about dishes and wine if the customer requests or desires.
5. Takes orders on check, turns or gives over with specification the order to the cooks with consideration to the timing of the preceding courses. Picks up all food and all other required items from various stations.
6. May carve meats, bone fish and prepare flaming dishes or desserts at guest's table. He may assist Senior Captain for the same.
7. May serve guests from plates to the guest's table.
8. Other tasks to be performed as determined by establishment from time to time.
9. Replenishes wine, water, butter, and bread as and when required.
10. Observes the guests in order to anticipate any additional request and to perceive when the meal has been completed.
11. After all the guests have finished each course and before the next one is served, the waiter/ waitress should remove all soiled dishes or ensure that the assistant stewatard does it.
12. When guests have finished the meal, the table is cleared and reset and ready for the next customer.
13. Performs other tasks as directed by the supervisor.

Depending on the restaurant, other less common duties may be required, such as singing birthday songs to customers who are celebrating a birthday. A theme restaurant may even require staff to dance (e.g. Joe's Crab Shack). There are now event caterers that outsource waiting staff to events and specific functions. Silver service staffs are specially trained to serve at banquets or high-end restaurants. They follow specific rules of service and it is a skilled / specialized job. They generally wear black and white with a long, white apron (extending from the waist to ankle).

Quality of Service Staff

The quality of service staff in any establishment reflects the quality of the establishment itself. No matter how good the food and ambience are, poorly trained, untidy or rude staff can antagonize customers. On the other hand, if the staffs are well-trained and eefficient, they can, to a certain extent, make up for other shortcomings in the services provided.

1) *Personal Hygiene and Appearance.* All members of the staff should be well-groomed and clean at all times, as this gives them a sense of well-being and confidence to do their job efficiently.
    - The hands of the waiting staff should be given special attention, as they are constantly under the scrutiny of the guests. Nails should be trimmed, and kept clean. Playing with one's hair and face should be avoided.
    - Chewing gum should be avoided in all public areas of the hotel.
    - Minimum jewellery should be worn by the service staff. A wrist watch, finger ring and plain earrings (for girls only) should be permitted.
    - If an employee has a skin problem, a doctor should be consulted immediately
    - Uniform should be clean and well-pressed. Shoes should be properly polished and well-fitting.
2) *Good Conduct.* All service staff should be well-mannered and respectful to guests, and to senior members of the staff. They should be calm and pleasant, even in the most tiring circumstances. They should be able to satisfactorily solve any problem that may arise. In case of difficulty, a senior and experienced member of the staff should be consulted. Tact, punctuality and honesty are admirable qualities among service personnel.
3) *Good Memory.* A good memory helps to improve performance. It also helps the service personnel to attend to small but important details such as remembering a guest's name or his likes and dislikes regarding food and beverage.
4) *Observation.* A keen sense of observation and an eye for detail will help a member of the staff to be more efficient at his job. An ability to correctly judge people is definitely an advantage. A sense of

anticipation in the service industry is an invaluable quality. The ability to anticipate what a guest or the management needs, even before it is asked for creates a very good impression.

5) *Concentration and Skill*. Waiting at a table requires concentration and skill. Service staff should develop a sense of urgency in the performance of their duties. Good service may not be commented upon, but bad service is surely noticed and talked about. Service should be prompt without the show of haste.

6) *Salesmanship*. Food and beverage service personnel are technical salespersons; hence they should have a thorough knowledge of the proper presentation and service of all the food and beverages served in the establishment. Waiters should be kept informed by their superiors of deletions or additions to the menu.

7) *Ability to Assume Responsibility*. All service staff should be able to cope up with the demands of the job and possess the ability to assume responsibility. They should be loyal to their employers, responsible to the guests and friendly towards their fellow workers. They should not consider any job as menial, and should be willing to perform all kinds of jobs efficiently. This will help the service staff to grow in their careers and at the same time enhance the image of the establishment in the eyes of the guests.

8) *Maximise Revenue*. Cutting down on costs and maximising the revenue of the establishment should be of prime objective to all members of the staff, even to those in junior positions.

9) *Punctuality*. Punctuality is all-important. If staff is continually late for duty, it shows a lack of interest in his work and a lack of respect for the management and customers.

10) *Local Knowledge*. In the interest of customers, the staff should have a certain knowledge of the area in which they work so that they may be able to advise the guests on the various forms of entertainment offered, the best means of transport to places of interest and so on.

11) *Personality*. Staff must be tactful, courteous, good humoured and of an even temper. They must converse with the customer in a pleasing and well-spoken manner and the ability to smile at the right time.

12) *Attitude to Customers*. The correct approach towards the customer is of the utmost importance. The staff must not be servile, but should

anticipate the customer's needs and wishes. A careful watch should be kept on customers at all times during the service without staring. Care should always be taken when dealing with difficult customers. Staff should never argue with customers as this will only aggravate the situation. All complaints should he referred to someone in authority in the food service area.

13) *Honesty*. This is all-important for the staff in dealings with both the customer and the management. If there is trust and respect in the triangle of staff, customer and management relationships, then there will be pleasant work atmosphere which encourages efficiency and a good team spirit among the food and beverage service operators.

PREPARING FOR SERVICE

Restaurants not only should attract potential customers but also should strive hard to entice them to become frequent and regular customers. This can be done in a number of ways, such as through the type of menu, the glamorous and attractive name of the place or atmosphere within the food service area.

The customer's first impressions of a restaurant are the most important and these are largely determined by the professionalism of the service staff and their preparations prior to service. These pre-service preparations are known as mise-en-place and are vital in that they create the right and pleasing environment by the setting and controlling of temperature, lighting and equipment

The serving food and beverage to the anxiously waiting customer needs professional expertise. The service should follow a sequence and have a plan of action based on the practices of the professional catering industry. The service staff should be expert performers of certain tasks before, during and after service. Deligent and courteous service would certainly transform a satisfied customer to regular customer.

Preparation Before Service

The service staff should check the following before service:

i) The tables and linen are clean.

ii) Tablecloths are evenly spread on the table.

iii) Chairs are dusted and properly arranged.

iv) The table set up is appropriate and pleasing.

v) The silver is polished and the china and crockery are spotlessly clean and befitting the occasion.

vi) Cruet sets, sugar bowls and flower vases are filled and placed on the table suitably.

vii) The floor / carpet is clean and dry.

viii) The restaurant and back area are in a state of readiness before the service session commences.

ix) The side station is fully equipped for service and the following should be checked:

- Condiments tray is cleaned and refilled.
- Napkins are folded and kept handy for the particular session.
- Salvers, extra linen, cutlery and service equipment necessary for the session are stacked up.
- Water jugs and ice buckets are filled and kept ready.
- Coffee pots ready with freshly brewed coffee / tea.
- Sugar cubes, butter and butter plates ready.

Preparation During Service

i) When the guests arrive greet them warmly, by wishing them the time of the day.

ii) Escort the guests to the table and seat them promptly by pulling the chairs out to ease seating. If need be, the table should be moved so that very little inconvenience is caused to guests when they seat themselves.

iii) Ensure that children have high chairs and special attention is paid to the elderly

iv) Serve water and present the menu card, if the captain Preparation for is busy.

v) If the order has to be taken, offer suggestions to the guests on the choice of food and beverages and repeat the final order to avoid possible errors.

vi) Do not leave the station unattended, as nothing annoys a guest more than not being able to find a waiter, when something is needed.

vii) If the table cloth has to be changed during service, the table top should not be exposed. Any articles on the table should be cleared to the side station and not placed on chairs or on the next table. The soiled cloth should be brushed using a service cloth and a crumbing tray or plate.

viii) Do not neglect little things such as lighting a guest's cigarette, responding to a request and showing interest in the guest's needs.

ix) Ensure that service is fast, efficient and pleasant.

x) Before serving dessert, clear and crumb the table.

Preparation After Service

i) Pull out the chairs or the table to enable guests to move out comfortably.

ii) Wish them warmly and request them to visit again, saying - Do visit again, sir / madam.

iii) Clear the table immediately and reset for the next guest.

iv) Have the side station cleared and restacked for the next sitting.

Mise-en-scene

Mise-en-scene, the French term means to prepare the environment of the outlet before service in order to make it pleasant, comfortable, safe and hygeinic. Before each service session, the restaurant should be made presentable enough to receive the guests. The supervisor or team of waiters should ensure the following mise-en-scene:

- Carpets are well brushed or hovered.
- All tables and chairs are serviceable.
- Table lights or wall lights have functioning bulbs.
- Menu cards are presentable and attractive.
- Tent carts or other sales material are presentable.
- Doors and windows are thrown open for sometime to air the restaurant. This should be followed by closing the windows and doors and setting the air-conditioning or heating to a comfortable temperature.
- Exchange dirty linen for fresh linen.
- Table cloths and mats are laid on the tables.
- Replace wilted flowers with fresh flowers.

Mise-en-place

Mise-en-place, the French term means to "putting in place" is attributed to the preparation of a work place for ultimate smooth service. It is widely used in the food and beverage service department in everyday hotel operations. Before service commences, the staff should ensure that the station is in total readiness to receive guests. A station comprises of a given number of tables which are attended by a given team of waiters. Thus a restaurant may have several stations, each with a team of waiters. In a large restaurant, each station may be headed by a Chef-de-rang. Mise-en-place involves:

- Side stations should be stacked with sufficient covers for resetting the restaurant after the first sitting is over. Extra linen, crockery, cutlery, glassware and ashtrays should be kept handy so that they are readily available for use.
- Cruet sets should be cleaned and filled on a daily basis.
- Sauce bottles should be filled and the necks and tops of the bottles wiped clean.
- Butter, condiments and accompaniments for service should be kept ready for use when needed.

Table Setting

Table setting refers to the way to set a table with tableware -such as eating utensils and dishware - for serving and eating. The arrangement for a single diner is called a place setting. The arrangement varies across various cultures. The rules for laying a table are not rigid. They are followed to facilitate dining and making the table neat. The basic rules for laying the tables are given below:

1) Table Linens: Table linen has to be laid properly. A white cloth is preferred but not mandatory. The only rule is to make sure that linen patterns and china patterns don't clash.
2) Chargers: Chargers or dinner plates should be placed on the table first. Chargers are decorative elements that are placed underneath plates to add color or texture to the table. Each plate should be set in the center of the place setting and each place setting on the table should be set equidistant. The rest of the components used to set a formal table will be set with the dinner plate in mind. If a charger is used, soup and melon bowls will be placed on top. The charger will generally be removed just before the main course

3) Napkins: Linen napkins should be folded elegantly and placed in the center of the dinner plate.

4) Silverware: Silverware is to be placed in order of use. In other words, the diner will start at the end and work his way in. The first course will use silverware farthest from the dinner plate, while the last course will utilize the silverware closest. Place all silverware an inch from the table's edge.

5) Knives: Set knives on the table to the right of the dinner plate. Technically, one should only use a knife if one is cutting meat; however, up to three knives can be placed on the table, in order of use. Blades should face inside, towards the table setting.

6) Forks: Forks are to be set to the left of the dinner plate in order of use. In most cases, there are three: one each for seafood, the main course and the salad. When dining formally, salads are generally served at the end of the meal.

7) Spoons: Spoons are set to the right of the knives in order of use. If there is a melon course, this spoon will be set closest to the plate with the soup spoon on the end. If there is a dessert spoon, this will be set above the plate. Coffee spoons are set on the saucer when it's time for dessert.

8) Glasses: Glasses are set above the plate to the right in order of use. From left to right: Water glass, red wine glass, white wine glass, champagne flute (if ordered).

9) Dessert: Dessert plates and coffee / tea cups will be set out after dinner. If a fork is to be used with dessert, this will be placed on the dessert plate. A dessert spoon should have already been set above the dinner plate. Coffee spoons should be placed on the saucer. Coffee / tea mugs aren't used for a formal dinner.

Points to Remember When Laying a Table

1) The table on which a tablecloth is to be spread, should be first covered with a baize base cloth, for the following reasons:

    a. To protect the diner's wrists and elbows from the table's sharp edges.

    b. To keep the tablecloth firmly in place.

c. To protect the surface of the table and prevent the rattling of crockery and cutlery.

d. To absorb moisture in case liquid spills on the table.

2) Based on the size of the table, appropriate linen should be used. The central fold of the tablecloth should be in the middle of the table and all the four edges should just brush the seats of the chairs. Soiled or torn linen should not be used. Three types of tablecloths namely cotton, linen and damask are used. Of these, damask is the best.

3) If a bud vase is used as a central decorative piece, it should not be very large or tall as that obstructs the view of guests sitting opposite each other. Heavily scented flowers should be avoided, as they affect the flavour of the food.

4) Each cover should be well-balanced. (A cover is the space required on a table for laying cutlery, crockery, glassware and linen for one person to partake of a meal).

5) Only the required cutlery, crockery and glassware should be placed on the table. On a normal dining table, the space required for one cover is 60 cm x 38 cm. The cover on the opposite side should be exactly similar, so as to give a well-balanced look.

6) Cutlery should always be laid from the inside to the outside of the cover, since the order of sequence in which they are to be used is always from outside to inside.

7) Knives and soup spoons should be placed on the right-hand side of a cover, while forks should be placed on the left-hand side. Dessert spoons and forks should be placed on top of the cover. The side knife should be placed on a quarter plate and kept on the left side of the cover. The cutting edge of all knives should face to the left.

8) Water tumbler should be kept to the right of the cover, at the tip of the large knife.

9) Napkins should be placed in the centre of the cover, in between the cutlery. Normally during a dinner session, napkins are arranged in empty water tumblers.

10) Cruet sets, a butter dish, an ashtray, meal accompaniments and a bud vase should be placed in between the covers at the centre of the table.

11) Crockery and cutlery should be spotlessly clean and the glassware well polished.
12) Chipped or cracked equipment should not be used. The hotel's monogram should be visible to the guest.
13) All cutlery and crockery should be placed about an inch from the edge of the table so that they are not accidentally tipped over.

Challenges of Catering Services

Some of the major challenges encountered by the catering department.

1. *Marketing the catering department's services.* A great deal of time must be spent in this effort to distinguish your facility in the minds of potential clients. Clients tend to perceive caterers as interchangeable as buses: There is always another one available who can handle their needs. You will need to battle this perception constantly.
2. *Excessive amount of time spent with clients.* Unfortunately, only a small number of persons and groups contacted will end up purchasing catered events. Moreover, once business is booked, a great deal of time must be spent planning and coordinating the events. Although some clients need more handholding than others, the wise catering executive will expect to devote much time to these tasks. To maximize available catering sales time, savvy caterers learn to determine how much time is necessary and/or appropriate to spend with a prospective client, who may be a serious buyer or merely a casual shopper for catering services.
3. *Unique demands.* All functions have unique demands. For instance, refreshment breaks are sometimes permanently set, but clients may not have a particular schedule in mind and merely wish to visit the refreshment area when time permits. This is especially true in conference centers, where attendees can break at will. Consequently, set-ups must to be freshened periodically, which requires an employee to be constantly alert to fluctuating needs.
4. *Difficulty in costing out and pricing certain functions.* Special requests and last-minute needs will cost more because of the special circumstances. The aforementioned refreshment breaks fall into this category. Because the demands these events present cannot always be predicted in advance, function hosts usually must wait until a final accounting is made by the catering department. This can cause ill will

among clients, especially those who are on a tight budget and would appreciate price guarantees.

5. *Ethical traps.* Sometimes a catering department may encounter conflict-of-interest dilemmas. For example, clients who need outside contractors, such as tour buses, entertainers, and decorators, may ask the caterer for a recommendation. The facility, always mindful of its image and reputation, will tend to recommend only a few outside contractors that can fill the bill adequately. However, such favoritism may be perceived by some as shady dealing.
6. *Responsibility greater than authority.* It is very important to determine in advance who is responsible for each part of an event. For instance, a convention may want to hire its own band but simultane-ously expect the facility to coordinate the details. This can easily lead to misunderstandings and client dissatisfaction unless everything is spelled out clearly.
7. *Time pressures.* The catering department is a pressure cooker. It seems as if everything must be ready "yesterday." Catering personnel must learn to work well within time constraints.
8. *Working with and coordinating with other departments and outside agencies.* Proper advance planning is necessary to avoid service glitches that could cause guest dissatisfaction. Caterers must cultivate the ability to communicate effectively.
9. *Maintaining qualified staff members.* Many catering departments experience severe volume swings. For instance, convention centers pose a unique challenge in terms of volume and staffing. One day you may have a breakfast for 5,000, which requires a lot of labor. But you may not have another similar function for two weeks; as a result, it is very difficult to keep qualified employees, many of whom prefer more predictable work schedules.

The lack of technical foodservice skills. Many caterers today, both men and women, have less knowledge about food than ever before. They are increasingly reliant on chefs and food and beverage directors for advice. This would not be a major problem if standardized menus were used consistently; however, things are more trendy these days, there is more competition, and many clients want custom menus and something special. This can make it difficult to respond quickly to unusual customer requests.

A potential client may become restless with the catering executive who needs to confer constantly with other food and beverage people in the organization. However, an executive's confidence and poise can transcend the bonds of ignorance. Instead of dismay, a potential client may be quite pleased with the executive who may not have the answer at the very moment, but who promises to get it quickly.

Catering: Health Safety Risks

Statistics have proved that bad management practices cause accidents and cost money, time and effort. Accident rates in the catering industry have been getting steadily worse over the last six years. The rate of major injury is now 54% higher than in 1986. Over 69% of major injuries result from slipping and tripping or falling on the same level or from contact with harmful or hot substances. The rate of accidents which are not major, but lead to three or more days off work has more than doubled over the last six years. These figures represent costs both in terms of pain and suffering for individuals and in direct costs to employers.

Recent studies across a range of industries suggest that for each accident resulting in an injury leading to three days off work there are seven less serious injuries and 189 accidents resulting in damage to property. Accidents can result in costs representing up to 8.5% of a company's turnover, and yet 70% of these accidents could have been prevented by improved health and safety management.

Individual workplaces will, of course, exhibit their own patterns of risk, but the main causes of accidents and ill health in the catering industry are:

- slips, trips and falls;
- lifting and manual handling;
- contact with hot surfaces and harmful substances;
- dermatitis;
- work-related upper limb disorders.

Most accidents can be prevented by good management and supervision combined with effective training, which makes accident prevention no different from any other aspect of running a successful business. Careful thought and planning applied to those areas of catering where the risks are highest should help to prevent accidents and reduce costs. It will also show enforcement officers that you are going down the right route towards complying with health and safety legislation.

Owners and managers have clearly defined legal duties about training employees. The law requires every employer and self-employed person to consider the health and safety training needs of themselves and all employees, including new recruits, part-timers and temporary or agency staff. It is important to appreciate that time and effort spent in ensuring staff are working safely and understand the reasons for good practices is likely to:

— save the business time and money: there will be less money and time wasted in staff accidents, damaged equipment, damage to premises and wasted resources;
— improve staff morale and feelings of security, leading to improved service, commitment and motivation.

Good management of health and safety can only be achieved with the co-operation of the workforce. It is vital that your employees know what is expected of them and are aware of any risks to their health and safety that may arise at work and any safe systems of work that are applied. The co-operation of the workforce is likely to be more constructive if you consult with them about developing health and safety measures. Where you recognise a trade union, safety representatives must be consulted about the health and safety arrangements before action is taken. Where trade unions are not involved the workforce should be encouraged to appoint its own safety representatives.

Involving safety representatives helps ensure that health and safety measures will be effective in practice. Health and safety will not be a burden if managed properly. Managing health and safety effectively:

— ensures it is not a burden;
— keeps costs to a minimum and can bring savings;
— prevents injury and ill health to your business' most important resource: people;
— reduces the likelihood of civil claims.

Effective management of health and safety can best be achieved by:

— realising it is an integral and essential part of business management;
— identifying the main risk areas and taking action on those first;

— setting yourself clear targets, for example to train staff and to clearly allocate responsibilities;

— supervising adequately;

— sconsulting staff at all stages.

In most catering situations, local authority enforcement officers are responsible for the enforcement of health and safety legislation. Inspectors from HSE look after health and safety in catering facilities in institutions such as hospitals, schools etc. The role of the enforcement officer is not just to enforce the law but also to promote health and safety, give advice on the law and how to comply with it and advise on other sources of information - for example, a series of booklets available from HSE. Additionally, many local authorities either arrange or facilitate health and safety training. So, enforcement officers are there to help businesses and promote health and safety.

References

Bradley, Alice, *Cooking for profit; catering and food service management,* Chicago: American school of home economics, 1922.

Casado, Matt A. *Food and Beverage Service Manual.* New York: Wiley, 1994.

Chmelynski, Carol Ann Caprione. *Opportunities in Food Service Careers.* Lincolnwood: VGM Career Horizons, 2000.

Whitehead, Jessup, *The steward's handbook and guide to party catering,* Chicago: J. Anderson & co. printers, 1889.

6

Bar and Beverage Management

Beverages are potable drinks which have thirst-quenching, refreshing, stimulating and nourishing qualities. By refreshing, one means the replenishment of fluid loss from the body due to perspiration. Simulation results in increase of the heart beat and blood pressure. This is due to the intake of spirits (alcohol) or tea (thein) and coffee (coffein). Nourishment is provided by the nutrients in the beverages, especially fruit juices.

Most of the beverages supply energy in the form of sugar or alcohol. They also provide other nutrients like mineral salts and vitamins. For example, milk gives calcium and citrus fruits give vitamin C.

Generally, people drink for one or more of six reasons; to quench thirst, to get drunk, to enjoy a social setting (social drinking), to enjoy the taste of the beverage, to feed an addiction (alcoholism), or as part of a religious or traditional ceremony or custom (proposing toast).

Classification of Beverages

A beverage is a liquid formulation specifically prepared for human consumption. The word "Beverage" has been derived from the Latin word "bever" meaning rest from work. After work, one tends to feel thirsty due to fluid loss through perspiration and one is inclined to drink water or other potable beverages to compensate fluid loss. Beverages can be broadly classified into two. They are

1. Alcoholic beverages and
2. Non-alcoholic beverages.

ALCOHOLIC BEVERAGES

An alcoholic beverage is a drink containing ethanol, commonly known as alcohol. Ethanol is a psychoactive drug, with a depressant effect. Significant blood alcohol content may be considered legal drunkenness as it reduces attention and slows reaction speed. Ethanol being a psychoactive drug, with a depressant effect, many societies regulate or restrict its sale and consumption.

Alcohol has been widely consumed since prehistoric times by people around the world, as a component of the standard diet, for hygienic or medical reasons, for its relaxant and euphoric effects, for recreational purposes, for artistic inspiration, as aphrodisiacs, and for other reasons. Some drinks have been invested with symbolic or religious significance suggesting the mystical use of alcohol. However Alcoholic beverages can be addictive and the state of addiction to ethanol is known as alcoholism.

Fermented Alcoholic Beverages

In fermentation process, certain yeasts decompose sugars, in the feed stock in the absence of oxygen, to form alcohol and carbon dioxide; method for production of ethanol, wine, and beer. Low-alcohol-content drinks are produced by fermentation of sugar or starch-containing products, and high-alcohol ones are produced by distillation of these low alcohol products.

Beer

Beer is alcoholic beverage made by brewing of fermenting cereals mash, especially malted barley, usually with the addition of hops as a flavoring agent (bitter taste) and a s a stabilizer. A great many beers are brewed across the globe. Local traditions will give beers different names, giving the impression of a multitude of different styles. However, the basics of brewing beer are shared across national and cultural boundaries. Ale and Lager are two main types of Beer. These are clear and sparklng. Another beer is stout which is stronger and coloured.

Wine

Wine is an alcoholic beverage produced through the partial or total fermentation of grapes. Other fruits and plants, such as berries, apples, cherries, dandelions, elder-berries, palm, honey and rice can also be fermented. Some popular type of wine are Table wine, Sangria, Sparkling wine, Champagne, Fortified wine, Port, Sherry, Vermouth etc.

Distilled Alcoholic Beverages

A distilled beverage is a consumable liquid containing ethyl alcohol (ethanol) purified / enriched by distillation from a fermented feed stock such as fruits, vegetables, or cereal grains. The word spirits generally refers to distilled beverages low in sugars and containing at least 35% alcohol by volume. Popular spirits include Absinthe, baijiu, brandy, grappa, rum, tequila, vodka, whisky, sake and traditional German schnapps. Short description of these are presented below.

Whiskey

Refers to a broad category of alcoholic beverages that are distilled from fermented grain mash and aged in wooden casks (generally oak). Different grains are used for different varieties, including: barley, malted barley, rye, malted rye, wheat, and maize (corn).

Brandy

It is a general term for distilled wine, usually containing 40–60% ethyl alcohol by volume. In addition to wine, this spirit can also be made from grape, pomace, or fermented fruit juice. It is normally consumed as an after-dinner drink. Brandy made from wine is generally coloured with caramel to imitate the effect of long aging in wooden casks; pomace and fruit brandies are generally drunk unaged, and are not usually coloured.

Rum

Rum is a distilled beverage made from sugarcane by-products such as molasses and sugarcane juice by a process of fermentation and distillation. The distillate, a clear liquid, is then usually aged in oak and other barrels. Rum is produced in a variety of styles. Light rums are commonly used in cocktails, while golden and dark rums are appropriate for use in cooking as well as cocktails. Premium brands of rum are also available that are made to be consumed neat or on the rocks.

Vodka

Vodka is one of the world's most popular distilled beverages. It is a clear liquid containing water and ethanol purified by distillation from a fermented substance such as potatoes, grain or sugar beet molasses, and an insignificant amount of other substances: impurities and possibly flavourings. Except for various types of flavourings, vodka is a colourless liquid. Vodka usually has an alcohol content of 35% to 50% by volume. Vodka is a Russian delight.

Saké

It is a Japnese wine made from rice and is very strong.

Compound Beverages

Distilled beverages with added flavorings and relatively high sugar content are generally referred to as compound beverages.

Liquer

A liqueur is a sweet alcoholic beverage, often flavored with fruits, herbs, spices, flowers, seeds, roots, plants, barks, and sometimes cream. The word liqueur comes from the Latin word liquifacere which means "to dissolve." This refers to the dissolving of the flavorings used to make the liqueur. Liqueurs are not usually aged for long periods, but may have resting periods during their production to allow flavors to blend. There are many categories of liqueurs including: fruit liqueur, cream liqueur, coffee liqueur, chocolate liqueur, schnapps liqueur, brandy liqueur, anise liqueur, nut-flavoured liqueur, and herbal liqueur, depending upon the flavouring agents used.

Gin

Gin is a spirit flavoured with juniper berries. Distilled gin is made by redistilling white grain spirit which has been flavoured with juniper berries. Compound gin is made by flavouring neutral grain spirit with juniper berries without redistilling and can be considered flavoured vodka.The most common style of gin, typically used for mixed drinks, is London dry gin.

Non-alcoholic Beverages

A non-alcoholic beverage is a beverage that contains no alcohol. Such drinks are generally drunk for refreshment, or to quench people's thirst. Non-alcoholic beverages can be mainly classified as hot and cold beverages.

Cold Drinks

Aerated

These beverages are charged or aerated with carbonic gas. The charging with carbonic gas imparts the pleasant effervescent characteristic of these beverages. Carbonation occurs when carbon dioxide is dissolved in water or an aqueous solution. This process yields the "fizz" to carbonated water and sparkling mineral water. Example: soda water, dry ginger, fizzy lemonade, ginger beer, coca-cola, pepsi, and others.

Spring water

Spring water is the water derived from underground formation from which water flows naturally (artesian) to the surface of the earth. Minerals become dissolved in the water as it moves through the underground rocks. This may give the water flavor and even carbon dioxide bubbles, depending upon the nature of the geology through which it passes. This is why spring water is often bottled and sold as mineral water.

Mineral water is the water containing minerals or other dissolved substances that alter its taste or gives it therapeutic value. Salts, sulfur compounds, and gases are among the substances that can be dissolved in the water. Mineral water can often be effervescent. Mineral water can be prepared or can occur naturally.

Squash

Squash is a highly-sweetened (and often fruit-based) concentrate, which is diluted with a liquid, most commonly water, before drinking. Typically, squash is created by mixing one part concentrate with four or five parts of water (depending on concentration and personal taste) directly into a glass or mug or into a jug. Squashes are also mixed with spirits or cocktails. The most common flavours are orange, apple and blackcurrant, lemon, peppermint, mixed fruit, summer fruits, and lemon-lime. Other flavours include peach, strawberry, passion fruit, custard apple and kiwi fruit.

Juice

Juice is prepared by mechanically squeezing or macerating fresh fruits or vegetables without the application of heat or solvents. Popular juices include, but are not limited to, apple, orange, prune, lemon, grapefruit, cherry, pineapple, tomato, carrot, grape, strawberry, cranberry, pomegranate guava, sapota and celery. It has become increasingly popular to combine a variety of fruits into single juice drinks. Popular blends include cran-apple (cranberry and apple) and apple and blackcurrant. Juices are also used for cocktails and mixing with spirits.

Syrup

Syrup is a thick, viscous liquid, containing a large amount of dissolved sugars (60 to 65% brix), but showing little tendency for crystalisation of dissolved sugar. The main use of these concentrated sweet fruit flavourings is as a base for cocktails, fruit cups or mixed with soda water as a long drink.

Some examples of syrup are orgeat (almond), cassis (blackcurrant), citronelle (lemon), framboise (raspberry) and cerise (cherry)

Hot Drinks

Tea

The most popular non-alcoholic beverage, tea is a stimulating and refreshing drink. All tea comes from the "Camellia sinensis", an evergreen shrub that may grow up to 60 feet in the wild. When cultivated for harvest, the tea bushes are kept to a height of about three feet. There are over 3000 varieties of tea each with their own specific characteristics. Tea leaves have a characteristic oval shape and serrated edge. Younger the leaves better the quality of the tea. The kind of tea obtained is determined by the manufacturing process and treatment. The principle flavour components of tea are caffeine, tannin yielding compounds and small amounts of essential oils. Caffeine provides the stimulating effect, tannin the colour, body and taste to the extract and the essential oils contribute the characteristic aroma. It is predominantly grown in India, Ceylon, China and Japan. Chinese tea contains less tannin than the other varieties.

Tea is mostly named after the region in which they are cultivated. Example: Assam tea is named after the Assam region in India, and Keemun is named after the Keemun region of China.

Types of Tea

The climate, soil conditions where the tea is grown, and how the tea is processed, determines the flavor characteristics of the tea. Tea is harvested after each flush - the sprouting of the top two leaves and bud. Tea pickers' motto is 'two leaf and a bud.' The top two leaves and bud are hand plucked and then processed into any of the four types of tea, which are Black, Green, Oolong, and White.

1. *Black Tea*: The leaves are withered, then rolled till they become soft and massy. This is done to break up the fiber and cells of the leaf to liberate the constituents so that their extraction is easy. The leaves are then fermented. During the process of fermentation some of the acid in the leaves oxidizes and is converted into less soluble forms while more essential oils develop. After fermentation is complete, the leaves are fired in a drying machine. Some of the popular black teas include English Breakfast, and Darjeeling.

2. *Green Tea.* Skips the oxidizing step. It is simply withered and then dried. It has a more delicate taste and is pale green/ golden in color. The chief difference between black tea and green tea is the former is fermented while the latter is not. Since the purpose of fermentation is to make tannin less soluble, an infusion of green tea has more tannin in it, astringent and slightly bitter to taste.
3. *Oolong tea.* It is popular in China, it is withered, partially oxidized, and dried. Oolong is a cross between black and green tea in color and taste.
4. *White tea.* It is the least processed. A very rare tea from China, white tea is not oxidized or rolled, but simply withered and dried by steaming.

The best tea generally produces a pale-coloured infusion and the depth of colour is not necessarily a 'sign of strength.' Freshly infused tea is harmless to normal digestion; continued infusion extracts the tannin, a bitter substance which is harmfull.

Storage of Dried Tea

1. Tea easily absorbs moisture and odors and so it is essential that it is kept in a cool dry place away from any strong smelling items.
2. Tea must be stored in an airtight container not exposed to light and used within a reasonable time. Because light breaks down the quality (photo-oxidation) of tea, glass containers are not suitable for the storage of tea unless stored away from light.
3. If the tea in chest, they should be kept off the ground and at 16 cm. or 6 inches away from the wafts. This allows a current of air to circulate round the tea chest and averts dampness.
4. Once a chest is opened it is advisable to put a close-fitting lid over it.

Preparation of Tea

Tea brewing or preparation is an art that is simple to perform but which also requires some care to do well. While essentially tea is brewed by adding boiling water to the dry leaf, the quantity of leaves, the temperature of the water and timing is of vital concern. The following is a guide for the preparation of tea. The basic rule of thumb to start is 'one teaspoon of loose-leaf tea per cup'.

1. Warm your empty tea pot by filling it with hot water. This will prevent the hot water from cooling too quickly when leaves are added.

2. Boil freshly drawn tap water. If the quality of your tap water is poor, try using filtered or bottled spring water. For black tea, use the water when it comes to a boil. Water left boiling too long will de-aerate. This will result in a flat tasting tea. For green tea, the water should be heated to a lower temperature (usually approximately 80 degrees Celsius), which may vary from tea to tea.
3. Empty the hot water from your tea pot and add 2.25g or one rounded teaspoon of tea leaves for each cup of water (or one heaping teaspoon per mug), placing the tea directly into the bottom of the pot or using a basket infuser. Tea ball strainers, while convenient, often yield poorer tasting tea as they are often too small to allow all of the leaves to fully unravel its contents. If you do use a tea ball, be sure to use one that is sufficiently large to pack the tea loosely.
4. Add the freshly boiled water over the leaves in the tea pot.
5. Brew tea for the appropriate length of time. Time needed to brew tea varies depending on the leaves being used and the drinker's individual taste. Careful timing is essential for brewing tea. A very general rule to follow is the smaller the leaf, the less time required for brewing. Broken grades of tea leaves and most Darjeeling teas usually only need 3-4 minuts. Beverages minutes to brew. Whole-leaf teas often need 4-5 minutes. All teas, however, will become bitter due to higher tannin extraction if brewed for longer than 5 or 6 minutes. When brewing tea, time with a timer, and not with your eyes. It is a common mistake to brew the tea until it looks a particular color or shade. The color of tea is a poor indicator of the tea's taste.
6. If you use a basket infuser or a tea ball, remove these promptly when the brewing time has expired. If you placed the tea directly into the pot, pour the tea into the cups through a strainer to catch the leaves. In this instance, if you do not wish to serve your tea immediately, pour your tea through a strainer into another pre-heated tea pot.
7. Tea sometimes is brewed with spices like fresh ginger, dried ginger powder or cardoms to enrich the flavor.

Milk and sugar should be added according to individual taste. Adding of milk first or last does not make any significant difference in the taste of tea - but many people have their choice some like to add milk first and some afterwards. Sugar must be added last.

Tea is also taken hot with sugar and slices of lemon. This is known as Russian Tea. For preparing iced tea: prepare strong tea. Pour over crushed ice on which placed a sprig of mint and topped with lemon slices.

Instant tea: Of late completely water soluble tea powder is getting popular. Another convenient method of preparing tea is to use tea bags.

Coffee

Coffee berries, which contain the coffee bean, are produced by several species of small evergreen bush of the genus Coffea. The two most commonly grown species are Coffea canephora (also known as Coffea robusta) and Coffea arabica. These are cultivated in India, Latin America, Southeast Asia, and Africa. Once ripe, coffee berries are picked, processed to remove the mesocarp, and dried. The seeds are then roasted, undergoing several physical and chemical changes. They are roasted to various degrees, depending on the desired flavor. They are then ground and brewed to produce liquid coffee which is also known as coffee decoction. Coffee can be prepared and presented by a variety of methods to cater the need of loca palate.

Coffee is always brewed by the user immediately before drinking. In most areas, coffee may be purchased unprocessed, or already roasted, or already roasted and ground. Coffee is often vacuum packed to prevent oxidation and lengthen its shelf life.

Processing of Coffee Beans

Coffee preparation is the process of turning coffee beans into a beverage. While the specific steps needed vary with the type of coffee desired and with the raw material being utilized, the process is composed of four basic steps; raw coffee beans must be roasted, the roasted coffee beans must then be ground, the ground coffee must then be mixed with hot water for a certain time (brewed), and finally the liquid coffee must be filtered off from the spent powder.

1. *Roasting.* Roasting coffee transforms the chemical and physical properties of green coffee beans into roasted coffee products. The roasting process is integral to producing a savory cup of coffee. When roasted, the green coffee bean expands to nearly double its original size, changing in color and density. As the bean absorbs heat, the color shifts to yellow and then to a light "cinnamon" brown then to a dark and

oily color. During roasting, oils appear on the surface of the bean. The roast will continue to darken until it is removed from the heat source. Coffee can be roasted with ordinary kitchen equipment (frying pan, grill, oven) or by specialised appliances. Some times, butter fat (melted butter / ghee) is added during roasting to enhance the flavour of the resultant powder.

2. *Grinding.* The whole roasted coffee beans are ground, which is also known as milling, to facilitate the brewing process. The fineness of grind strongly affects brewing, and must be matched to the brewing method for best results. Brewing methods which expose coffee grounds to heated water for longer require a coarser grind than faster brewing methods. Uniformly ground coffee is better than the mixture of sizes produced by a mill with chopping blades. Many coffee drinkers grind the beans themselves immediately before brewing. There are four methods of grinding coffee for brewing: burr-grinding, chopping, pounding, and roller grinding.

Methods of Preparation of Coffee

General methods of preparation of coffee is given below. This is followed by specific methods of brewing coffee which is given under appropriate headings.

1. *Brewing.* Coffee can be brewed in several different ways, but these methods fall into two main groups depending upon how the water is introduced to the coffee grounds.
   - If the method allows the water to pass only once through the grounds, the resulting brew will contain mainly the more soluble components (including caffeine).
   - If the water is repeatedly cycled through the beans (as with the common percolator), the brew will also contain more of the relatively less soluble, and bitter-tasting, compounds found in the bean, but for this coarse ground coffee will be required.
2. *Boiling.* Despite the name, care should be taken not to actually boil coffee for more than an instant because the decoction becomes bitter.
   - The simplest method is to put the ground coffee in a cup, pour in hot water and let it cool while the grounds sink to the bottom. This is a traditional method for making a cup of coffee

- "Cowboy coffee" is made by simply heating coarse grounds with water in a pot, letting the grounds settle and pouring off the liquid to drink, sometimes filtering it to remove fine grounds.The above methods are sometimes used with hot milk instead of water.

  Water temperature is crucial to the proper extraction of flavor from the ground coffee. The recommended brewing temperature of coffee is 93°C (199.4°F). If cooler, some of the solubles that make up the flavor will not be extracted. If the water is too hot, some undesirable, bitter, components will be extracted, adversely affecting the taste. If coffee is heated to boiling point only very briefly, the taste will be little affected; the longer it is kept at a high temperature the worse the taste becomes.

3. *Steeping.* A cafetière (or French press) is a tall, narrow cylinder with a plunger that includes a metal or nylon mesh filter. Coffee is placed in the cylinder and boiling water is poured on. The coffee and hot water are left in the cylinder for a few minutes (typically 4'-7') and the plunger is pushed down leaving the filter immediately above the grounds, allowing the coffee to be poured out while the filter retains the grounds. Depending on the type of filter, it is important to pay attention to the grind of the coffee beans, though a rather coarse grind is almost always called for. A plain glass cylinder may be used, or a vacuum flask arrangement to keep the coffee hot.
4. *Drip Brew.* Drip brew (also known as filter or American coffee) is made by letting hot water drip onto coffee grounds held in a coffee filter (paper or perforated metal). Strength varies according to the ratio of water to coffee and the fineness of the grind, but is typically weaker than espresso, though the final product contains more caffeine. By convention, regular coffee brewed by this method is served in a brown or black pot (or a pot with a brown or black handle), while decaffeinated coffee is served in an orange pot (or a pot with an orange handle).

Moka Pot Method

There is an art to making coffee in a moka pot that includes the amount of water, the amount and grind of the coffee, the compactness of the coffee grounds in the filter and the heat of the water used to brew it. It is possible to make excellent coffee without any acidity or bitterness in a moka pot if you follow simple procedures listed below:

1. Place your kettle of cold water on your stove burner and heat water until hot. Depending on the quality of your water, you may find that using filtered water significantly improves the taste of your coffee.
2. Grind your coffee. Grind just a little coarser than for an espresso machine (fine, espresso grind of dark roasted coffee). Just coarse enough so it doesn't go through the upper filter holes or block them.
3. Place hot water in the bottom section of the pot up to the level of the safety valve.
4. Insert the filter basket. Fill the filter basket with ground coffee until it is level and then level off with a knife. Do not compact the coffee, because as the water reaches the grounds they will expand effectively tamping your coffee for you.
5. Make sure the filter disk and gasket are in place in the top portion of the pot. Screw the top section onto the bottom section of the pot and tighten to obtain a perfect seal. If using a stovetop moka pot, place it on the stove on medium to medium-high heat. When hot, the air and water trapped inside the bottom tank expand due to the heat being applied the device. As this happens, it pushes the hot water up a tube, through the coffee grinds, and out of the spout into the top chamber of the pot.
6. When the water in the tank has been exhausted, that's when you hear the 'gurgle,' that signifies the drink is ready to pour (approximately 4-5 minutes). Brewing is completed when all the water has been percolated into the top chamber. Remove the moka pot from the stove.

Do not put the pot in the dishwasher. Wash the pot in mild detergent and water and dry thoroughly after each use. Always keep your moka pot scrupulously clean. Disassemble the moka pot after every use and clean the filter and top pot, being sure that you clean the underside of the top pot. Every few weeks, run some vinegar through the moka pot as if you were brewing coffee to get rid of any mineral deposits left behind by hard water.

Pot Method

i) Warm an earthenware pot or jug. Put in 3 level teaspoons of fresh coffee powder (coarse grind) for each 250 ml cup.

ii) Pour water which has started to boil over the powder and stir. Cover the pot and let it stand near the fire for 5 to 7 minutes.

iii) Pour the coffee through a fine meshed sieve or cloth. Add milk and sugar to taste.

Filter Method

Several types of filters are available. Stainless steel or brass filters are the best, but the latter should be properly tinned, or else the coffee will be spoilt. Glass or china containers are good but are fragile. Copper should not be used because of possible copper poisoning.

i) Put in 3 level teaspoons of coffee powder (fine or medium grind) to each 250 ml. or 8 oz. cup. Press the plunger down lightly over the powder.

ii) Pour water which has just come to boil over (the plunger in a circular motion. Let it stand for 5 to 7 minutes.

iii) Coffee can be poured out straight from the lower vessel and milk and sugar added as required.

Percolator Method

i) Place the ground coffee powder in the centre section of a clean warm percolator on a fine strainer fitted inside and resting on a paper filter (a pinch off salt is mixed with the coffee).

ii) Pour fresh boiling water slowly through the top section.

iii) The water passes through the coffee, is strained and collects in ihe bottom section of the apparatus.

Espresso or Caffè Espresso

Espresso is a concentrated coffee beverage brewed by forcing very hot, but not boiling water under high pressure through coffee that has been ground to a consistency between extremely fine and powder.

The defining characteristics of espresso include a thicker consistency than drip coffee, a higher amount of dissolved solids than drip coffee per relative volume, and a serving size that is usually measured in shots, which are between 25 and 30 ml (30ml=1 fluid ounce) in size. Espresso is chemically complex and volatile, with many of its chemical components quickly degrading due to oxidation or loss of temperature. Properly brewed espresso has three major parts: the heart, body, and the most distinguishing factor, the presence of crema, reddish-brown foam that floats on the surface of the espresso. It is composed of vegetable oils, proteins and sugars. Crema has elements of both emulsion and foam colloid.

Instant Coffee

A thick coffee decoction is prepared first and then it is either spray dried to a fine powder or freeze dried to granules. When added to hot water it dissolves completely leaving no residue.

Turkish Coffee

It is heavily laced with cardomom and is quite thick in consistency. It is a traditional after meal drink in many Arab countries.

General Rules for Storing and for Making Coffee

i) Coffee loses aroma and flavour with storage, as the volatile components evaporate. It should be roasted and ground immediately before brewing for the best possible drink.

ii) Roasted coffee bean can be stored for some time, and can be re-roasted briefly immediately before use. Ground coffee should be used within two or three days of grinding.

iii) Vacuum -packing extends storage life much. Roasted coffee, whether ground or not, can be kept in an airtight container in a freezer to lengthen shelf life.

iv) Fresh coffee is the best; so buy quantities to last not more than a week.

v) Use the exact quantity of powder required.

vi) Use freshly drawn and freshly boiled water.

vii) The coffee-maker must be rinsed with hot water before each use and thoroughly washed and dried before being put away. Never brew less than three-fourths of the coffee maker's capacity; use a smaller one instead.

Cocoa

Cocoa, besides being a stimulant, is also a food. It is prepared from the seeds (beans) of a tree called theobromo cacao, grown in South and Central America.the West and East Indies and along the Gold Coast and adjacent areas in Africa. Commercial varities are criolo (fine quality) and trinitario (medium quality). The pods are gathered in heaps and cut open with sharp rounded knives. The cocoa beans which are covered with a moist, glistening sweet white pulp (mucilage) are scooped out. Oxidation begins almost at once causing the beans to become brown. Therefore, as soon as possible, they must be placed on fermenting heaps and are spread in the sun to remove the moisture so that spoilage does not set in.

However, fermentation is necessary to get the finest possible flavor. This is accompanied by a rise in temperature and the transformation of natural sugars to acetic and other acids. After several days, this operation is complete and the beans are allowed to dry. They are then ready to be packed and shipped.

Cocoa contains theobromine and caffeine as well as starch fat, nitrogenous compounds and salts. So, apart from being a stimulating drink, it is also a food. Cocoa can be prepared in milk only, or in milk and water, mixed to suit the taste of the individual. The powder is mixed with sugar to avoid lumping. A little cold milk is added and a thick even paste made. Either hot rnilk or hot milk and water are poured over. The preparation is then allowed to boil for a few minutes which improves the flavour. A pinch of salt added at the beginning enhances the flavour.

Advantages of Beverages

1. *Refreshment:* Non-alcoholic beverages such as plain or carbonated water, lime juice, ginger ale and other bottled beverages, fruit juices and iced tea or coffee are refreshing drinks and are used to relieve thirst.
2. *Nourishment:* Pasteurized milk, butter milk, chocolate and cocoa drinks, eggnog made with rum, fruit juices, glucose water, lemonade provide nutrients and help in nourishing the body.
3. *Stimulant:* Tea, coffee, cocoa and chocolate beverages help in stimulating the system.
4. *Soothing Agent*: Warm milk and hot tea have a soothing effect and are used for this purpose.
5. *Appetizers:* Soups, fruit juice and alcoholic drinks in limited quantities increase an individual's appetite and thereby food consumption.

Bartending

A bartender is the person behind a bar in a pub, tavern, inn, bar, or restaurant that serves beverages, both alcoholic and nonalcoholic alike. Their job is to mix and serve cocktails, beer, wine,shots, and other alcoholic beverages to the bar's clientele. In regions where tipping is the norm, bartenders receive a low base wage and earn most of their money through tips.

In the United States Bartenders are frequently considered the aristocracy of the working class, revered by the blue collar worker. There is a mythos about the trade; the abilities of a bartender are expected to go far beyond the obvious drink making and food serving. Bartenders (Barkeeps, drinkslingers or simply: "tenders") provide solace to the downtrodden drinking man, company for the lonely, entertainment for the bored and useful information to visitors.

For example a bartender might be called upon to recommend a restaurant for dinner, a theater for a show, the day's sports scores, the marital status of women lounging in the bar area, as well as a wide breadth of general trivia regarding stocks, cars, wine, sports, politics and history.

In some states within the USA, you may need to become certified before taking a bartending job. This is not true in all states, but it is best to learn the laws concerning your area. There are stiff penalties, fines and even jail time if you get caught serving alcohol to a minor. Also, there are thousands of drinks to learn. In some regions a drink may go by different names than in other regions. So, learning what your locals call a popular drink is the key. Also, keeping up with new drinks takes a person with a really superior memory.

Flair Bartending

Flair Bartending is the practice of entertaining guests, clientele, or audience with the throwing/juggling of bar tools (eg; shaker tins) and liquor bottles in tricky, dazzling ways. Used occasionally in cocktail bars, the action requires skill due to the dangers of glass breakage and possible burn (high alcohol spirit in contact with a lit candle or cigarette can ignite).

It has become a sought after talent among venue owners and marketers to help advertise a liquor product or the opening of a bar establishment. Competitions have been organised by liquor brands to attract flair bartenders, and some hospitality training companies hold courses to teach techniques of throwing and catching. Plastic bottles have been created for learning and practicing.

"Flair", or "freestyle bartending", as it may be called can be divided into two styles; working flair or competition flair. The difference between the two being the level of risk and complication of the tricks are higher for competitions. Good flair should be light hearted and entertaining while making actual, drinkable cocktails. It is a form of showmanship for confident cocktail bartenders that differs from the ideas behind mixology and drink-orientated, or service-minded bartending.

Tips for a Good Bartender

It doesn't matter how long someone has been a bartender, they can always use good bartending tips, because within the vast world of bartending, there are a lot of tips that can be offered. Anything that will help someone's performance is always a good thing. Flaming for instance, is one of the bartending tips that a lot of people would appreciate.

- Flaming liqueurs is awesome, but can also be extremely dangerous. Most liqueurs with high alcohol content are really easy to flame, and continue to burn even if the flame isn't visible. Bacardi 151 rum is a good example of flaming alcohol. Here are a few tips on flaming your liqueurs.
- Simply warm your liqueur up in a sauce pan and have a pre warmed cocktail glass ready. After heating the glass, pour the rest or other alcohols into the glass to warm. The glass can be heated over an element or a flame, but use caution to avoid contact with the glass and element or flame as the glass will break or char easy.
- When the alcohol has been heated, ignite it and add it to the alcohol in the glass. If done correctly, the alcohol in the glass will be warm enough to flame also.
- When flaming liqueurs, be sure to keep any objects away from the glass. Flames can often shoot high up and ignite things in their way. If igniting liqueurs, use extreme caution and enjoy the fireworks.
- Something else associated with bartending tips that is always appreciated, is layering. Layering or floating liqueurs is one of the most difficult techniques in bartending.
- Although this bartending tip seems like a challenge, there is a very simple method that you can use. Each liqueur weighs differently and either floats or sinks when added to another.
- A lot of recipes are written with the heaviest liqueurs printed first. If all else fails, experiment and get used to the liqueurs that you most often use.
- To pour the liqueurs into the glass, simply use the rounded or back part of a spoon and rest it against the inside of the glass. Slowly pour down the spoon and into the glass.

- The liqueur should run down the inside of the glass and smoothly layer. This bartending tip takes practice, but can mastered by anyone.
- Make sure that the liqueurs are poured in order of their weight, starting with the heaviest first. The next thing that people tend to appreciate bartending tips with is shaking or blending drinks.
- This method is common with drinks containing fruit juices, cream, or eggs. In today's time, a blender is most often used to blend drinks, but the old fashioned shake method is usually the best.
- Fill the shaker to 2/3 with ice and add the ingredients. After adding the ingredients, cover the shaker and proceed to shake. This is usually done by shaking over your shoulder.
- Remove the cover and strain into the proper glass, allowing the drink to form a foamy head. Finish by garnishing and adding a straw.
- To assist you in understanding bartending words; A Taste of Texas offer you their Glossary of Bar Terms

And here are some more bartending tips for yourself and your bar.

- Even Professionals measures the ingredients. So don't guess to make a perfect drink every time; these are some Basic Bar Measures:
    - One Normal Shot Glass= 1oz.
    - Jigger = 1.5 oz-2 oz
    - Pony = 1 oz
    - Dash = 1/6 oz
    - Teaspoon = 1/8 oz
- Always put ice in the glass or shaker before pouring ingredients. That way, the liquids are chilled as they are poured over ice.
- Serve cocktails icy cold! Pre-chill glasses in the refrigerator or let them sit in shaved ice before using. It makes drinks tastier!
- When the recipe calls for a twist of lemon peel, rub a narrow strip of peel around the rim of the glass. Then twist the peel so that one small drop will go into the drink. Then drop the peel.
- If you want more juice from lemons and oranges if you soak them in warm water.
- When you shake a drink that requires an egg, use an ice cube. It breaks up the egg and helps it blend into the drink.

— When the drink consists of clear liquids, STIR! If the drink has a carbonated drink (soda, ginger ale), stir gently to preserve the bubbly! SHAKE drinks that contain fruit juices, sugar, eggs, cream or other ingredients difficult to mix. Really SHAKE - don't just rock!

— A clean piece of wax paper rubbed on the rim of a bottle will prevent dripping when you pour!

— For a "sugar-frosted" glass, moisten the rim of a pre-chilled glass with lemon or lime and then dip into powdered sugar (before alcohol is poured).

The following are some of the basic bartending tips:-

Building: Pour one on top of the other, allowing them to mix. Most highball drinks are made this way. For example, for a Rum and Coke, you would put ice in the glass, add the rum, then add the coke. The carbonation in the soda allows it to mix naturally. You always add the liquor first, followed by the mixer.

Another example is a Tequila Sunrise. Fill the glass with ice, add the tequila, fill almost to the top with orange juice, then top with grenadine. This gives the drink it's "sunrise" appearance. There's no special pouring technique as there is with layering, but the order is often important.

Blending: Add the ingredients with ice into a blender and blend until smooth. This takes practice to get right. Too much ice and the drink seems weak, too little and it seems runny. Usually, the liquids should fill about 1/2 to 2/3 of the way up the ice.

Shaking: This requires a cocktail shaker, also referred to as a "Boston" shaker. You can use the type that come with a lid for a more elegant appearance, or you can use the metal mixing cup/pint glass combo for more speed and flexibility. Fill the shaker with ice, then add the ingredients. Shake (away from your guests to avoid a tip eliminating accident) and then pour into a glass. Typically drinks that are shaken are also strained.

Stirring: Fill a large glass (typically a pint glass) with ice, add the ingredients, stir with a bar spoon, and pour or strain into the final glass.

Straining: After shaking or stirring, straining simply means to pour the liquid, leaving the ice. This prevents the drink from becoming diluted over time. Classic examples of this include the Martini and the Cosmopolitan.

Layering: This takes practice to do properly. By gently placing one liqueur on top of another you can create a layered effect where the liqueurs don't mix. To do this, you can tilt the glass and slowly pour one liquor on top of another, or you can pour over the back of a spoon as well. Either way, the liquor on top has to be less dense than the liquor on the bottom or they won't stay separate. If you pour sloppily you can just set it refrigerator. The layers will separate themselves.

Making Simple Sugar Syrup: Simple syrup, also known as sugar syrup, can be made into a variety of thicknesses for a variety of different uses.

— Cooled thin syrup (3 parts water to 1 part sugar) is useful for brushing onto cakes to add a bit of extra sweetness and moisture.

— Medium-thick syrup (2 parts water to 1 part sugar) is great for adding sweetness to teas and coffees.

— Thick simple syrup (1 part water to 1 part sugar) is excellent for candying fruits and veggies.

Pouring and Serving Draught Beer

When pouring beer from a tap, open the faucet all the way with a quick, smooth motion by grasping the tap handle at its base. Pulling the tap handle at the top opens the faucet too slowly, and beer will draw foamy. At the beginning of the pour, tilt the glass slightly and don't let the glass touch the beer faucet. Then straighten the glass as you pour, and top it with a collar of ½ inch to 1 inch of foam.

To make sure your glasses are "beer clean," a three-sink cleaning system is ideal. The first sink is for washing the glasses, the second for rinsing, and the third for sanitising the glasses. If you have a two-sink system, use the first for cleaning the glasses and the second for sanitising.

— Make sure you always use cleaners and sanitisers specifically designed for cleaning beer glasses.

— When drying the glasses be sure to allow airflow inside the glasses. Usually best to use a drying rack.

— Before pouring beer be sure to rinse the glass with cold water whenever possible.

— Ways to check if your glasses are beer clean.

— Wet the inside of the glass and turn upside down. If the water drops stick to the side it is not "beer clean."

— Bubbles will not form on the sides of a glass that is not "beer clean."

— Lacing from the head will only form on the sides of a "beer clean" glass as well

These are a few more quick bartending tips to help you along the way:-

— A 1/2 oz. of liquor equals 1 count.

— If you are using a pourer on your bottles, to measure 1-1/2 oz. of liquor, count

— "1-1,000...2-1,000...3-1,000"

— As you pour. You will eventually be able to do it by eye with practice.

— Cocktails & other shaken/stirred drinks

— Fill shaker half-full of ice.

— Most shaken drinks that contain light cream can also be made as blended drinks, substituting vanilla ice cream for the light cream.

— To make blended drinks:-

  — It is always best to add your liquor(s) and juice(s) prior to adding the ice.

  — That assists with less ice melt that will only water down the drink and make a soupy, flimsy slush.

Also a good rule of thumb, each scoop of ice that goes into the liquor-filled-blender-pitcher equals roughly the number of drinks you wish to make.

— For Lowballs (drinks made in an old fashion or rock glass)

— Fill the glass about half-full of ice before pouring the drink.

— For Highballs

— Fill the glass with 2/3 of ice before adding liquor. Always pour liquor in before the mixer.

— Never stir drinks containing carbonated mixers until after the mixer has been added.

— Always keep fruit juices and other mixers refrigerated.

— Always use fresh fruit in fruit drinks, e.g. strawberry margaritas, banana daiquiris.

— Always be a responsible drinker/bartender.

— Above all never drink and drive

And here is a good bartending tip for being efficient:-

Bartending Tools

Some tools aid in bartending, while some are required. There are hundreds of different ones out there, while each one serves its own unique purpose. If you didn't have a bottle opener, you probably wouldn't be able to open most of the bottles within a bar.

This tool is required for any type of bar to operate.If you were to go into a bar during operation, you would see a lot of utensils being used by the bartender. The bartender knows how to use each one, and exactly how each it will benefit him.

— There are some implements, that don't really require usage, but will help the user out a lot. These types save a lot of time, and a lot of effort when properly used.

— The blender is an extremely essential bartending tool. While some bars operate without a blender, most have one. A blender saves a lot of time and work when drinks called for crushed or blended ice.

— All the bartender has to do is pop some ice into the blender, and within seconds he has what he needs to make the drink. The old traditional way will work, but it takes time.

— Glasses are required bartending items. Without a glass, you would have nothing to hold your drink. Glasses come in all different shapes and sizes, depending upon what you're drinking.

Frosted glasses are excellent when drinking beer; they give the beer that fresh out of the fridge look and feel. A lot of bartending tools, come in different sizes and colours.

— The different look of these tools provides a certain look of fashion when using it around the bar. While the different colours don't really matter when using the tool, they make the look of it better when compared to a plain old white item.

— You could order bartending devices in sets, or separately. If ordering them in sets, you usually get many different tools within that specific set. This could save you a lot of money, when you compare the set with buying each piece by itself.

— Some tools can be quite expensive, but when sold in a set, the cost of expensive implements almost always seems to weigh itself out. There are a lot of places that deal with bartending tools.

— If you know a certain tool that you need, it's a good idea to see if it is sold in a set. Bartending tools are good to have, and make the environment of the bar work and look that much better.

The most important assets for any profession are the right tools. You need basic bar tools to mix, serve, and store your drinks. Whether you're stocking a home bar or working as a professional, your basic tools are a wine opener, cocktail shaker, measuring glass, and strainer.

Wine Opener

The best wine opener is a waiter's wine opener (Figure 1). It has a sharp blade, a corkscrew (also known as a worm), and a bottle opener. This wine opener can be found in most liquor stores or bar supply houses.

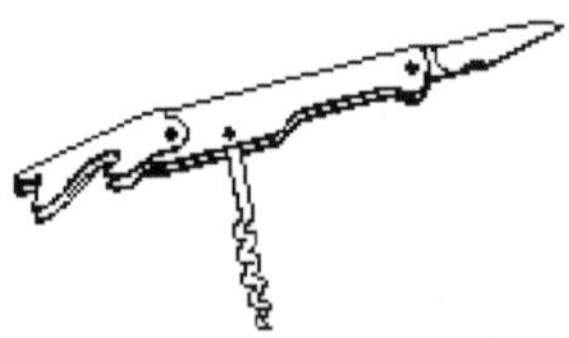

Figure 1. A waiter's wine opener

Cocktail Shaker

Two types of shakers are shown in Figure 2. The Boston shaker is the one that most professional bartenders use. It consists of a mixing glass and a stainless steel core that overlaps the glass. The Standard shaker usually consists of two or more stainless steel or glass parts and can be found in department stores or antiques stores. Many of these shakers come in different shapes and designs.

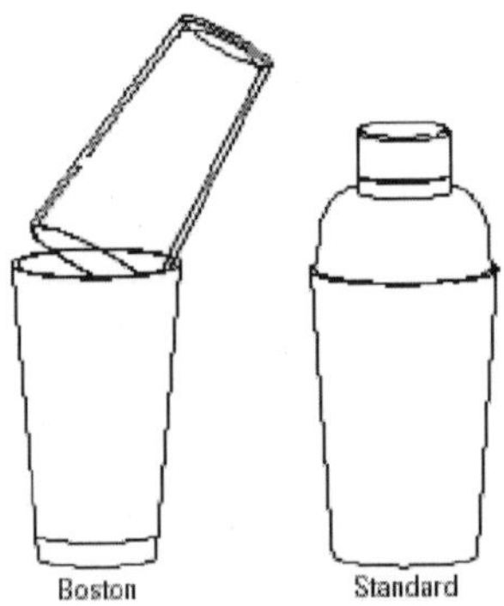

Figure 2. A Boston shaker and a Standard shaker

Strainer

A couple of different types of strainers are available, but the most popular is the Hawthorn, shown in Figure 3. The Hawthorn is a flat, spoon-shaped utensil with a spring coil around its head. You can use it on top of a steel shaker or a bar glass to strain cocktails.

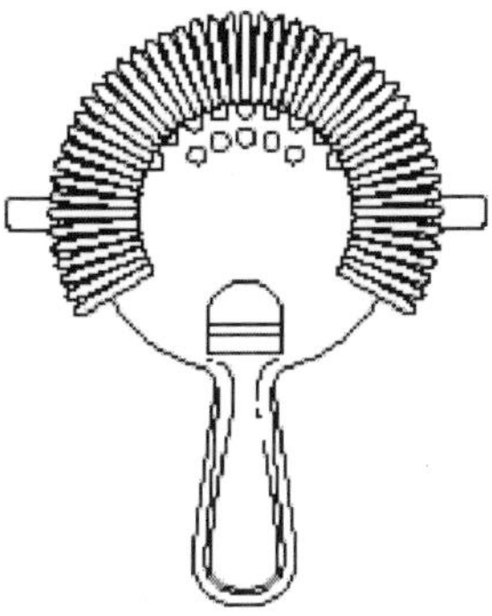

Figure 3. The Hawthorn strainer

Other Tools

Many of the following tools are shown in Figure 4

— *Bar spoon*: A long spoon for stirring cocktails.

— *Blender*: Many types of commercial or home blenders with various speeds are available. Always put liquid in first before switching it on when making a drink. This will save your blade. Some blenders (but not all) can be used to make crushed ice. Check with the manufacturer or buy an ice crusher.

— *Coasters or bar napkins*: Coasters prevent rings from developing on your bar and other tables. Napkins also help your guests hold their drinks.

— *Ice bucket*: Pick one that's large enough to hold at least three trays of ice.

— *Ice scoop or tongs*: A must for every bar. Never use your hands to scoop ice.

— *Jigger or measuring glass*: A small glass or metal measuring container that usually has a 1.2 oz. measurer on one side and a 2 oz. measurer on the other.

Figure 4: A collection of bar tools: (1) bar spoon, (2) blender, (3) tongs, (4) ice scoop, (5) ice bucket, (6) jigger or measuring glass, (7) knife and cutting board, (8) muddler, and (9) pourer.

— *Knife and cutting board*: You need a small, sharp paring knife to cut fruit.

— *Large water pitcher*: Someone always wants water.

— *Muddler*: A small wooden bat or pestle used to crush fruit or herbs.

— *Pourer*: This device gives greater control to your pouring. A variety of different types is available, including some with a lidded spout, which prevents insects and undesirables from entering the pourer.

— *Stirrers and straws*: Used for stirring and sipping drinks.

— *Large cups or bowls*: Used to hold garnishes, such as cherries, olives, onions, and so on.

People generally expect certain drinks to be served in certain kinds of glasses. The problem is that there are more standard bar glasses than most people (and many bars) care to purchase.

Tips for Bar Management

During the past 20 years, bars have experienced a roller coaster of statistics. Although people still gather to socialise in bars, just as they have for hundreds of years, other factors have come into play for the industry as well.

Problems with driving while intoxicated have changed the drinking patterns of people in all over the world. The growing concern with health and fitness toward the end of the 20th century took its toll on the bar industry. Keeping tabs on this industry requires a look at statistics of the alcoholic beverage industry as a whole—what people buy in the store doesn't differ much from what they buy in a bar. According to the Distilled Spirits Council of the United States, sales of distilled spirits declined considerably from 1980 to 1985 but turned around to a growth period in the late 1990s. Sales of white spirits (vodka, rum, gin and tequila) increased 0.6 percent from 1993 to 1997. They rose again from 1997 to 1998 1.6 percent. Sales of brown spirits, on the other hand, did the opposite, although the decline slowed in the late 1990s. From 1993 to 1997, sales of brown spirits dropped 3 percent and declined 1.5 percent from 1997 to 1998.

You can see how certain social issues have taken their toll on the sales of alcoholic beverages. Now let's take a look at the "state of the union," so to speak, for the United States bar industry as a whole. In the mid-1990s, the total number of operating liquor licenses in restaurants and bars exceeded 225,000 and beer and wine licenses reached more than half a million. Generally, the number of liquor licenses distributed is based on the population of the county.

In 1996, food and beverage workers held 4.6 million jobs, with 390,000 of those being bartenders. So what does all this mean to you? Well, it means you have some tough competition out there. But you're not just competing with the other bars in your area these days. You're competing with every entertainment option from which your customers can choose.

Successful new bars can be in the black within the first six months, and they can go on to recover their initial investment within three to five years. However, like many new businesses, the statistics aren't in favour of the startup. About 80 percent of new businesses fail within the first five years, and the bar business faces the same kind of statistics. Why do they fail? The first reason is they didn't have enough capital to keep the business going. The second reason is a lack of knowledge about the business.

From a personal perspective, you need to ask yourself if you're really the type of person who wants to own and run a bar. Of course, you don't have to run it if you own it, but you'd better make sure you have a team of good, trustworthy managers working for you if you plan to be "hands off." In the beginning, you will probably have to be greatly involved no matter whether or not you plan to be an active owner. If you're the kind of person who would rather deal with paperwork or sit in an office where you don't have to talk to people, this business is not for you. You will need to be out there talking to people and shaking hands. Getting to know your patrons, even if it's just to say "Hi" can go a long way for your customer service.

Another thing you should consider is the time commitment and time of day. If you're an early riser, you might not enjoy having to work until 3 or 4 a.m. at your bar. If you have a family, you need to discuss how owning a bar will affect them and your personal situation. Many times you will have to be at your bar from the time you wake up—say, around 10 or 11 a.m.—to the time you go to sleep—say, around 4 or 5 a.m.

As you can see, this could take its toll on your family life. Eventually, you'll probably be able to have a saner schedule, once your managers and staff are well-trained, but it may take six months to a year to reach that point. If this could cause problems for you or your family, you may want to reconsider the idea of owning a bar. From a business standpoint, however, a bar can provide an excellent return on investment.

Before you get started on the actual nuts and bolts of creating your dream bar, you have to decide what kind of establishment you'd like to own. Let's take a trip through the various kinds of bars—from neighbourhood bar to large-scale nightclub—and see which one is right for you.

Neighbourhood bar: Conceptually, the neighbourhood bar is still an American version of the English pub. You'll find them everywhere in the United States. If you own this kind of place, you can expect to know a great deal of your regular customers. As on the TV show "Cheers," you may find yourself taking phone messages for customers or cashing their paychecks. It's because of the friendly "home away from home" atmosphere that neighbourhood bars are successful. Some of these pubs open as early as 6 a.m., and they sometimes close earlier than other bars—depending on the clientele. This type of bar is perfect for small-scale entertainment options, such as darts, pool tables, video games and jukeboxes.

Across the country, this is probably the most popular type of bar you'll find. But there are a lot of neighbourhoods out there, so you might find that there is room for one more in your area. According to the experts the start-up cost for this kind of bar can range anywhere from $20,000 to $200,000, depending on the size and concept. The amount of revenue these businesses produce varies greatly depending on geographical location—big city or small town—and the size of the bar.

Sports bar. Depending on the establishment's capacity, sports bars can be a specific version of the neighbourhood tavern, or they can take on a life as big as a nightclub. You may have the latter in mind, but your market research may point to the former. It's important to do your homework!

Generally, sports bars offer some kind of menu options, such as sandwiches, burgers, pizza and appetizers. Since the main attraction is sporting events, sports bars have televisions in view of every seat, sometimes all tuned to different channels. Audio and video technology comes into play, with some owners spending a large percentage of their revenue on keeping up with the latest in technology—from satellites to big-screen TVs. The startup costs and revenue potential reflect basically the same numbers as a neighbourhood bar.

Brewpub or beer bar. Studies have shown that although consumers are drinking less alcohol, their tastes are becoming more discriminating. As a result, microbrews are becoming more and more popular. In a brewpub, you can brew your own beer right on the premises. In a beer bar, you can offer a large selection of different types of beer, including microbrews produced elsewhere. It's often easier to get a liquor license for a brewpub or beer bar than a full-scale liquor license since you don't need a fully stocked liquor bar.

Most brewpubs only sell their own beer options on tap (draft beer), with a few selections of bottled beer options, too. Since you're creating your own product in a brewpub, you also have the ability to control what you make and sell—from quality to quantity. The startup costs of a brewpub can be quite high—from $100,000 to $1 million—because of the brewing equipment you need to have. If you produce a popular beer, you have the opportunity to grow into a very successful operation to make two or three times your startup costs.

Beer bars tend to have lower startup costs, which can often mean obtaining a less expensive, fixed-price license from your state government. Beer bar startup costs range from about $20,000 to $100,000, depending on size and location. The revenue potential depends on the geographical location and drinking trends in the community.

Wine and champagne bar: This kind of bar often gives guests the opportunity to taste a variety of different kinds of wines and the ability to learn more about their qualities. Wine and champagne bars tend to stay small and intimate in size and are located in more sophisticated neighbourhoods.

Again, because you only need a beer and wine license to open this type of bar, your licensing fees drop considerably. Depending on the type of product you serve and the extent of your decor, you can expect to find the cost and revenues close to the amounts for a beer bar.

Nightclub: Like the neighbourhood bar, nightclubs can take on a number of different personalities. You can open a small "cocktail lounge" with a jukebox or a tinkling piano in the corner. A medium-sized nightclub might look like a neighbourhood bar during the lunchtime hours, then spring to life with a popular band at night. Or if you have a big enough budget, your nightclub might be a large dance club where the most fashionable people and hippest celebrities hang out every weekend. Whichever path you take, you must be prepared to spend a great deal of time and money on promotion to create your "buzz." Nightclubs can make plenty of money if they're managed properly.

As a bar owner, you need to embark on the same kind of relentless detective work to profile your customers before you start investing large sums of money in your business. The majority of the research material you need is probably already available to you. You simply have to compile it. You can go about developing your customer profile in several different ways, then compare the results to determine your direction.

— *General demographics*: Your bar's concept may go in a totally different direction if you're in a college town with a high percentage of young, single students than if you're in a quiet, conservative suburb populated with families.

— *Alcohol trends*: National and regional alcohol suppliers keep records of how their product fits into the market. Your potential suppliers can provide valuable information about your customers and what they like to drink. Generally, they are glad to help. If you do your research and have a successful bar, your suppliers will profit, too.

— *Other important statistics*: Visit your local public library or university library. Many libraries have business departments that have a wealth of information about demographics, income levels and spending trends.

— *Lifestyle trends*: Call the lifestyle and entertainment editors at your local newspaper and regional magazines, as well as the advertising and marketing departments of local radio stations. They can give you information about your competitors and tell you more about the establishments that have been successful in the area.

— *Your customers and the competition:* You can discover a ton of information about your customers using internet resources. Besides general demographics, you can surf the web for information about other bars in the area. Pop into chat areas and newsgroups to find out where the action is and which bars are the hot spots.

Once you've compiled all your research, you can devise a concrete profile of your clientele. For example, you may decide your target customers are professionals between the ages of 30 and 50 who have incomes of more than $35,000 and like jazz music. Whatever you set as your target market will affect all the decisions you make from here on, so make sure you get it right!

Once you have your profile, you can develop your menu and bar inventory based on what customers like. Look for trade magazines and industry associations that provide data on food and beverage spending patterns. Keep in mind that you may have more than one profile to work with. You may have a conservative professional clientele during the daytime and a rowdy college crowd at night. If you use your research wisely, you can develop a bar that caters to both profiles for even more business.

The bar/tavern industry can be a pricey undertaking. Because of the high failure rate, you may come across desperate bar owners willing to take a low purchase price just to get out of the business. You'll also find that startup costs for bars vary depending on size, location and target market.

Your bar's size, location, type and concept will make your startup cost as individual as your business. Again, you could buy an existing bar that would nullify all the numbers on our low-end chart, or start a large-scale nightclub that's off the map from our high-end numbers. You'll have to do some research to find out what your bar will cost based on your concept, size and location.

The groundwork you lay to operate your bar includes the systems you use to track liquor and food. How much does the customer owe the server/ bartender, and in turn, how much do they owe you? Also, what liquor and food do you sell the most? The systems you choose depend on the type and size of bar you have.

In most bars, only the bartenders and servers handle money. Cashiers or takeout staff may also have cash-handling responsibilities. Factors to consider when choosing an accounting system include the level of sales you expect, both from alcohol and food, and the efficiency needed for your staff to operate at its full potential. Also, look for holes that your accounting system might leave open for theft at all levels, not just servers and bartenders. No one thinks they are hiring a thief. Many people who might steal if the opportunity arose do not consider themselves thieves, either, so they don't come off as such.

If you use the cash-and-carry system, where the drink is ordered by the server verbally and then paid for before the bartender or server rings it up, you might find many "forgot to ring it up" drinks, as well as a few given away for free. It is the nature of the system. If your inventory controls are so tight that you will notice when too much has been used, or if your manager, who shares in the profits anyway, is your bartender, then you can use this system without much fear.

Select Perfect Location

Your choice of location will depend on how you want your bar to look, what you want your bar to contribute to the community, and the kind of clientele you want to patronise it. Then you need to decide whether you want to buy the location or sign a lease. Again, that depends on your budget. Finally, you need to figure out how to fuse your concept with both your name and your location to your best advantage.

People who know this industry well have polar opinions on the concept of location. Some owners and experts put enormous importance on the bar's location while others refuted its significance altogether. It all depends on what you want your bar to be and what your strengths are as an owner. If you want your bar to get impulsive neighbourhood traffic in a particular area, then you should be closest, and most obvious, to them.

If you'd rather spend the time and money, saved by more affordable real estate, to develop your establishment's concept and create your own buzz and destination, your actual location won't matter so much. You should consider factors such as safety, parking, accessibility to customers—even the history of the site—when choosing a location.

The word "location" can refer to two different things—what area your bar is in (downtown, uptown, suburbs, etc.) and where you are in relation to your customers. Are you on their way home from work? Or do they have to make it a point to get to you? Michael O'Harro, a National Bar & Restaurant Management Association board member, explains how he took a bar location nobody wanted in Virginia and made it work. "It was in an alley," he says. "It was a 15-foot-wide alley, and we were 128 feet away from the street. No one would go up the alley—[people] were afraid of it. So the building sat empty for 50 years. But the bar at the end of the alley was spending $20,000 a month in rent, while my rent was $500.

Naming

When it comes to naming a bar, experts generally fall into two major schools of thought. The first says your bar is your dream—your hard work—so you should name it anything you want. The second approach to naming says your moniker is the first and greatest form of advertising for your drinking establishment.

Now that you have your entertainment in place and ready to go, it's time to start planning how you're going to get people into your bar to enjoy it. Just like any other aspect of operating your bar, marketing is an ongoing process. Many bar owners think marketing is the most fun and exciting aspect of running a bar.

There are still ways to get some advertising and marketing out there without spending a ton of money. But anytime you reach into your own pocket to buy advertising for a bar, it's not good. Your employees love working there. They are talking and saying great things about the place, and that is passed on to your customers. The customers love being there, and they tell other customers. If you can get to that point, it's just priceless." You can create special promotions for your bar, launch a direct-mail campaign with a newsletter for regular customers, develop a web site, and any other creative marketing techniques you can dream up.

Promotional Events

After you bar is up and running, you'll have a better idea of what nights need a little boost. Most bars are busy on Friday and Saturday nights, with Thursdays coming in third place. You might decide you need to pump up business on Monday or Tuesday, so pick one day and keep it going until you have established enough regular business to move the promotions to a different day. Here are some ideas to keep in mind when you're working on promotional events.

— *Prepare*: Work out a budget. If your promotion continues for more than one day, budget for the entire time you want it to run. A good goal to shoot for is to make a profit that's three times the cost of the promotion.

— *Make a schedule*: Design a planning calendar at least eight weeks before the promotion. Depending on the size and magnitude of the promotion, you may want to start advertising it at this point, too. Never advertise an ending date, though, so you can cut it early if it doesn't do as well as you planned, or you can extend it if it really takes off.

— *Maintain the energy level*: On the day of the promotion, don't stop the action to give away prizes or make announcements. You can turn the music down, but don't turn it off. This will keep the energy level high and consistent. If you absolutely have to turn off the music, never keep it off for more than 10 minutes, or you risk people getting impatient and leaving.

— *Party all night*: Schedule your prize giveaways, contests and entertainment to run throughout the night. If you have a grand prize to give away or a finale planned, don't do it until after midnight so your guests stay in your bar as late as possible.

Promoting your bar can be fun and creative. During a promotion and after it's over, ask your customers and your employees for feedback and critiques. Of course, your sales will give you a lot of the information you're looking for, too.

References

Borgstrom G., *Principles of Food Science*, 2 vol., 1968.

Cichy, Ronald F. *Managing Service in Food and Beverage Operations.* Lansing: Educational Institute of the American Hotel and Motel Association, 1998.

Desrosier N. W., *The Technology of Food Preservation*, 3d ed. 1970.

Ninemeier, Jack D. *Planning and Control for Food and Beverage Operations.* Orlando: Educational Institute, 1998.

Sims-Bell, Barbara. *Career Opportunities in the Food and Beverage Industry.* New York: Facts on File, 1994.

Waller, Keith. *Improving Food and Beverage Performance.* Oxford: Butterworth-Heinemann, 1996.

7

Food and Beverage Cost Control

Control is a process by means which managers attempt to direct, regulate and restrain the actions of people in order to achieve desired goals. An obvious first step is to established goals for the enterprise. Probably the most common goal for all private enterprise is financial success, although this is by no means the only- range goal of business. Others might relate to preserving the environment, promoting better health among the population or etc. To achieve the goals, management must setup any number of sub goals compatible with its long-range plans. These tend to be more specific and usually more immediate in nature. For example, to achieve the goal of preserving the environment, it would be necessary to make rather immediate plans to process or dispose of waste materials in appropriate ways.

The total responsibility for the operation of any food and beverage enterprise rest ultimately with management. A number of factors, including nature and scope of operations, will determine the extent to which the management exercise directs control as opposed to delegating responsibility to a subordinate. In general, the large the operation, the more likely it is that one or more subordinates will supervise and direct control procedures. The authors will assume the existence of both a food controller and a beverage controller each of who will be responsible for the supervision of all procedures in that single area. By the same token, we will assume that the manager will personally retain direct control over labor cost.

The food and beverage business can be characterized as one that involves raw materials purchased, received, stored and issued for the purpose of manufacturing products for sale. In these aspects many similarities exist between the hospitality industry to achieve the goal of profitable operation. This will entail a discussion of how costs and sales are controlled in food and beverage operations. The means employed by foodservice managers to directly, regulate and restrain the actions of people, both directly and indirectly, in order to keep costs within acceptable bounds, to account for revenues properly, and make profits.

Definition of Cost Control

The process whereby manager attempt to regulate costs and guard against excessive costs in known as cost control. It is on going process and involves every step in the chain of purchasing, receiving, storing, issuing and preparing food and beverages for sale, as well as scheduling the personnel involved. Exact methods for cost control will vary from place to place, depending in part on the nature and scope of operation; but the principle behind varying methods will be constant. The obvious governing power over costs in all areas in order to keep costs within acceptable bounds, to account for revenues properly, and make profits.

Two of the principal causes of excessive costs are inefficiency and waste. For example storing food in refrigerators that are not cold enough, or liquor in bottles that are not tightly closed, will lead to spoilage and hence to excessive cost. So will the preparation of an inedible beef stew or an undrinkable martini. When the stew is thrown into the garbage can or the martini poured down the drain, costs of operation are increased but sale are not. Since profit is essentially the difference between sales and costs, it is apparent that any increase in costs that does not lead to corresponding increases in sales can only have the effect of reducing profits. Clearly, management must take steps to guard against the occurrence of these excessive costs.

While cost control is critically important to the profitable operation of any business, it alone will not ensure profitability. Additional steps must be taken to ensure that all sales in appropriate income to the business.

Industry Wide Variations in Cost

Cost percents vary considerably from one foodservice operation to another. Some factors contributing to these variations would be type of service, location, and type of menu.

1. Fast food – those that operate at a low margin of profit per item served and depend on relatively high business volume.
2. Fine dining – those operations that operate at a relatively high margin of profit and therefore do not require such high business volume.

Types of Cost

There are various types of cost which are:

1. The actual cost is what a cost or expenses actually was. For example, the payroll records and check made out to employees will indicate the actual labor cost for that payroll period.
2. A budgeted cost is what a cost expected to be for a period time. For example, for an anticipated level of sales for a month, we might budget or forecast what the labor cost should be for that period. Later, that budgeted cost would be compared with the actual labor cost in order to determine the causes of any differences.

Are costs that can be changed in the short term. Direct costs are generally more easily controllable than indirect costs. Variable costs are normally controllable. Certain fixed costs are controllable, including advertising, promotions, utilities, repairs, etc.

Non-Controllable Cost

Are those costs that cannot be changed in the short term. These are usually fixed costs. These typically include items such rent, depreciation, and taxes.

Fixed Cost

Are those that are normally unaffected by changes in sales volume. The term fixed should never be taken to mean unchanging, merely to indicate that any changes that may occur in such costs are related only indirectly to changes in sales volume. Examples: Rent, Utilities, Insurance Premiums

Variable Cost

A variable cost is one that varies on a linear basis with revenue. Are those that are clearly related to business volume. Directly variable costs are those that are directly linked to volume of business, such that every increase or decrease in volume brings a corresponding increase or decrease in cost. The obvious variable costs are food and beverage. The more foods and beverage sold, the more that have to be purchased. If revenue is zero, then the cost should also be zero. As business volume increases, so do these costs. As business volume decreases, so do these costs.

Direct Cost

Direct cost is a cost that is the responsibility of a particular department or department manager. Most direct costs will go up or down, to a greater or lesser degree, as revenue goes up and down. Because of this, they are considered to be controllable by, and thus the responsibility of, the department to which they are charged. Examples of this type of cost would be food, beverages, wages, operating supplies and services beverages and linen and laundry.

Indirect Cost

An indirect cost is commonly referred to as an undistributed cost or one that cannot easily be identified with a particular department or area, and thus cannot be charge to any specific department. For example, property operation, maintenance and energy cost could only be charged to various departments (such as linen or food and beverage) with difficulty. Even if this difficulty could be overcome, it must still be recognized that indirect costs cannot normally be made the responsibility of an operating department manager. Indirect costs are also sometimes referred to as overhead cost.

Joint Cost

Is a cost shared by and the responsibility of two or more department or area. The cost of dining room waiter who serves both food and beverage is an example. His labor is a joint cost and should be charged to the food department and to the beverage department. Most indirect costs are also joint costs.

Sunk Cost

A cost that has been incurred and cannot be reversed. Also referred to as "stranded cost." A worn-out piece of equipment bought several years ago is a sunk cost because the cost of buying it cannot be reversed.

Opportunity Cost

The cost of not doing something or the profit lost. An organization can invest its surplus cash in marketable securities at 10 percent, or leave the money in the bank at 6 percent. If it buys marketable securities, its opportunity cost is 6 percent. Another way to look at it is to say that it is making 10 percent on the investment, less the opportunity cost of 6 percent, therefore the net gain is 4 percent.

Standard Cost

A standard cost is what the cost should be for a given volume or level of revenue. For example, a standard cost can be develop by costing the recipe for a given menu item. If ten of these menu items are sold, the total standard cost should be ten item the individual recipe cost. Another illustration would be personnel cost (wages) for cleaning at dining area. If the area attendant is paid RM4.00 an hour, and it takes one half hour to clean the area, the standard labor cost for cleaning the area would be RM2.00. While, if the service person take 7hours for clean the area, total standard cost would be RM28.

Prime Costs

Is a term used in the food and beverage industry to refer to the cost of materials and labor.

Prime Cost = Food Cost + Beverage Cost + Labor Cost

Historical Costs and Planned Costs

Historical costs are figures that have already happened and can be found in the business records.Planned costs is made by using historical costs in the present to determine what is likely to happen in a future period to come. These numbers are also used in budgeting.

Standard Food Cost

The usefulness of control information can be increased by establishing standards for each revenue center within the food and beverage operation. For example, instead of computing a standard food cost covering all outlets, a property might establish separate standard cost levels for its coffee shop, dining room, service, and banquet operations. An advantage of this alternative is that each outlet can be evaluated separately based on its own set of anticipated costs. However, food and beverage managers realise that as a standard becomes more specific, more time is required to develop and monitor it. The longer the time needed to collect information on which to base the standard, or later to measure actual results, the less practical managers may judge the task; and as a result, the less likely they may be to undertake the control activity. In addition, the more complex the development of standard costs becomes, the more likely the task will be met with resistance by those who must collect the information.

Therefore, an ideal control system must strike a balance between the time and effort spent developing the control system and the usefulness of the results the system provides. The principles for establishing standards are the same regardless of whether the property is commercial or institutional, large or small, fast food or gourmet, hotel or restaurant.

Systems for developing food and beverage standards must begin with the menu. The menu should be designed to implement the property's marketing plan as it relates to the food and beverage operation. Because it establishes which food and beverage items will be served, the menu is the most basic and important control tool. Once a menu is created, five standard cost tools can be developed:

Standard Purchase Specifications

A purchase specification is a concise description of the quality, size, weight, count, and other factors needed to describe a desired item. The specified factors should be described in sufficient detail to properly guide the company's suppliers and receiving personnel in the delivery and receipt of the desired products. Management should establish standard purchase specifications based on menu requirements and the operation's merchandising and pricing policies. Once developed, standard purchase specifications should be given to those responsible for purchasing, the property's suppliers, and receiving personnel. In this way, all of the parties involved in ordering, supplying, and receiving will have the necessary written guides to permit the operation to consistently obtain the quality and kind of food and beverage items desired.

In addition to providing a knowledge of what is required by the operation, standard purchase specifications offer several other advantages:

— Fewer products may be required. Analysing the menu may suggest ways to duplicate product use (use an ingredient for several menu items) so that fewer ingredients have to be purchased.

— Reduced purchase costs are possible if proper quality items are purchased. Developing purchase specifications based on the needs of the menu means that the property will not have to pay a higher price for a product of greater quality than necessary.

— If purchase specifications are properly established, more than one supplier will likely be able to quote prices and compete for the operation's business.

The development of specifications involves time and effort. Time is needed to create the specifications and then to monitor the need for changes as the operation's business evolves. Furthermore, their use will create increased duties for the receiving staff. Finally, since specifications establish the minimum quality expected, over time they may become the maximum quality that will be purchased.

However, considering the many advantages to the use of purchase specifications relative to the few disadvantages, it should be clear they are a critical standard cost control tool. It is only through carefully developed and rigidly enforced specifications that the operation can help assure that the" right" quality product is consistently available for production and service. Remember, however; use of standard purchase specifications will not, alone, guarantee that products of the correct quality will be received unless effective receiving control procedures are in use.

Standard Recipes

A standard recipe is a formula for producing a food or beverage item. It provides a summary of ingredients, thc required quantity of each, specific preparation procedures, portion size and portioning equipment, garnish, and any other information necessary to prepare the item. The advantages of standard recipes are equally relevant in both food and beverage preparation. The primary advantage of following a standard recipe is that, regardless of prepares the item, when it is prepared, or to whom it is served, the product will always look, cost, and taste the same. The consistency in operations provided by the standard recipe is at the heart of all control, and many marketing, systems.

There are several other reasons to use standard recipes in addition to the advantages of consistency in appearance, cost, and taste:

— When managers know that the standard recipe will yield a specific number of standard-size portions, it is less likely that too many or too few items will be prepared.

— Since standard recipes indicate needed equipment and required production times, managers can more effectively schedule food production employees and necessary equipment.

— Less supervision is required since standard recipes tell the employees the quantity and preparation method for each item. Guesswork is eliminated; employees need only follow recipe procedures. Of course, managers should routinely evaluate the quality of items produced and ensure that standard recipes are followed correctly.

— If the chef is ill or the bartender doesn't show up, a product can be produced if a standard recipe is available. Granted, inexperienced employees will be slow and may make mistakes. However, if the recipe is in the head of an absent employee instead of on a standard recipe card or available for printout, management will be in an even more awkward position.

Many persons think about the importance of standard recipes for food production; as suggested above, however, they're also critical to control the consistency (quality and cost) of beverages. Today in the U.S. it is critical that standard recipes specifying ingredient and portion sizes of alcoholic beverages be available in consistent use. Liquor liability concerns often arise when standard recipes are not available and or when standard portion controls are not in use. It is always necessary to be able to verify the actual quantity of alcohol (not just number of drinks!) that has been consumed by a guest.

Using a standard recipe does not requite that the recipe be physically in the work area during production times. After a cook prepares a menu item several times, or a bartender mixes a drink several times, he or she will-remember ingredients, quantities, and procedures. It would obviously be impractical if, before preparing a drink, a busy bartender had to refer to a standard recipe. A standard recipe must always be followed and must always be available, but it does not always need to be read.

Developing Standard Recipes

Developing standard recipes does not require throwing out existing recipes and starting over. Rather, it often requires standardizing existing recipes according to a series of steps. Select a time period for standard recipe development. For example, you may choose to standardize three recipes at each weekly cooks' meeting, or spend one hour each week with the head bartender to develop standard beverage recipes. At these meetings, ask the cook or head bartender to talk through the preparation of the item.

Record the recipes in a standard format that will be helpful to those preparing the items. For example:

— Decide on the desirable yield. If 25 portions of a food item are normally prepared for slow periods and 60 portions are needed for busy times, recipes should be designed to yield these servings.

— List all ingredients in the order they are used.

— Decide whether to use weights or measures or both. Weighing is always more precise than measuring, and it is just as practical to weigh liquids, flour, etc., as it is to measure them. Avoid confusion by using consistent abbreviations throughout all the standard recipes you are developing.

— Whenever possible, express all quantities in amounts that are practical for those preparing the item. For example, convert all measures into the largest possible units. Change 4/8 cup to ½ cup, four cups to one quart, or three teaspoons to one tablespoon. At this point you need to be sure that the proper equipment is available. It does little good to specify a three-ounce quantity when an accurate measuring scale is not available. Also, when applicable, recipes should be developed that call for standard-size pans and other equipment.

— Record procedures in detailed, concise, and exact terms. Avoid ambiguous statements. For example, what does" one cup whipping cream" mean? Does it mean one cup of cream that has been whipped or does it mean one cup of cream that must be whipped? When mixing is called for, tell how to mix (by hand or by machine) and provide the exact time and speed if a machine is used. State the size and type of equipment and small wares such as pans or bowls needed and always list exact temperatures, cooking times, and other necessary controls.

— Carefully consider potential sanitation problems which can arise in each step of recipe production; note these and incorporate food handling precautions directly into the recipe. For example, if the operation uses a hollandaise sauce (this sauce is potentially hazardous and is highly susceptible to contamination by microorganisms), a last step in the recipe for hollandaise sauce might state: "Hollandaise sauce is a potentially dangerous food which can become contaminated by microorganisms; always prepare in small batches and do not hold on the serving line for more than one hour."

— Provide directions for portioning. Indicate the type and size of the serving dish. Also, indicate portioning equipment, such as ladle or scoop, and specify the expected number and size of portions. Be sure all required portioning equipment is available for use. If garnishes or sauces are needed, these should be listed.

After the standard recipes have been recorded, share them with other production staff. Solicit their ideas about accuracy and possible refinements. Finally, test the recipes to be certain that they yield products of the desired quantity and quality. After successful testing, the recipe may be considered standardised. Despite the advantages of using standard recipes, there may be some difficulties encountered in implementing them. Cooks or bartenders, for example, may feel that they can no longer be creative in the kitchen or behind the bar. They may resent the need to put things down on paper. Other difficulties may be related to concerns about time. It takes time to standardise existing recipes, and it takes time to train production employees to precisely follow them.

These concerns, however, are minor when compared to the points already noted in favor of using standard recipes. In addition, managers can minimise difficulties with implementing standard recipes by explaining to employees why standard recipes are necessary and by involving them in developing and implementing the recipes.

Standard Yields

The term yield means the net weight or volume of a food item after it has been processed and made ready for sale to the guest. The difference between the raw or "as purchased" (AP) weight and the prepared or "edible portion" (EP) weight is termed a production loss. In general, there are three steps in the production process. The first step is preparation, which includes such activities as meat trimming and vegetable cleaning. The second step is cooking. Holding, the third step includes the portioning of those products that have not been preportioned. A "loss" can occur in any of these steps.

A standard yield results when an item is produced according to established standard production procedures outlined in the standard recipe. They serve as a base against which to compare actual yields. For example, if the standard purchase specifications are adhered to and a meat item is properly trimmed, cooked, and portioned, the actual yield should closely approximate the standard yield.

Determining Standard Yield

Standard yields are determined by conducting a yield test. Ideally, everything that does not have a 100 percent yield should be tested. However, from a practical standpoint, yield tests are typically performed only on high-cost items or on lower-cost products used in large quantities.

The yield from a product depends upon several factors, including the grade, original weight, and preparation and cooking methods. Therefore, it is helpful for a food and beverage purchaser to compare the yields for similar products from different suppliers. It may be possible to substitute a product with a lower cost per unit that provides a yield similar to that of a higher cost product, without compromising the operation's quality standards.

Since the AP weight is already known, the meat must next weighed when it is removed from the oven after cooking. By subtracting the cooked weight from the original weight, you determine the loss in cooking-in this example, an average pounds, 14 ounces per beef rib. Next the fat cap and bones must be removed, and the remaining meat weighed. This edible portion or servable weight-in this example, an average 11 pounds, 3 ounces per beef rib. Subtracting the edible portion (servable) weight from the cooked weight indicates that the in carving and bones averaged 5 pounds, 3 ounces.

Cost per servable pound

Once the edible portion (servable) weight is determined, a per servable pound can be determined. To find the cost per servable pound, first establish the yield percentage. The yield percentage (sometimes called yield factor) is the ratio of servable weight to original weight and is calculated by dividing the servable weight by the original weight (normally both weights are expressed in ounces; there are 16 ounces in one pound), multiplying by 100 to change the decimal to a percentage.

The cost factor

The cost factor is a constant value that may be used to convert new AP prices into a revised cost per servable pound, assuming that the standard purchase specifications; standard recipe, and standard yield remain the same. The cost factor is obtained by dividing the cost per servable pound, calculated as part of the yield test, by the original AP cost per pound. Anytime the AP cost changes from the amount used to calculate the original cost per servable pound in the yield test, a new cost per servable pound can be rapidly computed. This is accomplished by multiplying the cost factor by the new AP price.

Adjusting Standard Recipe Yields

The yield from a standard recipe can be easily increased or decreased by using an adjustment factor. An adjustment factor is found by dividing the desired yield by the original yield. Each recipe ingredient is then multiplied by the adjustment factor to determine the amount needed for the desired yield.

Standard Portion Sizes

Each food and beverage standard recipe indicates a standard portion size. This is the fourth standard cost tool for ensuring consistency in operations. Because a given menu item or drink will be the same size each time it is portioned, no guest will get a larger or smaller portion or a stronger or weaker drink. The benefit is twofold: portion costs for the same food and beverage items will be consistent, and the guest will always receive the same value for the dollars he or she spends. Value is the relationship between price and quality. Basing the selling price of the food or beverage item, at least in part, upon its cost will help to establish a fair selling price, or value, from the guest's perspective.

Assume that an operation does not provide a standard portion size. On one occasion, a guest may receive a very large portion-a great value. Returning at a later time, the same guest may receive a smaller portion at the same selling price-a lesser value and a disappointment for the guest. Consistency, then, in terms of value perceived by guests, is a primary advantage of standard portion sizes. Portion control tools must be available and used every time a recipe or beverage is prepared.

Portion control tools include such items as weighing and measuring equipment, ladles and scoops to portion food, jiggers and shot glasses for beverages, or automated beverage-dispensing equipment. Employees must know about portion sizes in order to follow them. Required portion sizes from each standard recipe should be posted in production areas for cooks and bartenders to refer to. In addition to these lists, some operations use pictures of each item. When these are posted in serving line stations, employees can see how the item should look or how it is placed on the plate.

STANDARD PORTION COSTS

After standard recipes and standard portion sizes have been developed, a standard portion cost-the fifth standard cost toolcan be calculated. A standard portion cost is, simply, the cost of preparing and serving one portion of food or one drink item according to the standard recipe. The process of establishing this cost is called precosting.

A standard portion cost is determined by dividing the recipe's total ingredient costs by the number of portions the standard recipe yields. For example, if the cost to prepare a recipe is $75.00 and it yields 50 portions, then the standard portion cost for one item is $1.50 ($75.00 + 50 portions). The prices for ingredients listed in standard recipes can be obtained from current invoices. Today, many operations use computerised precosting systems to keep the per-portion cost of standard recipes current. For example, if the price of ground beef increases, the new cost is entered into the menu management system and all recipe costs in which ground beef is an ingredient are automatically adjusted to reflect the price increase.

Calculating Standard Dinner Costs

Many food service operations combine individual menu items to create dinners or other meals that are casted, priced/ and sold as one selection (although some operations such as cafeterias offer items a la carte-each item individually priced). Because the vegetable varies from day to day (the term du jour for vegetable mcans of the day, and because guests have choices in the potato, dressing, and juice categories, it would take an impractical amount of time to determine the standard dinner cost for all the different dinner combinations that are possible. For the categories in which the guests have a choice, managers can choose the cost of the most popular item in the category to determine the dinner cost.

For example, if baked potatoes are chosen most often by guests, then the portion cost of baked potatoes might be used when calculating the standard dinner cost. It is also possible to select the item with the highest portion cost in a category and use this when determining the standard dinner cost. In addition, managers can track the actual number of each item chosen for several days, and then calculate an average cost that can be used when determining the standard dinner cost.

Regardless of the method used, planners should be aware of the item cost which is used in calculating the standard dinner cost. Then, when additional items are considered, they can better assure that the per portion cost of the new item will be in line with that used in earlier cost calculations. The worksheet provides four more columns for calculating the standard dinner cost when the standard portion costs of items change (due to a change in an ingredient's price on the item's standard recipe). When this occurs, the new standard portion cost is added to the unchanged costs of the other dinner items to arrive at a revised standard dinner cost. Increasingly, computerised menu management systems are used to update the costs of menu items. These systems are also used to calculate possible food costs when managers consider changing menu prices.

Standard Portion Cost for Beverages

Establishing a standard drink cost for beverages is relatively simple because usually there are few ingredients. Most alcoholic beverages are sold by the liter rather than by the ounce. Therefore, because recipes and bar equipment typically use ounces as a unit of measure, it is usually necessary to convert liters to ounces before making recipe extensions or costing calculations.

Standard cost tools for beverage control

The five standard cost tools-standard purchase specifications, standard recipes, standard yields, standard portion sizes, and standard portion costs-are necessary to establish performance standards for both food and beverages. However, two additional standard cost tools are important to the beverage operation: standard glassware and standard ice size. Standard Glassware. Glassware obviously affects portion size, quality, and perceived value. In too small a glass, highballs made with mixers such as soda, tonic, or water will be too strong since less mixer can be added to the standard portion of liquor.

Conversely, in too large a glass, the drink will taste weak since the greater amount of mixer dilutes the standard portion of liquor. Therefore, the standard drink recipe should specify a standard glass size, which should be determined when the beverage recipe is standardized. A standard glassware review sheet, should be posted in the work area. The same style and size of glass should be used every time the drink is prepared. This means, of course, that sufficient quantities of all necessary glassware must be available at all times.

Glassware is also important in marketing to help carry out an atmosphere theme and to influence the appearance and presentation of the drink. However, while glassware affects presentation (marketing) concerns, it is wise to limit the number of different glasses in inventory. For example, the same glass might be used for ice water, soft drinks, milk, and highballs. If this can be done, problems with the costs of glassware, storage space behind the bar, and training time for bartenders and servers may be reduced.

Standard Ice Size. It is easy to ignore the effect of ice size on drink quality. Although any size ice is suitable for most food service purposes, drink standardisation must consider ice cube size. Bigger cubes leave more empty space in the glass because they do not clump together as smaller cubes do. This space must be filled with something. In a liquor-only drink, such as a martini, the amount of beverage appears smaller, unless a larger portion is served. In a mixed drink, the drink will be diluted by adding more mix. On the other hand, small cubes or shaved ice fill up a glass more completely before a beverage is added, but both melt more quickly. Therefore, a delay in serving or consuming the drink may create a diluted taste. Management must therefore consider its operating procedures to determine the proper size of ice cubes for the operation.

Recipe management software

Recipe management software maintains three of the most important files used by an integrated food service computer system: an ingredient file, a standard recipe file, and a menu item file. Most other management software programs must be able to access data contained within these files to produce special reports for management.

Ingredient file

An ingredient file contains important data about each purchased ingredient. Ingredient file data generally include ingredient code numbers and descriptions, as well as each ingredient's:

— Purchase unit and cost per purchase unit

— Issue unit and cost per issue unit

— Recipe unit and cost per recipe unit

A sample ingredient cost list produced from some of the data contained in an ingredient file. This report is useful for detailing unit expenditures at current costs and monitoring relationships among various product units (such as purchase, issue, and recipe units of the same ingredient). Some ingredient files may specify more than one recipe unit. For example, the recipe unit for bread used for French toast is by the slice; the recipe unit for bread used for stuffing may be by the ounce.

The initial creation of an ingredient file and the subsequent file updates (daily, weekly, monthly, etc.) are often challenging tasks for many food service managers. However, the benefits of an ingredient file often outweigh the cost of creating and maintaining the file. When the ingredient file can be accessed by other management software programs (especially by inventory software), ingredient data can easily be transferred (rather than reinputted) to appropriate management software programs. Since other management software programs rely on data maintained by the ingredient file, it is important that data contained in the file are accurate. If errors are made when initially entering data, all subsequent processing will be unreliable and system reports will be relatively worthless.

Standard recipe file

Computers can assist in generating standard recipes by simplifying many of the calculations needed. Numerous software programs that calculate recipe quantities based upon estimated unit sales and then print the standard recipe are available. Standard recipe conversion information generated by recipe management software. The software converts recipe ingredient amounts to weights and then to ingredient costs. It can also determine nutritional information for an entire meal (or other period) and define applicable preparation areas.

Some recipe management software programs provide space within standard recipe records for preparation instructions (also referred to as assembly instructions) that are typically found on standard recipe cards. This can be a useful feature when the number of portions yielded by a particular standard recipe has to be expanded or contracted to accommodate forecasted needs. For example, if a standard recipe is designed to yield 100 portions but 530 portions are needed, it may be possible (depending on the particular menu item) to instruct the system to proportionately adjust the ingredient quantities. A recipe for 530 portions can be printed that includes preparation information, thus providing a complete plan for the new recipe's production.

Few restaurants purchase all menu item ingredients in ready-touse or preportioned form. Some ingredients are made on the premises. This means that the ingredients within a standard recipe file may be either inventory items or references to other recipe files. Recipes that are included as ingredients within a standard recipe record are called sub-recipes. Including sub-recipes as ingredients for a particular standard recipe is called chaining recipes. Chaining recipes enables the food service computer system to maintain a single record for a particular menu item that includes a number of sub-recipes. When ingredient costs change, recipe management software programs must be capable of automatically updating not only the costs of standard recipes, but also the costs of sub-recipes that are used as ingredients in other standard recipes.

Menu item file

A menu item file contains data for all meal periods and menu items sold. Important data maintained by this file may include the menu's identification number, descriptor, recipe code number, selling price, ingredient quantities for inventory reporting, and sales totals (by unit).

This file also stores historical information about the actual number of items sold. Generally, after a meal period, the actual number of menu items served is manually entered into the menu item file, or automatically transferred from an electronic cash register (ECR) or point-of-sale (PaS) system through an interface to the restaurant management system. This data can be accessed by management or by sophisticated forecasting programmes to project future unit sales, determine the number of ingredient quantities to purchase, and schedule needed personnel.

In addition, computer-based sales analysis applications access data in the menu item file to produce various sales analysis reports for management. When menu items, prices, or tax tables need to be changed, the menu item file is accessed and appropriate changes are entered according to procedures indicated in the user's manual provided by the system's vendor.

Actual Sales Records

The information necessary to determine standard food cost may come from actual sales records citing the number of each menu item sold during one or more prior periods. If a sales history has been kept, the total number of each item sold can easily be transferred to the worksheet.

If there is no record of past item sales (for example, if an entirely new menu is introduced), items sold must be tallied daily during the study period. An accurate tally of the number of each a la carte and complete meal item sold during the trial period must be made. The information may come from an analysis of the guest checks created each day during the study period or from a management report generated by most electronic cash registers or point-of-sale systems. The worksheet has space for only 16 days. Because accuracy increases as the number of days increases, two or more forms can be used to tally item sales for at least one month.

By recording this information on a worksheet, total sales (number of units) and total food costs for the trial period can be easily tracked. With this information, an overall food cost percentage can be figured. Because each food item is likely to have a different food cost percentage, calculating the overall food cost involves determining a weighted average food cost. Items with a high food cost raise the average food cost percentage; items with a low food cost reduce it. It is this weighted average food cost that will be used as the standard against which to measure actual food costs.

— The item sales price is the actual selling price of each menu item as printed on the menu.

— Total food revenue represents the total revenue expected from sales of the individual menu items.

— Item food cost is the standard portion cost. If the item is sold individually, this figure can be taken from the pre-casted standard recipe.

— Total food cost is the total cost of all food used to produce the number of items sold.

— The food cost percentage is calculated by dividing the food cost by the sales price and multiplying by 100. The standard food cost percentage for the soup is: While the standard food cost percentage for each individual item is of some interest, one more step is needed to arrive at the overall standard food cost percentage.

— To calculate the standard food cost percentage against which to compare actual food costs, the sum of the total food cost column is divided by the sum of the total food revenue column and multiplied by 100.

The effort needed to calculate an overall standard food cost percentage can be simplified by using one of the many electronic spreadsheet programmes available for a personal computer. The number of each menu item sold can be entered on a daily basis. The computer can calculate total revenue and total costs along with the item's standard food cost percentage and the overall standard food cost percentage.

Standard Costs per Meal

Properties offering more than one menu, such as lunch and dinner, must decide whether to develop standard food costs by meal or across all meals. If by-meal food costs are desired, calculations for each meal must be done on a separate worksheet. There are two advantages to a separate listing. First, when food cost standards are separated by meals, it is easier to compare any differences between standard and actual costs. Second, since corrective action can focus specifically upon the meal period contributing, higher than expected food costs, the reasons for losses can more quickly be identified and brought under control.

There is, however, one serious disadvantage to overcome when standards are established for each separate meal period. To effect control, actual food costs must also be assessed separately for each meal. Even with the use of point-of-sale equipment, the process of determining how much of each food item is used for breakfast, lunch, or dinner is very time-consuming. For example, a manager might know the cost of food that should have been used during a meal period (number of items sold times each item's standard food cost). But if some food was wasted or improperly portioned during preparation, the actual cost of food used would be greater than that determined from the tally of sales. Many food and beverage managers, therefore, find it more helpful to spend time identifying problems common to all meal periods, such as ineffective purchasing, receiving, storing, and issuing, or problems in production and service, rather than searching for problems applicable to a specific meal period.

Standard beverage costs are calculated for exactly the same reason as standard food costs. The manager wants to establish a goal-base of comparison-against which to measure actual results of the beverage operation. The standard beverage cost becomes the goal. The steps in calculating standard beverage costs are:

— Establish all standard cost tools: standard purchase specifications, recipes, yields, portion sizes, portion costs, glassware, and ice.
— Select a time period for the analysis. As with standard food costs, more time and effort spent on determining standard beverage costs will generally produce more accurate cost calculations. However, no system

can provide data with 100 percent accuracy. The best time schedule will allow observation of all phases of the beverage operation, including both slow and busy times, or shifts with high, low, and/ or regular prices. At a minimum, the review should cover two or three weeks in succession. Operations with several beverage outlets need a longer observation period for sales to reflect an average volume and a variety of drinks served.

— Inform all affected staff members-bartenders, food and beverage servers, and others-about the study. They will want to know:
  — The reason for the study-to determine cost expectations for accounting, record keeping, management, and control purposes.
  — Why the study is important-management wants to assess how well the beverage programme is operating.
  — What's in it for them-the results of the study will help staff members know what's expected of them, and cost savings may be shared with the staff.
  — Implications of the study-results of the analysis have no bearing on employment status; no one's honesty or competency is being reviewed or questioned.
  — Procedures for the study-there will be minimal, if any, disruption in on going operations.
— Set rules for the study period, emphasizing that during the trial study employees must very carefully follow all standard procedures. The purpose is to ensure that accurate and reliable information is collected.
  — Standard beverage recipes are to be used whenever drinks are prepared.
  — Portion control tools (shot glasses, jiggers) and standard glassware are to be used in preparing every drink.
  — Management personnel might work behind the bar whenever possible during the study to better assure that required procedures are followed consistently. When not working the bar, managers should carefully supervise operations to ensure compliance with all standard operating procedures.
  — At the beginning of each shift, the manager should remind personnel that the property is involved in the beverage study and that careful compliance with all procedures is important.

  - Revenue from all drinks served must be collected. Management must approve all complimentary drinks. Personnel must save all drinks returned because of mistakes. Special precautions to minimize the possibility of guest" walkouts" and errors in guest checks should be used.
- Before the study begins, take careful inventory of the quantity of liquor behind the bar.
- Maintain a record of the cost of all liquor issued to the bar during the trial study.
- Record any beverages transferred from the bar and any food transferred to the bar.
- Calculate the standard beverage cost. Close supervision and efficient operations during the study period should yield a reasonably accurate standard beverage cost. That is, with continued use of the standard cost tools, a lower beverage cost percentage most likely could not be achieved without measures such as raising prices, reducing portion sizes, or revising basic operating procedures.

As with the standard food cost percentage, the standard beverage cost percentage is a goal that managers of the beverage operation should work toward. There are, of course, many factors that affect actual practice. For example, errors may occur, control of the beverage operation may gradually become looser, or changes in policy may require revised procedures. These and similar factors reinforce the valuc of recalling the standard beverage cost percentage when examining actual operating results. The beverage manager should understand that when actual beverage costs exceed standard beverage costs, a problem may exist.

Costing of Dry Herbs and Spices

The Dry Herbs and Spices table uses relatively small measures because these foods are often used in fairly small amounts. The key measures are:

- Number of tablespoons per ounce
- Number of ounces per tablespoon
- Number of ounces that a cup of the item weighs
- Count per ounce (such as whole bay leaves)
- Count per tablespoon (such as whole peppercorns)

Costing fresh herbs

Fresh herbs can be used as garnishes of whole leaves or whole leafy stems. They are also used whole in stocks and some roasting recipes. When stemmed and chopped, they find their way into recipes as flavorings and again as garnishes.

Fresh herbs are often sold by the bunch, but it is important to keep in mind that the size of the bunches will vary for one reason or another. One supplier may ship smaller bunches than another, and even if you only buy from one source, the size of a bunch can vary as seasons change. To help you in this regard, the Fresh Herbs table gives you yield information based both on a bunch and on an as-purchased (AP) ounce. To cost whole leaves or volumes of chopped leaves, you first determine the cost of the as-purchased (AP) ounce.

Costing chopped fresh herbs

This was calculated by measuring the number of cups of cleaned, stemmed, and chopped leaf obtained from one bunch. That number was then multiplied by 16 (there are 16 tablespoons in 1 cup), and dividing that result by the AP ounces in the bunch. For curly parsley, the number of chopped tablespoons obtained from 1 AP ounce is shown as 6.62.

Controlling Food Costs

Controlling food costs starts with inventory organisation and control. Over and over we have found that reducing inventory levels and organising food storage areas will significantly reduce food costs. It is a simple axiom: When you have excess and disorganisation you have waste.

Best Guess Inventory/Order System

This system works best when your chef/kitchen manager has been able convince you that ordering is a complex procedure that you the manager/owner should not get involved in. Only someone with his/her many years of experience can understand the obscure secrets of food purchasing. The system works like this:

— In the middle of the lunch hour rush a waitress runs out of crackers. (Side station stocking problem?)

— She rushes to the store room but does not see the crackers because two cases are hidden under other things. (Poor organisation problem?)

— She then rushes to the chef, who is busy on the line, and tells him you are out of crackers.

— The chef was to busy to leave the line and check the storeroom.

— That afternoon whatever salesperson walks in first will get an order for crackers. (Forget price, we need them now!) And because we ran out the chef doubles the order to four cases.

— Now we have six cases of crackers that will sit in the storeroom for who knows how long. (Your money is sitting on a shelf earning nothing)

— Murphy's Law says it is only a matter of time until someone stacks a couple of cases on #10 cans on top of the crackers.

— Chances are good that before you can use up all those crackers, you will have one or more cases of cracker bits and crumbs.

Helpful Hint

In many instances we have eliminated 20% to 50% of the shelves and storage areas to encourage the kitchen to keep their inventory lean and mean. In some cases of extreme overstocking this alone has resulted in reducing food costs by more than 10%.

A rule of thumb we have found to work well is: Order to bring your inventory up to a two order period par level. That is: If you order an item daily, such as produce, order enough to have a two day supply including the inventory you have on hand. If you order dry stores weekly, subtract the inventory you have on hand from what you expect to use over the next two weeks and order the difference.

With this simple concept you should never run out of product, and never have more than a two order period inventory on hand.

Food Storage

Many restaurants still loose product to freezer burn, contamination and spoilage because of improper storage procedures. Even worse are those restaurants who loose customers because they serve less than fresh meals.

Want to know what improper storage is costing you?

— On the sly, after all your employees have left, take an inventory of everything in your freezer and walk-in that is not properly wrapped, covered or date marked.

— In the next day or two take a second inventory to see how many of these items are still not properly stored. Check for rotation to see if the oldest items are used first.

— Now cost out the items that are still improperly stored. Multiply this by 365 days. Bet that number gets your attention.

— Give your kitchen crew a break by assuming that half of those items will be used up before they spoil. Chances are that even half of your annual spoilage cost will get you thinking what you could do with all that extra money.

Portion Control

Advance preparation can have a critical impact on food costs. Just as you would not stop to drain the swamp when the alligators are nipping at your butt, your cooks will not worry about portion control when deluged with orders during a rush. Advance preparation and portioning not only saves food cost dollars, it also results in a more efficient kitchen, with a more consistent product and faster service to your customers.

Purveyor Shopping

Regularly scheduled requests for bids/quotes from both your current suppliers and new suppliers can loop some more off your food costs. This is an area where you can delegate, up to a point.

— Have one or more of your employees make the calls, using the specifications from your inventory/order form. If a new supplier offers a good price, ask for samples.

— Do not let the employee change your specified supplier on the inventory/order form without your approval.

— Review the price offered and check the quality of the sample before changing purveyors. If you have any doubts, check their service and the consistency of their quality with other restaurants in your area.

— Have a receiving procedure that checks price, quality and quantity at your door. One way is to post your inventory/order form on a clipboard at the back door. The person receiving the delivery certifies that price and quantity of the delivery matches the inventory/order form as well as checking for quality. Exceptions can be noted on the back of the form, and signed by the delivery driver, with management follow-up.

— A double check is to have your bookkeeper check invoiced prices and quantities against quoted prices and amount ordered quantities on the inventory/order form

Lowly Dishwasher

Being the lowest in the pecking order in a restaurant, the dishwasher's potential for profit maximising is often overlooked. More than anyone else he/she can tell you what is coming back from your dining room. How much of your food costs are going into the trash because of excessive portions or just because customers do not like an entree, vegetable or condiment?

Changing a garnish, eliminating a vegetable or reducing a portion may allow you to reduce the menu price, making you more price competitive with the same profit.

The Back Door

The back door is where a good portion your profits can go, if you let it.

— The most obvious step is to keep your back door locked. This will require you to install a door bell outside for deliveries. In addition local fire codes may require an emergency exit bar on the door. Be sure it includes an alarm that must be deactivated by management or designated kitchen personnel before the door can be opened.

— Keep the area outside your back door clean and tidy. As much as is practical you want to eliminate places where stolen food product can be hidden until the thief gets off shift.

— Check your garbage. It is a common trick to wrap a couple steaks up and hide them in the out going garbage. You may also realise considerable saving in lost linen and silverware costs by checking the garbage.

— If you are designing a new kitchen, locate your freezers and walk-ins, where you keep high cost items like meat and seafood, as far from the back door as possible. Make it harder to sneak things out.

How to Make it all Workable

Just like everything else in your restaurant, you are the key to making food cost control work. We favor the two person spot check and prosecute method.

— *The Two person check*—Designate whoever has authority to open the back door to check all garbage before the dishwasher carries it out. If the inspector does his/her job theft will be reduced by requiring two person collusion.

— *The spot check:* This is where management insures the inspector is doing his/her job. This is also where management gets their hands dirty and spot checks the garbage at unexpected times. This clearly establishes you are committed to controlling back door theft. It also validates that you do not ask your employees to do anything you will not do.

— *The prosecution:* You may choose not to go through the hassle of calling the police and actually prosecuting a thief. What you can do is:

  — If your cook/garbage inspector catches a dishwasher taking food out with the garbage, establish that the dishwasher is actually the thief and fire him/her. After a severe reprimand the first time, the same dishwasher caught taking food out again is reasonable proof of his/her guilt in our minds.

  — If you wait outside and find stolen food in the garbage after your cook has inspected the garbage, fire the cook.

  — It is very possible the cook who allows stolen food to go out the door is negligent rather than a thief. No one likes to root through garbage. By firing this cook you will insure that the next cook/ inspector will really check the garbage.

  — Help your cook/inspector. Provide heavy vinyl or rubber gloves and apron for use while inspecting the garbage.

Tricks to Reduce Breakage and Spoilage

— The very first step in breakfast preparation should be to set a supply of eggs out to temper, even before the grill is turned on. Egg yokes are less likely to break if the egg is cracked at room temperature.

— If you use frozen portion cut steaks, layer the steaks in a shallow hotel pan then cover them with clean cooking oil. With this simple procedure:

— The steak's cooler shelf life will be doubled. And, you will have better tasting steaks because the oil prevents the steaks flavorful juices from draining off.

- When broiled the oil seals in the steaks flavor, without leaving any after taste.
- With a longer shelf life you can keep more steaks defrosted, eliminating the need to defrost in a microwave, or attempt to broil a frozen steak if you sell more than expected.

Effective Food Cost Control

It is very important to use clear, properly prepared reports to analyse food cost results. Often, the reports become the focal point due to errors and omissions. Once the report has lost credibility, a meaningful discussion of operational issues is difficult.

A properly prepared food cost report should have a brief summary at the top of the page. Basic operating statistics should be highlighted. We need to know the period of time (week, month, quarter or year) and the ending date. Operating results should include the period sales and purchases, beginning and ending inventory values, food cost and the food cost percentage.

Supporting the summary information, you should include a recap of purchases, inventories and cost of sales by category (e.g. meat, seafood, produce, etc.). Budget comparisons are useful as well if the budgets were thoughtfully prepared. Try to put the current period in context. Show how well the performance was compared to other benchmark periods (e.g. previous month, last year, current year budget, etc.). The comparison section should show in which direction the operation is headed.

Supporting the management summary page, insights and concerns regarding specific components need to be reported. For example, if there was significant waste due to spoilage of produce, the purchasing manager can concentrate on ordering fewer cases (or splitting cases if necessary). Rising prices of gas and corn has impacted the cost of many commodities. Calculate the impact of your meat and dairy price increases on net profits. Bring any other significant findings to management's attention.

Seven Steps to Food Cost Control

1. *Ordering:* The first step is to order right. Having detailed recipes, designing purchasing specifications, doing comparative shopping based on those specifications, and comparing quality, price and service, etc. Oh yes, don't order too early in order to avoid spoilage, wasted storage

space and lost interest on your money. Don't order too late, so premium costs and delivery charges accrue.

2. *Receiving:* The fundamentals are obvious: count; weigh; inspect for condition and quality; verify against the purchase order; keep the receiving area clean and uncluttered; limit access to the receiving area; train the person receiving and make him or her responsible. Get credit memos from the delivery driver.
3. *Storing:* Is the method and place of storage for the various items appropriate for the item? Is it secure from pilferage? Are the shelves strong enough for the product, allow air circulation and easy to clean? Are all items stored at a temperature appropriate for that product? Are items dated (with year, in some cases) and priced? Is the storage area orderly and clean? Should shelves be labeled and maybe even stocking quantities noted?
4. *Issuing:* What is issuing based on? Who has access and or authority to issue or take things from the secured store rooms and walk-ins? Are issues being made in appropriate quantities and at appropriate times? Is there a relationship to volume or reasonable par stocks? Are issues being accounted for? Is a perpetual inventory or sign out sheet designed specifically for your operation or a particular store room in use?
5. *Preparation:* Phrases that come to mind include: trim properly; use trimmings for stock pots and other recipes. Proper tools, sharp knives, clean and neat working area, enforcing a policy of following recipes, and having photos of finished products available and used regularly are also critical.
6. *Cooking:* Proper temperatures, proper cooking times, following recipes carefully, using photographs of finished products, correct size, material, and type of utensils and cookware, clean work area.
7. *Serving:* Serving is not only about portion control, it is also about decisions made regarding portion size and presentation. With a buffet, it is obvious. Proper serving utensils, proper holding/serving equipment, right presentation order, plate sizes, etc. In a bar its easy, too. Jiggers or other measuring and control devices and very strict discipline. Dining room service should be easy to control using good kitchen supervisors, trained cooks, photographs for both cooks and servers, etc. Watch what comes back from bused tables to see if portions are proper. Marketing

decisions may drive large portions but if the patrons are not eating it or taking it home, the portion size or the recipe should be reconsidered. Proper china for each item served is important for both presentation and portion control.

Work hard on your cost controls and be consistent about them. One element of controlling food cost covers all seven categories: thorough training. Give your staff the ability and knowledge and confidence to do their jobs properly and to your specifications. Inconsistency and failure to enforce procedures will drive costs skyward. Failure here is like throwing money away.

Budgetary Control

In non-commercial food and beverage operations, budgets are just as important. They help to ensure that planned expenses do not exceed anticipated revenues and, if required, that an operating surplus (”profit”) can be generated. An operating budget is not an obstacle to efficient performance to be prepared and followed only when top management insists. In fact, operating budgets are critical for planning the profit requirements of food and beverage operations.

The budget is your best forecast for the future. Operating budgets are an excellent source of estimated revenue and cost information, which can represent planned performance standards. Actual operating data can be compared against budgeted information to determine the extent to which financial plans are attained.

An operating budget is a plan that estimates how much revenue will be generated and what expenses will be incurred to meet financial requirements and goals. There are several different types of budgets-for example: long- and shortterm, capital and cash. The type of budget most useful to a food and beverage operation is a shortterm, (one-year) operating budget, which covers items affecting the income statement. The budget is a constant reminder of the amount of revenue planed. And, just as crucial for purposes of control, information stemming from the budget limits the amount of allowable expenses. If these limits are exceeded, budgeted profits decrease unless expenses are reduced in other areas and/ or revenue increases beyond the anticipated level.

Once developed, the budget becomes an important part of the control process. The budget plan tells managers how much money can be spent in each expense category. When actual revenue falls below forecasted levels and/ or when actual expenses exceed budget estimates, managers know there may be problems. Corrective action can then be implemented on a timely basis. A current period's budget is used to develop the budgets for the next fiscal period. Information from the current budget is the basis for beginning the budget process for the next fiscal year.

Because the budget provides anticipated revenue and cost figures, it enables the calculation of a budgeted food cost percentage (budgeted food cost divided by budgeted food revenue multiplied by 100) and a budgeted beverage cost percentage (budgeted beverage cost divided by budgeted beverage revenue multiplied by 100). In a similar way, benchmarks for all other expenses-such as labour and energy costs-can also be calculated. These budget percentages can later be compared with percentages representing actual operating results to measure the food and beverage manager's effectiveness in meeting budget goals.

Managers have two special concerns when they establish operating budget standards. The goals set for revenue, profit requirements, and operating expenses must be attainable and must not compromise established quality requirements. H standards are impossible to attain, personnel may get frustrated and the operation could deteriorate. For example, if food costs have averaged 45 percent, achieving a budgeted goal of 38 percent may not be possible, at least within a single fiscal period. Furthermore, food and beverage managers are concerned about quality standards.

Management should set minimum quality standards based upon the expectations of the target markets. This helps ensure that standards will not be compromised as the budget plan is developed and implemented. When necessary, management can use the budget not only to evaluate past efforts but also to plan corrective action for the future. Since the budget helps define responsibilities, management personnel can be held responsible for meeting revenue goals and keeping all operating costs within budgeted limits.

When budget figures are exceeded or underspent, responsibility can correctly be assigned to the manager in charge. In small food and beverage operations, the owner/manager generally develops the budget. In larger operations, other staff members provide important help. For example, department heads, whose performance will be judged by the extent to which they attain budget goals, might be assigned to plan expense levels for their areas of responsibility, in consultation with senior management personnel.

In still larger operations, a budget committee may review department revenue and expense plans before a final property-wide budget is approved.

Budgeting in Multi-Unit Operations

There are basically two methods used to develop operating budgets in multiunit operations. The most common method uses a bottom-up budgeting approach m which operating budgets are assembled at the unit level and are "rolled" up the organisation. Another approach is referred to as top-down budgeting. With this plans budgets are developed at the corporate level and are then passed down to lower organisational levels with each successively lower level becoming responsible for a specific segment of the budget.

The main advantage of using bottom-up budgeting is that budget plans are specifically geared to the individual operation. When budgets are developed for a specific operation by the unit manager, the lower level participation yields a budget that is "our plan," not a plan thrust upon lower management by higher organisational levels. The "ownership" this creates helps the unit manager recognise the importance-and feasibility-of the operating budget. Likewise, bottom-up budgeting enables budget planners to focus on specific units and special problems that are likely to be encountered.

Unfortunately, corporate-level managers encounter a problem when the sum of profits anticipated by individual units generating their own operating budgets, does not equal the profit requirements of the corporation. For example a restaurant company may be owned by a parent organisation that mandates a profit contribution larger than that which is planned to be generated by the individual units. This points to an advantage of top-down budgeting.

In addition to helping plan for corporate-level profit expectations top-down budgeting has other potential advantages. For example, unit managers in specific properties may not be aware of marketing commitments advertising campaigns menu charges and other factors that can have a significant impact upon operating budgets within an individual unit.

In actual practice budget planners in multiunit organisations use a give-and take method that first develops tentative budget plans and then modifies them to be realistic expectations for individual properties. Psychological aspects of budget development must also be considered and incorporated into budget development strategies. For example unit managers may wish to send conservative estimates "up the organisation," and conversely, top-level managers may wish to suggest more aggressive budget goals.

Budget Reforecasting

Budgets are developed several months before the start of the food and beverage operation's fiscal year. As such future events that affect revenue and expense levels cannot be accurately forecasted. Since the operating budget is a critical control tool it is important to have updated information against which to compare actual operating results.

Many food and beverage operations use a method of reforecasting to update budgets. For example if revenue trends are significantly different than expected revised revenue estimates for the budget may be developed. This same approach is used to consider realistic expense estimates based upon actual performance during the earlier parts of the budget year. Reforecasting is most easily accomplished when all expenses are expressed as a percentage of revenue. Then, as revenue estimates increase or decrease, affected operating expenses can be adjusted accordingly.

When reforecasting is done, food and beverage managers can use information from income statements to compare actual operating results with:

— Budgeted revenue and expense levels-both for the current period and for cumulative to-date results during the operating year.

— Reforecasted revenue and expense information-both for the month and fiscal year-to-date.

Steps of Budget Development

There are three major steps in the process of developing a budget. First, forecasts of expected revenue are determined. Second, required profit levels for the food and beverage operation are calculated. Third, an appropriate method is used to calculate projected costs incurred in generating the forecasted revenue. Although it is useful to divide the process of budget development into these three steps, the last two steps really belong to the same phase of budget development because the profit requirement can be regarded as one of the" costs" assessed in calculating expenses.

Step 1: Calculate Projected Revenue Levels

The first step in the budget development process is to estimate revenue levels. fu hotel and restaurant operations, forecasts are normally made separately for food and beverage revenues. This helps managers pinpoint operating problems during the budget period. When budgets are based on combined food and beverage revenues, managers may not be able to easily identify operating problems during the budget period. However, when accurate guest check averages are available, some managers combine food and beverage revenues when developing budgets. In this case, revenue forecasts are based on the number of guests anticipated for the period covered by the budget. Revenue forecasts are determined by multiplying the number of anticipated guests by the amount of the average guest check. Depending on a number of other factors, this forecast may be increased (for example, if selling prices are planned to increase during the period covered by the budget) or decreased.

Projected revenue calculations should be made at least monthly. Calculating revenue projections on a weekly basis would provide even more specific information and perhaps increased accuracy. Individual estimates can then be combined into an annual revenue forecast. By using either monthly or weekly projections, actual revenue can later be compared with budgeted revenue-and actual expenses with budgeted expenses-in time for corrective action, if necessary. Generally figures for past revenue levels can be obtained from monthly income statements. Collecting revenue figures is made relatively easy by today's common use of computerised systems that list monthly cumulative "todate" statistics. This also makes it easy to notice trends between fiscal periods.

There are many factors that affect the development of revenue forecasts. In fact anything that can influence revenue levels also affects the development of revenue forecasts. For instance, internal sales promotion plans or scheduled remodeling could have a strong impact on revenue. Consequently, projected revenue for the coming fiscal period may need to be adjusted to account for these plans. Important factors to consider in determining revenue estimates include revenue histories, current factors, economic variables, and other factors.

Revenue histories: Useful forecasts for the new budget period can be developed by analysing past revenue levels and identifying trends. For example, if examining revenue histories shows that food and beverage revenue has increased by an average of eight percent for each of the past five years, then revenue for the upcoming period could be estimated by simply adding eight percent to the current revenue level. This assumes that the revenue growth of the past will continue in the future.

Current factors: There are many factors over which the property has little or no control that may affect revenue during the new budget period. For example, new competition, street improvement projects, or even the weather may have a strong impact on revenue levels. Social issues, such as liability laws regarding the sale and service of alcoholic beverages, may affect alcoholic beverage revenue. Budgeted revenue figures that are based on revenue histories and trend studies would need to be adjusted if any of these factors currently affect the property.

Economic variables: As costs increase during periods of high inflation, selling prices for food and beverage products must also be increased. At the same time, the public's habits and lifestyles are affected by economic conditions. When inflation rises, guests may demand greater value for their money. Some guests may "trade down" and replace their usual dining experiences with less expensive meals in lower-priced restaurants. Other guests may simply "trade out" and enjoy more meals at home with their families.

Other factors: Properties offering both food and beverages must estimate total revenue levels for both services. As noted previously, when making projections for food and beverage operations, revenue and expenses should normally be kept separate so that, subsequently, each can be controlled separately. Many lodging properties use the concept of derived demand, in which estimates of room revenue are used to help project revenue from food, beverages, and other revenue centers based upon guest spending patterns that have been developed from in-house studies. The hotel food and beverage manager must still calculate the impact of banquet operations and local community spending patterns separately to determine the total operating budget for the food and beverage department.

Forecasting beverage revenue: Few small beverage operations develop specific budget revenue estimates for individual beverage products such as beer, wine, liquor, and soft drinks. Rather, they assume that each beverage product will generate the same percentage of total beverage revenue in each budget period. For example, if liquor has been responsible for 70 percent of beverage revenue in past years, beverage managers may assume that it will continue to contribute 70 percent of future beverage revenue. However, beverage managers should carefully review trends in these percentage-of-revenue statistics. Wine sparkling water, and nonalcoholic specialty drinks are generating an increased proportion of beverage revenue in many places. Where this is true, other products, such as liquor, will contribute a reduced percentage of revenue.

Decisions regarding the percentage of total beverage revenue applicable to each product are relatively easy to make when electronic cash registers or other point-of sale devices are used to record information about beverage revenue by category. In operations that do not use computerised equipment or keep records on this basis, it may be necessary to base product revenue percentages on administrative judgment. In this case, perhaps a trial period for keeping careful product revenue records may provide some hard data to back up estimates of product revenue percentages.

Step 2: Determine Profit Requirements

There are two basic ways to treat profit when budgets are developed: (1) regarding profit as "what is left over from revenue after subtracting expenses," and (2) treating profit as if it were a "cost." The traditional approach determines profit by deducting estimated expenses from forecasted revenue:

$$\text{Profit} = \text{Revenue} - \text{Expenses}$$

A better approach treats profit as a "cost." This approach determines profit requirements before estimating expenses so that, in effect, the property pays itself first. Money remaining after profit requirements have been deducted from revenue is then used to pay for the operation's expenses. While the traditional method uses estimated expense levels to determine profit, this approach uses forecasted revenue and required profit levels to determine allowable expenses:

$$\text{Revenue} - \text{Required Profit} = \text{Allowable Operating Expenses}$$

With this formula, the food and beverage manager is concerned about achieving budgeted profit levels while at the same time assuring sufficient revenue to meet expenses. Using this plan for developing a budget, the food and beverage manager wants to (a) generate revenue, (b) plan for the desired operating profit, (c) have sufficient money remaining to meet the expenses required to generate the revenue, and (d) achieve all this without sacrificing quality requirements.

For a freestanding restaurant or other food service operation, the principles behind the determination of profit can be understood in terms of the accounting concepts of "return on investment" and/or "return on assets." Investors require that the property provide them with a reasonable return on their investment and that management safeguard the assets they have invested in the operation. This entitles investors to require additional profit to help compensate for the risk of their investment. In light of the high rate of restaurant failures, this risk is often great and, therefore, required returns are often high.

In lodging operations, investment requirements can be generated from the moms department, food and beverage department, and perhaps other revenue centers as well. The owner, working with the general manager, must first determine the amount of profit required from the lodging operation. Then, the staff must allocate profit responsibilities among the different departments based on expected levels of departmental revenue. The food and beverage manager will ultimately be responsible for generating a required amount of profit and will spread this responsibility between revenue-producing centers such as dining rooms, banquets, beverage operations, and room service.

Step 3: Calculate Projected Expense levels

Once revenue volumes are estimated and profit requirements are determined, expenses required to generate the projected level of revenue can be estimated. These expenses include: cost of food sold, labour expense, supplies expense, utilities, marketing expense, rent expense, depreciation expense, insurance expense, and many other expenses as well. Budget planning requires that management examine how these expenses are affected by changes in revenue volume. Fixed costs are costs that remain constant in the short run, even though revenue volume may vary. Common examples of fixed costs are: management salaries, rent expense, insurance expense, property taxes, depreciation expense, and interest expense.

Variable costs are costs that vary in relation to changes in the volume of business. If variable costs are strictly defined as costs that vary in exact proportion to arta revenue, then few costs, if any, are truly variable. However, several costs come dose to this definition and may legitimately be considered variable costs. For example, food and beverage costs increase as revenue volume increases simply because more food and beverage products must be purchased to prepare and serve the additional meals and drinks. Other examples of variable costs are labour costs for waged personnel and the cost of some supplies used in food production and service areas.

Mixed costs are costs that contain both fixed and variable cost elements. These costs are also referred to as semi-variable or semi-fixed costs. Although, in practice, the variable element of a mixed cost may not be directly proportional to usage or revenue volume, this assumption is generally accepted. An example of a mixed cost is telephone expense. One portion of this expense would be the fixed cost of the system, the other portion would be the variable cost of calls made during a specified period. Managers must consider each of these types of expenses as the budget is developed. The best method for estimating expense levels is, of course, the one that is most useful to the individual operation. Several widely used methods are described' in the following sections.

Simple Mark-Up Method

Perhaps the most common method of estimating food and beverage operating expenses is the mark-up method, which is based on the current expense level. This amount is then increased (or perhaps decreased, though this is rare) to arrive at the expense level for the new operating budget. For example, if the current month's food cost is $135,000, and a 12 percent cost (.12, as a decimal) increase is anticipated for the next budget period, the adjusted food cost for the new budget period is:

Budgeted food costs for each month are totalled to arrive at the estimated food cost for the new budget year. Total projected costs for the entire food and beverage operation are then determined by combining similar calculations for beverage and all other expense categories.

One problem with this method is that, by basing projections on current expense levels, it assumes all costs were reasonable during the current year. If in fact, some costs were too high because of waste, theft, or some other reason that inefficiency is extended into the new budget.

Percentage Method

Another frequently used method of estimating food and beverage operating expenses is the percentage method, which is based on the percentage of each expense relative to revenue. Food and beverage cost percentages are calculated by dividing food or beverage cost by food or beverage revenue and multiplying by 100. The percentage method for forecasting food and beverage expenses assumes that the same cost percentages from the current period will continue to apply to the projected revenue for the new budget period. For example if the current beverage cost percentage is 24 percent, when the new budget is developed, 24 percent of the estimated beverage revenue is allocated for beverage costs. Like the mark-up method, the percentage method assumes that the current cost percentage is reasonable. This has the potential disadvantage of continuing an inefficient operation if the current budgeted cost percentage is higher than it should be. Close analysis to ensure that the budget allows for the planned profit goal can offset this disadvantage.

Zero Based Budget Calculations

A third method, zerobased budgeting, avoids the disadvantages of the other two by starting over from zero instead of extending costs or cost percentages transferred from the current period. This method takes more time and involves starting at a zero expense level for each category of cost and building up to new budgeted expense levels, justifying each step along the way. As a result, it yields expense information designed specifically for the period covered by the new operating budget. Forecasting costs in this way provides a very useful control tool for later comparing budgeted costs with actual costs. However because it requires a significant commitment of time to justify each cost estimate, the zerobased budget is not frequently used in commercial food and beverage operations.

Estimating Beverage Expenses

Separate costs for different beverage products may be considered in budget development. For example, suppose 70 percent (.70) of beverage revenue is estimated to be from liquor, and the beverage cost for liquor is 28 percent (.28) of its revenue. If beverage revenue equals $100,000, the total cost of liquor is:

% of Beverage Revenue X Total Beverage Revenue
X Beverage Cost = Total Cost

However, management must also consider the impact of other expenses such as labour, supplies, and advertising-on the entire budget. The same basic procedures can be used to estimate costs for all other expenses allocated to the food and beverage department.

For example, labour costs represent a significant expense for all types of food service operations. Managers must take the time to objectively assess likely labour cost levels based on estimated revenue. Energy and advertising expenses are other examples of costs that are generally significant and, therefore, demand attention during budget development. However, some categories of expense, such as office supplies, may have little financial impact on the food and beverage operation. Simple mark-ups are likely to be a fast and reasonably accurate way to budget for these expenses.

Computers and the Budget Process

Computers are now in common use for both routine and advanced budgeting applications in all but the smallest operations. The programmes designed to best per form these activities are termed electronic spreadsheet software. Electronic spreadsheets are simple in concept, but possess powerful computation capabilities.

Electronic Spreadsheets

Electronic spreadsheets resemble a traditional accounting worksheet since they are organised by rows and columns. The border along the worksheet's left margin typically contains numbers to designate row locations while the top margin contains letters depicting column locations. The intersection of a row and column forms a cell. A cell address is defined by its respective row and column indicators.

It is important to note that unlike an accountant's worksheet, which is very limited in size, electronic spreadsheets are stored in the computer's extensive memory. Spreadsheets are often so large that their size prohibits them from being displayed in their entirety on a display screen or monitor. At any point in time, the user views only a section, referred to as a window, of an otherwise enormous spreadsheet. The terminal keyboard contains cursor (arrow) keys enabling the user to move from cell to cell and from window to window.

Cell Contents

The food and beverage manager customizes a generic spreadsheet by defining the content of its cells. Electronic spreadsheet cells can contain a label, a number, or a formula. When textual information is entered into a cell it is referred to as a label. Spreadsheet software automatically identifies labels since they are entered from the terminal's typewriter keyboard. Labels assist in the organisation of data input and in the comprehensibility of output information. Headings, titles, chart of account lists, and the like typify budgeting labels.

Numeric values, used to produce calculated results, are entered into cells from the keyboard's number keys. The software is capable of identifying numeric input coming from the numeric keys) similar to the manner in which it recognises text characters for labels.

Formulas are preceded by special characters (for example, +) or words (for example, sum). These are used so that only the results and not the formula will appear in the addressed cell. Perhaps the most important benefit of spreadsheet software is its ability to maintain a formula that relates specific cells. For example, consider the spreadsheet below. Numeric values appear in cells B4, C4, 04, E4, B5, C5, OS, and E5. The results of stored formulas are presented in calls 07, E7, and B9. The formula used to produce the output in B7 is +B4 / B5. Cell C7 is generated from formula + C4/ C5. The calculated average food cost percentage found in B9 is computed from this formula: + B7 + C7 +07 + E7/ 4.

Formulas, capable of referencing various cells and constants, illustrate the usefulness of spreadsheet programmes. They enable someone who has only basic computer skills to direct the computational efforts of a powerful machine.

Recalculation Feature

The budgeting process generally requires many calculations. Moreover, whenever data is altered or extended, numerous recalculations are necessary. Spreadsheet software significantly enhances and streamlines this process since it contains for mulas composed of cell addresses and possesses a unique recalculation feature. Spreadsheets can be configured to automatically recalculate all numeric values whenever one value changes. Recalculations are performed in a chaining fashion. As a cell is modified, any and all cells related to it are also changed. In Exhibit 7, formulas in cells B7, C7, 07, and E7 relate corresponding row 4 and 5 elements. The formula in cell B9, however, depends on the calculated outputs of B7, C7, 07, and E7. Assume week two's food cost was erroneously entered.

The data in cell C4 should have been 3200, not 3000. When the cursor is moved to cell C4 and the figure 3200 is entered (replacing 3000), all subsequent computations dependent on this cell data (C7 and B9) will automatically be recalculated. In a manual process, these recalculations would require a working knowledge of the relationship among all data, and would take considerable time to accomplish. There would also be an increased opportunity for making errors in the recalculations. Budget reforecasting is becoming an increasingly used tool to help the food and beverage manager monitor the operation. The recalculation feature of electronic spreadsheet software enables food and beverage managers in all sizes and types of operations to quickly update budget projections by reforecasting revenue levels or expenses when necessary.

Food and beverage managers tend to appreciate spreadsheet output options as much as they do the usefulness of cell contents and automatic recalculations. Many electronic spreadsheet programmes provide both text (worksheet) and graphic output formats for any portion of the spreadsheet. Text output consists of a printed copy of me spreadsheet as it appears on the display screen.

The data on a spreadsheet can also be displayed graphically. Graphic options include bar charts, pie charts, or line drawings. Often, a visual presentation of the same data improves comprehension and understanding.

Cost-Volume-Profit Analysis

Cost-volume-profit (CVP) analysis is an analytical process used to determine the revenues required at any desired profit level. Also referred to as "breakeven analysis," CVP reviews the relationships among costs, revenue, and profits associated with alternative plans. CVP analysis is used to help managers answer such questions as:

— How many guests must the operation serve to meet budgeted profit goals?

— When fixed or variable costs increase, how many additional guests must the operation serve to meet budgeted profit goals?

— How profitable would it be for the restaurant to expand its hours of operation?

— Should the restaurant remain open during predictably slow meal periods?

— Graphs or equations can be used to conduct the analysis. Use of equations is likely to be faster and more accurate, and this procedure will be used in the discussion and examples that follow.

CVP Assumptions and Limitations

Like all mathematical tools, CVP analysis is based on several assumptions. If these assumptions are not relevant to the actual situations being analysed, the results of the analysis may be flawed. Some of the more basic assumptions behind CVP analysis include the following:

— Fixed costs remain constant during the period being analysed. Over time, fixed costs do change. However, it is reasonable to assume that fixed costs remain constant over a short time span.

— Variable costs vary directly with revenue during the period under study. In other words, if variable costs equal a certain percentage of revenue, and revenue increases, the new level of variable expenses will still equal the same percentage of revenue.

— Revenue relates directly to volume. For example, CVP analysis assumes that as business volume (the number of guests served) increases by a certain percentage, revenue will then increase by that same percentage. This means that decisions made from CVP analyses must be reviewed if, during the timeperiod in question, the sales mix changes. A change in the sales mix usually affects the amount of the guest check average. A higher average guest check results in higher revenue at the same level of business volume.

— All costs can be properly divided into two components: fixed costs and variable costs (which vary directly with revenue).

— Only quantitative factors are considered by the CVP model. Qualitative factors such as employee morale, guest goodwill, and so forth are not considered. Therefore, food and beverage managers must carefully consider these qualitative factors before making any final decisions.

References

Dahl, J. O., *Planning profitable restaurant advertising,* New York: J. O. Dahl, 1933.

Marvin, Bill. *Guest-Based Marketing: How to Increase Restaurant Sales Without Breaking Your Budget*. New York: John Wiley, 1997.

Robert, Phil. *Service That Sells!: The Art of Profitable Hospitality*. Denver: Pencom International, 1998.

Sackler, Warren. *Foodservice Cost Control Using Microsoft Excel for Windows.* New York: Wiley, 1996.

Wenzel, G. L., *Handbook of restaurant costs: how to maintain a 40% food cost and a 25% payroll,* Austin, Texas: G. Wenzel?, 1948.

Bibliography

Albert Pick & Company (Chicago), *Equipment for cafeterias, lunch rooms, restaurants and dining rooms, kitchen equipment,* Chicago: The Company, 1920.

Anderson, Kenneth. *International Dictionary of Food & Nutrition.* New York: Wiley, 1993.

Angelo, Rocco M. *An Introduction to Hospitality Today*. Orlando: Educational Institute, American Hotel & Motel Association, 1998.

Bradley, Alice, *Cooking for profit; catering and food service management,* Chicago: American school of home economics, 1922.

Brown, Douglas Robert. *The Restaurant Managers Handbook: How to Set Up, Operate, and Manage a Financially Successful Restaurant.* Lauderhill, Atlantic Pub., 1991.

Bryson, McDowell. *Concierge: Key to Hospitality: A Training Manual.* New York: Wiley, 1992.

Casado, Matt A. *Food and Beverage Service Manual.* New York: Wiley, 1994.

Chesser, Gerald. *Art and Science of Culinary Preparation: A Culinarian's Manual.* St. Augustine: Educational Institute of the American Culinary, 1992.

Chmelynski, Carol Ann Caprione. *Opportunities in Food Service Careers.* Lincolnwood: VGM Career Horizons, 2000.

Cichy, Ronald F. *Managing Service in Food and Beverage Operations.* Lansing: Educational Institute of the American Hotel and Motel Association, 1998.

Cournoyer, Norman G. *Hotel, Restaurant, and Travel Law: A Preventive Approach.* Albany: Delmar Publishers, 1993.

Dahl, J. O., *Planning profitable restaurant advertising,* New York: J. O. Dahl, 1933.

Desrosier N. W., *The Technology of Food Preservation*, 3d ed. 1970.

Frooman, Abraham Arthur, *Five steps to effective institutional food buying, by A. A. Frooman,* Chicago, 1948.

Gray, Madeline and Vass De Lo Padua, *How to cook for profit; a complete guide to food in quantity, from order pad to diner's table.* New York: Greenberg, 1947.

Hoke, Ann, *Restaurant menu planning,* New York, London: Harper & brothers, 1940.

Horwath, Ernest B. and Louis Toth, *Hotel accounting, including departmental control, food costing, and auditing,* New York: The Ronald press company, 1928.

Janet McKenize Hill, *The Up-to-Date Waitress*, Boton: Little, Brown, and Co, 1906

John Love, *McDonald's behind the Arches*, Toronto: Bantam Books, 1986

Katsigris, Costas. *Design and Equipment for Restaurants and Foodservice: A Management View*. New York: Wiley, 1999.

Leon Gottlieb, *The Best of Gottlieb's Bottom Line*, New York: Lebhar Friedman, 1980.

Livingstone, Helen, *Food service; for restaurant, coffee shop, hotel, cafeteria, home,* Blooming Ill: McKnight and McKnight Pub. Co., 1950.

Raymond J. Goodman, Jr., *The Management of Service for the Restaurant Manager*, 2nd Edition

Scanlon, Nancy Loman. *Marketing by Menu*. New York: John Wiley, 1999.

Searing, Fred, *Profit building ideas for food and food service,* Stanford, Conn.: Dahl Pub. Co., 1947.

Wadhams, Caroline Reed, *Simple directions for the waitress or parlor maid,* New York: Longmans Green and co., 1917.

Waller, Keith. *Improving Food and Beverage Performance*. Oxford: Butterworth-Heinemann, 1996.

Walsh, Joseph F., *Sound spending, with special reference to the operating cost of institutions, schools, colleges, hospitals, orphanages, convents, monasteries, etc., seminaries, parishes,* Cleveland: Seminary press, 1935.

Ware, Richard. *How to Open Your Own Restaurant: A Guide for Entrepreneurs.* New York: Penguin Books, 1991.

Wenzel, G. L., *Handbook of restaurant costs: how to maintain a 40% food cost and a 25% payroll,* Austin, Texas: G. Wenzel?, 1948.

West, Bessie Brooks and LeVelle Wood, *Food service in institutions,* New York; London: J. Wiley & sons inc; Chapman & Hall limited, 1938.

Whitehead, Jessup, *The steward's handbook and guide to party catering,* Chicago: J. Anderson & co. printers, 1889.

Wigger, G. Eugene. *Themes, Dreams, and Schemes: Banquet Menu Ideas, Concepts, and Thematic Experiences.* New York: John Wiley, 1997.

Wilkinson, Jule. *Complete Book of Cooking Equipment*. Boston: CBI Pub. Company, 1981.

Woods, Robert H. *Quality Leadership and Management in the Hospitality Industry.* East Lansing: Educational Institute of the American Hotel & Motel Association, 1996.

Zaccarelli, Herman E. *Food Service Management by Checklist: A Handbook of Control Techniques*. New York: Wiley, 1991.